TASTELESS LISTS

TASTELESS LISTS

Karl Shaw

This is a Parragon Book published 1999

Parragon
Queen Street House
4 Queen Street
Bath BA1 1HE, UK

First published in the UK as *The Mammoth Book of Tasteless Lists*
by Robinson Publishing, 1998

A copy of the British Library Cataloguing in Publication Data
is available from the British Library

ISBN 0-75253-542-0

Printed and bound in the EC

10 9 8 7 6 5 4 3 2 1

CONTENTS

Chapter One: Entrances & Exits

Chapter Two: Food & Drink

Chapter Three: Art & Entertainment

Chapter Four: Health & Beauty

Chapter Five: Saints & Sinners

Chapter Six: Odds & Sods

Chapter Seven: Crime & Punishment

Chapter Eight: Ad Nauseam

1
ENTRANCES & EXITS

10 Falling Between Stools: Lavatorial Deaths

1. Roman emperor Heliogabalus (204–222 AD) was hacked to death by the praetorian guard as he sat on the lavatory, and his body thrown down a Roman sewer.
2. The Saxon king Edmund Ironside had his reign curtailed when he sat on a wooden lavatory: an assassin hiding in the pit below twice thrust his longsword up the king's anal passage, embedding the sword in his bowels and killing him instantly.
3. Russia's empress Catherine the Great died of heart failure while straining to overcome constipation.
4. King George II, according to his German *valet de chambre*, was a loud and garrulous farter. One evening he heard a roar from the palace privy which he judged to be "louder than the usual royal wind" and found the king slumped dead on the floor. George had fallen off the toilet, smashing his head on a cabinet as he fell.
5. Sussex's messiest death occurred in 1856 when Matthew Gladman fell into a Lewes High Street cesspit. He had apparently entered a water closet in the dark, unaware that the floorboards had been removed in order to empty the chamber below. Doctors tried to revive him with electric shock therapy but failed. He died of asphyxiation by methane gas.
6. The 36-year-old Hollywood screen actress Lupe Velez, the "Mexican Spitfire", attempted to commit suicide by

overdosing on sleeping pills in 1934. Ms Velez underestimated the dosage, however, and suddenly felt violently sick. As she made a dash for the bathroom she slipped on the tiled floor and was flung head first into her toilet. Her maid found her the next day with her head jammed down the bowl, drowned.

7. In 1957 King Haakon VII of Norway slipped on some soap in his marble bathroom and smashed his head on some taps, fatally fracturing his skull.
8. Elvis Presley died of heart failure in 1977 and was found face down in his bathroom.
9. In September 1990 a joint reception in honour of the double wedding of two Jordanian brothers and their brides ended when the dance floor gave way, catapulting the entire wedding party into a cesspool below. Thirteen people died, including both brides.
10. A 41-year-old German, Heinz Schmitzer, fell into an outhouse cesspit in 1994 and drowned in raw sewage while attempting to retrieve his wallet.

Lovers of "the Virgin Queen" Elizabeth I

1. The Duke of Alençon.
2. Robert Dudley, Earl of Leicester.
3. Robert Devereux, Earl of Essex.
4. Sir Christopher Hatton.
5. Thomas Heneage.
6. Edward de Vere, Earl of Oxford.
7. Sir William Pickering.
8. Sir Walter Raleigh.

10
Most Adulterous British Prime Ministers

1. Sir Robert Walpole (PM 1721–42). The marriage of Britain's first prime minister to Catherine Shorter was a sham. He took numerous mistresses, most famously Maria Skerrett. After his wife's death he quickly married his favourite mistress, but she died in childbirth shortly afterwards.
2. The Earl of Bute (PM 1762–3) was variously alleged to have had an adulterous affair with the Prince of Wales's wife Augusta and a homosexual relationship with her son, the young King George III.
3. The Duke of Grafton (PM 1767–70). The first British prime minister to flaunt his mistress in front of the reigning monarch, and the first known to have slept with his mistress, Nancy Parsons, at No. 10 Downing Street.
4. George Canning (PM 1827) almost certainly had an affair with Caroline, the Princess of Wales, while she was estranged from her husband and living at Montague House, Blackheath, in 1799.
5. The Duke of Wellington (PM 1828–30) had numerous affairs throughout his marriage to Kitty Pakenham. Wellington's famous retort "Publish and be damned" was in response to the blackmailer Joseph Stockdale, who threatened to print the memoirs of Wellington's former mistress, Harriette Wilson. Stockdale did publish, and so the whole of London was able to read about the Iron Duke's prowess between the sheets, which according to the high-class tart was "most unentertaining" and "very uphill work". Wellington's stance wasn't quite as brave as it is often

painted: he threatened to sue for libel, but the writ never materialized. The Duke of Wellington was still having affairs at the age of 83.

6. Lord Melbourne (PM 1834, 1835–41). Queen Victoria's first prime minister suffered at the hands of his scandalously unfaithful wife Lady Caroline Lamb, but was also involved in two court actions brought against him by the husbands of Lady Brandon and Caroline Norton. It is believed that Lord Melbourne was addicted to flagellation.
7. Viscount Palmerston (PM 1855–8, 1859–65). An habitual womanizer who was cited as co-respondent in a divorce case at the age of 79. Palmerston also tried to rape one of Queen Victoria's ladies-in-waiting while he was visiting Windsor Castle. He defended his behaviour by claiming that he was blind drunk on port and had entered the wrong bedroom. The whole matter was hushed up, but Victoria never believed his story nor did she forgive him.
8. Herbert Henry Asquith (PM 1908–16) admitted to "a slight weakness for the companionship of clever and attractive women": a slight understatement as he was a compulsive womanizer. At the age of 62 he had an affair with the 27-year-old friend of his daughter.
9. David Lloyd George (PM 1916–22) lived a scandalous double life, spending half his time with his wife and the other half in the bed of his secretary Frances Stevenson. The press turned a blind eye to the affair even when he fathered an illegitimate daughter. He also slept with his daughter's governess, who was about half his age. When Lloyd George's son once answered a phone call enquiring whether the mistress of the house was available, he replied, "Which mistress?"
10. Ramsay MacDonald (PM 1924, 1929–35). The first Labour prime minister was accused of being a class traitor when he had an affair with a leading Tory "hostess", the Marchioness of Londonderry.

10 Deaths Without Dignity

1. In July 1994, a 39-year-old motorcyclist in Commerce City, Colorado, was killed when a 40-pound dog fell off an overhead bridge on to his head, causing him to lose control of the bike and collide with a truck.
2. Pickles the dog, who discovered the Jules Rimet Trophy under a bush after it was stolen before the World Cup finals in 1966, strangled himself on his own lead while chasing a cat.
3. Sir Arthur Aston, Royalist commander during the English Civil War, was beaten to death with his own wooden leg by Cromwell's men.
4. The French composer Jean-Baptiste Lully accidentally stabbed himself in the foot with his baton and died of gangrene.
5. Sandra Orellana from Texas fell to her death from the eighth-floor balcony at the Industry Hills Sheraton, where she staying during a business conference in 1996. Police said Orellana fell accidentally as she and her boss Robert Salazar were having sex against a handrail, and she changed positions.
6. In October 1973, in accordance with his last wish, a Swedish confectionery salesman from Falkenberg, Roland Ohisson, was buried in a coffin made entirely of chocolate.
7. The jazz musician Joe "Poolie" Newman, trumpet-player with the likes of Count Basie and Lionel Hampton, was a notorious womanizer. In 1989 Newman, determined to live up to his reputation, tried to his enhance his flagging sex life with a penile implant. Unfortunately, a build-

up of pressure caused his member to explode one evening while he was in a restaurant, and he haemorrhaged to death.

8. An Icelandic funeral parlour was fined in 1993 after the bereaved family of Henri Labonte complained to local authorities that the deceased had been dressed for his 26 December funeral in a Santa Claus costume and was wearing a fake beard.
9. Elizabeth, the wife of the poet and painter Dante Gabriel Rossetti, died in 1862 after overdosing on the laudanum she was taking for her neuralgia. Rossetti, himself an alcoholic and a morphine addict, was grief-stricken, and as a token of his love had a pile of his unpublished manuscripts wrapped in her golden tresses and buried with her in her coffin. Seven years later, however, he had a change of heart and decided that he wanted them back. Up came Elizabeth, and the poems were dusted off and published to great critical acclaim.
10. When King Francis I of Naples died, his corpse was embalmed and lay in state on display for three days, in accordance with royal custom. On the third night the two sentries on duty beside him were startled by a thud: after closer inspection of the cask they deserted their post and ran screaming into the night. Apparently one of the king's arms had dropped off.

10 PRESIDENTIAL PECCADILLOES

1. George Washington (pres. 1789–97) was an inveterate womanizer who spent very little time with his wife Martha. Among the women with whom the president is known to have had adulterous relationships were Kitty Greene, Lucy Flucker Knox, Mrs Clement Biddle (the wife of an army general), Elizabeth Gates (also a general's wife), Theodosia Prevost Burr, Lady Kitty Alexander Duer, Phoebe Fraunces, Eliza Powell, Mrs William Bingham and Mrs Perez Morton. Throughout the War of Independence the British made propaganda out of Washington's sex life, alleging that he kept hordes of mistresses, both black and white. He was involved in only one sex scandal, however, known as the "Washerwoman Kate Affair". A friend of Washington's, a Congressman named Harrison, acted as his procurer in Philadelphia while Washington was at the front. One day Harrison sent a letter to Washington informing him of his latest "find", but the highly compromising note was intercepted and found its way into the *Boston Weekly News* and later the *Gentleman's Magazine* in London. The story eventually became the inspiration for a Broadway play with the epic title *The Battle of Brooklyn: A Farce of Two Acts: As It Was Performed on Long Island, on Tuesday the 27th Day of 1776, by the Representatives of*

Americans, Assembled at Philadelphia. Washington was a flirt, and he didn't spare his wife's feelings. A French officer noted, "he does it quite openly, and before his wife, who does not seem to mind at all." In 1799 Washington died of a chill which he caught, according to the official version, riding his horse in the snow. According to a more likely interpretation, however, he caught his chill jumping out of a window trouserless after an assignation with an employee's wife at Mount Vernon. He left no direct descendants: though his wife Martha had four children by a previous marriage, Washington never sired a child to continue his line.

2. Thomas Jefferson (pres. 1801–9). His presidency was dogged by persistent allegations that he slept with black slave girls. At the centre of the scandal was Jefferson's relationship with a slave girl named "Dusky Sally" Hemmings, who came into Jefferson's possession in 1773. While officially employed as his "chambermaid" she bore him five children who were kept as slaves, including a light-skinned boy named "Yellow Tom" who bore a conspicuous resemblance to him. Mrs Francis Trollope, mother of novelist Anthony, wrote a bestseller in 1832 which asserted that Jefferson was the father of "unnumbered generations of slaves". One of the sons, Eston Hemmings, was able to pass himself off as a member of the white community and even married a white woman. Later Jefferson also had an affair with Maria Cosway, wife of the famous English painter of miniatures Richard Cosway.
3. James Garfield (pres. 1881) declared his marriage to his wife Lucretia "a great mistake" and vowed to spend as much of his time as he possibly could far away from her

on business trips. In 1862 he had an indiscreet affair with an 18-year-old reporter from the *New York Times*, and during the 1880 election there were press stories about his visits to a New Orleans brothel.

4. Grover Cleveland (pres. 1885–9, 1893–7). The *bon viveur* Cleveland weighed around 18 stones and it was said that the only exercise he took apart from hunting and fishing were occasional trips to local brothels. He provoked a scandal when, at the age of 49, he married a 21-year-old. During the 1888 election Cleveland's political enemies circulated a leaflet accusing him of bestiality and wife-beating, and newspapers published stories warning Cleveland's young slip of a bride that having sexual relations with her obese husband could be life-threatening.
5. Warren G. Harding (pres. 1921–3) maintained two regular mistresses throughout his marriage and attended regular drunken orgies with chorus girls at the home of a friend, Harry Daugherty. Harding's women were rewarded with well-paid government jobs, although once he was blackmailed for $15,000 by a woman who held some love letters written to her by the president. When his wife Florence went into hospital for the removal of a kidney in 1905, Harding took up with Mrs Carrie Phillips, the wife of a friend, and kept up the relationship for the next 15 years. It appeared that Harding and Mrs Phillips got off on the excitement of having sex virtually under the noses of their respective partners. He acquired a second long-term mistress, a 16-year-old schoolgirl named Nan Britton, when he was 57. Harding was usually able to pass her off as his niece, although once they attempted to check into a Chicago hotel as man and wife, only to be told by the incredulous clerk that if they could prove they were

man and wife he would let them have the room for nothing. Harding later became recklessly indiscreet and flaunted his young girlfriend on the streets of Washington. Miss Britton later revealed that they had made love on numerous occasions in a small closet in a White House anteroom. In 1919 she gave birth to his daughter, Elizabeth Ann. Harding never once saw the child and bought his girlfriend's silence by paying her $20,000 plus a monthly allowance. He died of a fatal cerebral thrombosis four years later.

6. Franklin D. Roosevelt (pres. 1933–45) went to elaborate lengths to hide affairs with two of his secretaries, first Lucy Page Mercer and later Marguerite "Missy" LeHand, including a retreat in Warm Springs, Alaska. Eleanor Roosevelt knew of the affairs, however, and took her husband's regular infidelities in her stride, perhaps partly because she herself was enjoying a lesbian liaison with the pipe-smoking Lorena Hickock, a news reporter who covered Roosevelt's 1932 campaign trail. Ironically, the only occasion upon which Roosevelt was in any way tainted by a sex scandal in the White House was when it emerged that his special envoy and Under-Secretary of State Sumner Welles was homosexual and had been caught propositioning porters on a Pulman train.
7. John F. Kennedy (pres. 1961–3) was an astonishingly energetic and reckless womanizer: his wife Jackie often organized seating arrangements at White House dinners

so that one or more of her sexually incontinent husband's lovers were seated next him; thus, she reasoned, she could at least reduce his access to new conquests. Ninety minutes before the famous first live televised debate with Richard Nixon, Kennedy disappeared into a nearby hotel room with a prostitute; he emerged 15 minutes later. Kennedy was apparently so pleased with his confident and relaxed TV performance that he subsequently repeated the trick before all of his TV debates. The arch-snooper and head of the FBI, J. Edgar Hoover, kept a bulging file on Kennedy which detailed his liaisons with New York prostitutes and his private suite in a Washington hotel, nicknamed "Kennedy's play-pen". During the 1960 election Kennedy spent time in Las Vegas with Frank Sinatra, and the FBI watched dozens of showgirls come and go from Kennedy's hotel room. He made love with women on the floor of his office in the Senate Office building, and from 1960 onwards even shared a lover, Judith Campbell, with the Mafia boss Sam Giancana. He had a string of affairs with famous actresses including Jayne Mansfield, Gene Tierney, Angie Dickenson, the stripper Blaze Starr and Marilyn Monroe. Kennedy always wanted to get rid of Hoover, but the head of the FBI knew his own job was safe so long as he still had the tapes of Kennedy and Monroe talking and having sex at the beach house of one of Kennedy's closest friends.

8. Lyndon B. Johnson (pres. 1963–9). According to his press secretary, Johnson "had the instincts of a Turkish sultan". He openly boasted his credentials as a sexual athlete and felt aggrieved that JFK's reputation as a stud was greater than his: "I have had more women by accident than he has had on purpose," he complained to his

friends. Johnson had six White House secretaries and claimed he had sex with five of them, including one session on the desk in the Oval Office. He was once caught by his wife copulating with a blonde secretary on a couch in the Oval Office. Johnson also maintained two long-term relationships throughout his marriage to Claudia "Lady Bird" Johnson: one with Alice Glass, a girlfriend he shared with the US newspaper tycoon Charles E. Marsh; the other with Madeleine Brown, who bore Johnson a son called Steven. As had been the case with Roosevelt, the only government sex scandal during his presidency involved someone else: a homosexual senior White House official, Chief of Staff Walter Jenkins, was twice caught in public sex acts with men, the second time with a 60-year-old man in a YMCA toilet.

9. Richard M. Nixon (pres. 1969–74) had an eight-year-long affair with a Hong Kong tour guide, Marianna Liu, a girl about 20 years younger than the long-married Nixon. Both the FBI and British Intelligence took a special interest in Nixon's liaisons with Liu, as she was suspected of being a Chinese communist spy. She later became a permanent US resident after Nixon personally rushed through her visa, and she settled in Nixon's home town in California. When Nixon tried to sack J. Edgar Hoover, as others had before him, Hoover simply showed him the Nixon/Liu file and emerged from the meeting with a grin on his face and his job intact.
10. Bill Clinton (pres. 1993–) has had to withstand more White House sex scandals than any of his predecessors. In 1992 a cabaret singer from Little Rock, Gennifer Jones, was the first of Clinton's alleged former lovers to hit the headlines when she revealed to *Penthouse* intimate details

of their 12-year affair, forcing the Clintons to own up to marital problems on TV. A trooper who had been detailed to guard Clinton during his days as Governor of Arkansas estimated that Clinton had slept with hundreds of women. Subsequent allegations of sexual misconduct included affairs with the wife of a judge, a sales clerk from a Little Rock department store cosmetics counter and a prostitute called Bobbie Ann Williams, who claimed that Clinton had fathered her child. A former Miss Arkansas, Sally Perdue, claimed she too had an affair with Clinton, which ended with the offer of a $40,000-a-year job if she kept her mouth shut, and the offer of broken legs if she didn't. In 1994 a typist from Arkansas, Paula Jones, accused Clinton of sexual harassment, claiming that he had dropped his trousers and indecently exposed himself to her at a Democrat conference at Little Rock three years earlier. Her affidavit contained explicit substantiating details about the president's genitalia.

12 Celebrity Body Parts

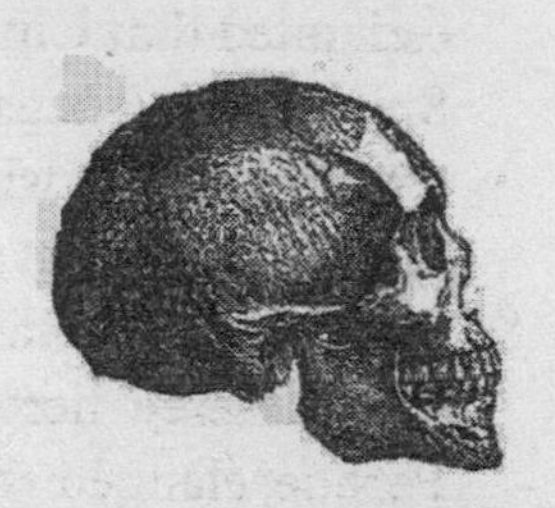

1. Albert Einstein's eyes. Removed by his ophthalmologist Dr Henry Abrams during the autopsy in 1955 and stored in a safety deposit box. The eyes were put up for auction in 1994.
2. Napoleon Bonaparte's penis. Removed at autopsy by a team of French and Belgian doctors. When first put up for auction in 1972 at Christie's, the member was observed to be approximately one inch long and was listed as "a small, dried-up object". It failed to measure up to the reserve price and was withdrawn, but was bought five years later by an American urologist for $3,800.
3. Hitler's teeth. Used to positively identify his charred remains, which were discovered by Soviet soldiers in a shallow grave outside his Berlin bunker in 1945. They have remained locked away in an archive somewhere in Moscow ever since.
4. Elvis Presley's wart. Perhaps the most unique item of Elvis memorabilia, currently owned by Joni Mabe of Athens, Georgia.
5. Joseph Haydn's head. For nearly 60 years the head of the Austrian composer was stored in a cupboard in the Museum of the Vienna Academy of Music. Haydn was buried without it after two of his best friends bribed the gravedigger to let them keep it.
6. Rasputin's penis. Following his assassination by a group of Russian noblemen, his manhood was hacked off and

preserved in a small velvet-lined box. The current whereabouts of this artefact are not known.

7. Sir Walter Raleigh's head. After his execution in 1618 it became the Raleigh family heirloom. His widow Elizabeth kept it for 29 years before willing it to their son Carew, who looked after it until 1666, when it went with him to his grave.
8. Oliver Cromwell's skull. An item which has changed hands many times since he lost exclusive use of it in 1658. After the restoration of the monarchy in 1660, Cromwell's corpse was exhumed from Westminster Abbey and hanged at Tyburn. He was then taken down from the scaffold and decapitated; his body was thrown into a pit beneath the gallows and the head set on a spike above Westminster Hall. The head remained there until 1703, when it was dislodged in a violent storm and was found lying on the ground by a sentry. He took it home and kept it hidden in his chimney, and on his death left it to his daughter. In 1710 the head reappeared, this time in a freak show. By 1775 it had been sold to an actor named Russell, who in turn sold it in 1787 to James Fox, an antique-dealer. Fox sold it for £230 to three men who put it on display in Old Bond Street, London, and charged half a crown per viewing. By 1865 it had passed into the possession of a Mr Williamson of Beckenham. His family donated it to Sidney Sussex College, Cambridge, in the 1960s. At one time there were even two authentic Cromwell skulls on sale in London simultaneously. The owner of the second, smaller skull explained that his version was obviously that of Cromwell when he was a young lad.
9. King Charles XII of Sweden's skull. Now on permanent public display in Stockholm, complete with the large

bullet hole which made the exhibition possible in 1718.

10. Beethoven's hair. In 1994 two collectors paid Sotheby's £4,000 for a four-inch-long lock of the composer's hair, allegedly snipped by Beethoven's dad in 1827. They said they planned to have it DNA-tested to confirm suspicions that the composer had African blood and suffered from syphilis.
11. Cancerous tissue from the jaw of US President Grover Cleveland. This resides in the Mutter Museum of Philadelphia, which specializes in bizarre medical curiosities, along with the B.C. Hirot Pelvis Collection, the Sappey Collection of mercury-filled lymphaticus, the Chevalier Johnson collection of foreign bodies removed from lungs, and the joined liver of Chang and Eng, the original Siamese Twins.
12. King Charles I's fourth cervical vertebra. The novelist Sir Walter Scott liked to break the ice at parties by introducing dinner guests to his novelty salt cellar, made from a relic stolen by a surgeon during an autopsy on the royal corpse when Charles's long-lost coffin was rediscovered at Windsor Castle in 1813. Scott kept it on his dining table for 30 years until Queen Victoria got to hear about it. She was quite unamused and ordered that it be returned to St George's Chapel.

9 Historical Figures who Died during Sexual Intercourse

1. Attila the Hun. Although short, squat and extremely ugly, Attila had a dozen wives. He burst an artery on his wedding night with his 12th.
2. Pope Leo VII (936–9) died of a heart attack during sex.
3. Pope John VII (955–64) was bludgeoned to death by the cuckolded husband of the woman he was making love with at the time.
4. Pope John XIII (965–72) was also murdered by an irate husband who discovered His Holiness on top of his wife.
5. Pope Paul II (1467–71) allegedly died of a heart attack while being sodomized by a page boy.
6. The Duke of Orleans, Regent to the French boy-king Louis XV. In 1721 the depraved and elderly duke took a new mistress who was nearly 30 years younger than him, against the advice of his doctors. He was found slumped by the fireplace of his drawing-room one day dying from a massive stroke.
7. French president Félix Faure (1841–99) died during sex in a Paris brothel. Faure's death sent the woman into shock and his member had to be surgically removed from her.
8. Lord Palmerston, British prime minister (1855–8, 1859–65) died of a heart attack while having sex with a young parlour maid on his billiard table on 18 October 1865.
9. Nelson Rockefeller, a former US vice-president, died aged 71 while copulating with his mistress.

10 Aphrodisiacs

1. At one time Chinese emperors were required keep 121 wives – a precise number thought to have magical properties – 10 of whom the emperor was expected to make love to every night. A Taoist manual advised that this could be made possible by applying sheep's eyelid marinaded in hot tea to the imperial penis.
2. Menstrual blood as a food or drink additive (Germany, eighteenth century).
3. Live monkey brains (Malaysia). The monkey was forced into a tight container to prevent it from escaping, and a bowl fitted to its head. The live monkey suffered agony while its scalp was cut open and peeled back to reveal the exposed brain. The brain was then scooped out with a spoon or sucked through a straw.
4. Toad excrement (France, eighteenth century). This method was also once used by Louis XIV's ageing mistress Madame de Montespan to revive the Sun King's flagging interest in her.
5. Lion testicles or arsenic (Regency London).

6. Penis and scrotum of a vanquished enemy warrior (Brazilian Cubeo tribe, nineteenth century).
7. Dolphin's testicles (Japan). Chicken testicles are preferred in Taiwan.

8. Pigeon dung and snail excrement (medieval England).
9. Animal hormone. To maintain Adolf Hitler's impaired virility, his personal physician Dr Theodore Morell injected the Führer with a compound containing hormones from crushed animal genitalia.
10. Chilli and hot spices: banned from Peruvian prison food because they are likely to arouse passions "unseemly in a single-sex environment".

Remains of the Day: 9 Celebrity Grave-Robberies

1. General Kitchener was sent to avenge the death of General Gordon, killed at Khartoum by the Mahdi's troops in 1885. As the Mahdi was already dead, however, Kitchener had to content himself with a spot of gratuitous desecration by blowing up the Mahdi's tomb at Omdurman and throwing his bones into the River Nile. Kitchener planned to keep the Mahdi's skull as an inkwell, but when Queen Victoria heard about Kitchener's trophy she ordered him to return it.
2. In March 1978 the body of Charlie Chaplin was stolen from its grave in Vevey, Switzerland, and held for a 600,000-franc ransom by a Pole, Roman Wardas, and a Bulgarian, Gantcho Ganev. The body-snatchers were finally arrested and Chaplin's remains were retrieved from a cornfield a few miles away. They said they needed the money to start a garage business.
3. In 1876 an American gang was apprehended while attempting to steal the remains of Abraham Lincoln. The plan was to hold it for ransom in return for the release of a convicted forger, Ben Boyd. Lincoln's coffin was subsequently embedded in steel and concrete.
4. In November 1888 the remains of the Spanish artist Francisco Goya were exhumed from the cemetery in Bordeaux, France, when he had lain for 60 years, so that they could be returned to his native country for re-burial. When the coffin was opened, however, Goya's head was missing. Its whereabouts are still unknown to this day.
5. The tomb of King William the Conqueror, situated at Caen

in Normandy, France, has been raided twice. In 1562 it was desecrated by Calvinists during the French Wars of Religion, when the king's bones were left scattered around the churchyard. In 1793 the tomb was robbed by French revolutionaries. All that remains today is a stone slab marking his last known resting place.

6. In 1790 the grave of the English poet John Milton, at St Giles, Cripplegate, London, was raided by souvenir-hunters. Gravedigger Elizabeth Grant was later found to be charging visitors sixpence a time for a viewing of Milton's teeth and part of his leg.
7. The tomb of King Richard I at Westminster Abbey in London had a hole in it, through which visitors could actually touch his skull. In 1776 a schoolboy stole the king's jawbone. It was kept as a family heirloom until its eventual return to the Abbey in 1906.
8. When King Henry VIII was interred in the royal vault at Windsor Castle, a workman removed one of his finger-bones and used it to make a knife handle.
9. The hands of the Argentinian president General Juan Peron were amputated in 1987 and were held for a £5 million ransom. Fortunately, Peron had no further use for them as he had already been dead for 13 years.

Safe Sex: History's 10 Most Original Contraceptive Devices

1. Pessaries made from crocodile dung (ancient Egypt) or from goats' bladders (ancient Rome).
2. Sixteen tadpoles fried in quicksilver, to be swallowed quickly by the woman immediately after intercourse (ancient China).
3. Spitting three times in the mouth of a frog, or eating bees immediately after intercourse (Dominican Church, thirteenth century).
4. Mashed pomegranate mixed with rock salt and alum (ancient Arabia).
5. Drinking raw onion juice (Europe, sixteenth century).
6. Ingesting cabbage immediately after intercourse (Europe, seventeenth century).
7. Jumping backwards seven or nine times immediately after sexual intercourse (Islamic, eighteenth century).
8. Condoms made from animal offal (Europe, eighteenth century). The original condoms were made by slaughterhouse workers from sausage skins. The modern variety did not become popular until Mr Goodyear vulcanized rubber in 1843. In Japan, men continued to wear sheaths made from leather or tortoiseshell.
9. Because he hated using condoms, Casanova placed his faith in a technique by which he inserted into his partner three gold balls, purchased from a Genoese goldsmith for about £50. He claimed that this method had served him well for 15 years. A more likely explanation for his run of luck is that he was infertile.

10. In some Third World countries the use of cola as a douche is one of the most common and successful forms of contraceptive. Scientifically controlled tests at Harvard Medical School proved that although regular cola has a 91 per cent success rate as spermicide, the diet variety is 100 per cent effective.

10 Causes of Death of British Monarchs since the Hanoverian Succession

1. George I: paralytic stroke, possibly brought on by indigestion after bingeing on melons while suffering the after-effects of seasickness, near Osnabrück, Germany.
2. George II: burst coronary blood vessel, aged 76, at Kensington Palace.
3. George III: senile decay, aged 81, at Windsor.
4. George IV: heart disease and alcoholic cirrhosis of the liver, aged 67, at Windsor.
5. William IV: arteriosclerosis and alcoholic cirrhosis of the liver, aged 71, at Windsor.
6. Victoria: cerebral haemorrhage, aged 81, at Osborne, Isle of Wight.
7. Edward VII: pneumonia and heart failure, aged 68, at Buckingham Palace.
8. George V: morphine injection in his jugular vein, aged 70, at Sandringham.
9. Edward VIII: throat cancer, aged 78, in Paris.
10. George VI: lung cancer, aged 56, at Sandringham.

10 All-Time most Disastrous Royal Marriages

1. Emperor Joseph II of Austria married his second wife, Josepha, in 1765. There were no children, nor was the wedding ever consummated. The empress suffered from a terrible skin complaint which made her so physically repulsive to the emperor that he had the balcony connecting his room to hers partitioned off. He explained, "If I could put the tip of my finger on the tiniest point of her body that is not covered with boils, I would try to have children".
2. Queen Isabel II of Spain was married to Francis, Duke of Cadiz in 1846. It was one of the most politically contentious arranged weddings of the nineteenth century, as every one of Europe's great powers had a vested interest in the Spanish queen's choice of husband. Isabel was finally pressured into marrying her first cousin, although it became necessary to get her very drunk beforehand because she had made it clear that she found him instantly repellent. Her intended, the homosexual Duke of Cadiz, was known as "Paquita", or, roughly translated, "Fanny". He was dwarfish, had a high-pitched voice, and was so effeminate that it was generally assumed that he would be incapable of consummating the marriage. On the day of the wedding, at the moment when they were pronounced man and wife, it was noted that they burst

into tears simultaneously. When Isabel was asked years later about her wedding night, she replied: "What can I say about a man who wore even more lace than I did?"

3. Philippe, Duke of Orleans, brother of Louis XIV of France, was married to his second wife, the Bavarian Princess Elizabeth, in 1760. Although the duke was one of history's most famous homosexuals, French court etiquette required that he had to have not only a wife, but also a full-time, fully paid official court mistress. It was a terrifying prospect for Philippe, as his new wife stood at least 18 inches taller than him. Most of the time the statuesque Princess Elizabeth was consigned to the edge of the bed, from where she regularly crashed to the floor. However, the couple were able, for dynastic purposes only, to produce three children. Philippe revealed afterwards that this had only been possible because he had on each occasion rubbed his penis with a holy medal for luck.
4. King Frederick I of Prussia was married to his third wife Sophia in 1708. The House of Hohenzollern, the royal family of Prussia and later of Germany, believed in a family ghost. According to legend a "white lady" would appear before the head of the household when it was time for him to die. One night the king's mad young wife charged head-first through the glass door to his bedroom and appeared before him in her white underclothes, splattered in blood. The old king took her for the family ghost, had a heart attack and died a few days later. The queen, a complete lunatic, had to be maintained at huge expense for another 20 years.
5. King Frederick II the Great of Prussia was married to Princess Elizabeth Christine of Brünswick-Beyern in

1733. The marriage had been arranged by his psychopathic father, King Frederick William I, who was determined to force his heir into an early marriage because he suspected that his son was gay. Prince Frederick was horrified when he found out whom he was expected to marry, as the Princess Elizabeth was conspicuously ugly and extremely smelly. The young Frederick announced that he would "rather marry the biggest whore in Berlin than this dumb princess", and threatened to commit suicide if the wedding went ahead. His father sent him a terse note to the effect that suicide wouldn't be necessary, because if he didn't do as he was told he would be executed anyway. The marriage was not consummated and the couple went their separate ways immediately after the wedding night.

6. King Ferdinand I of Naples married his wife Caroline in 1768. When Ferdinand was asked on the morning after his wedding night how he liked his new bride, he replied: "She sleeps like the dead and sweats like a pig."
7. Czar Peter III of Russia was married in 1745 to Catherine, a German princess who later became Empress Catherine the Great. Although Peter's new bride went on to become famous for her consistently hyperactive libido, Peter found his collection of toy soldiers a much bigger attraction than his wife. Every night he played with his wooden soldiers, miniature cannons and toy fortresses under the bedclothes, taking up the whole bed with war games and

imitating the sound of blazing canons, while his virgin wife lay motionless beside him. He also took to rearing hunting dogs in his bedroom, and Catherine found herself sharing their bed with 10 spaniels. Her complaints about the continual barking and the stench fell on deaf ears. Peter was, in fact, incapable of sexual intercourse, as he suffered from an abnormality of the foreskin. After years of sexless marriage, he finally consented to a simple corrective circumcision. The operation passed off without a hitch, but to test that everything was in full working order, a "trial run" was organized for him in the form of a poor widow named Madame Groot. Ten years after his wedding day, Peter finally fulfilled his obligation and slept with his wife. By this time, Catherine was already quite heavily pregnant by her lover Serge Saltykov, but she was able to convince her inexperienced husband that he was taking her virginity. This was the only time that Catherine and Peter had any sort of conjugal relationship, and she eventually had him strangled.

8. Emperor Ferdinand I of Austria was married to the 17-year-old Princess Maria Anna of Sardinia in 1831. Thanks to centuries of Habsburg royal inbreeding, Ferdinand was severely physically and mentally handicapped, and was both epileptic and encephalitic. His only recorded coherent remark on any subject was: "I am the Emperor, and I want dumplings." As nineteenth-century medical scientists mistakenly believed that epilepsy was hereditary, it was with some amazement that the rest of Europe received the news that the emperor's physicians had allowed him to marry and attempt to produce an heir. During the wedding night alone he had five epileptic fits. There were no children.

9. Leopold II, King of the Belgians, was married to Marie Henrietta, a Habsburg duchess, in 1853. Leopold was too ill to attend his own wedding, so the Austrian Emperor's brother, the Archduke Charles, stood proxy. Unfortunately for Marie Henrietta, Leopold was sufficiently recovered to attend the honeymoon. "If God hears my prayers," she told a friend after her wedding night, "I shall not go on living much longer." Although Queen Marie Henrietta's honeymoon had been such a personal nightmare, she did not pass on the benefit of her experience to either of her two daughters, neither explaining the facts of life to them nor preparing them for the loss of their virginity. When her eldest daughter Louise was betrothed at the age of 17 to the debauched Prince Philip of Saxe-Coburg, a man 14 years her senior and the owner of a huge private collection of pornography, Louise went to her wedding bed armed only with instructions to submit to her husband's wishes. The events that followed were such a shock to her that when he got up in the night to use the lavatory she fled and hid in one of the palace greenhouses. A palace sentry found her at dawn hiding behind some shrubbery, and led her back to bed.
10. The Russian czar Ivan the Terrible was consistently unlucky in love. The first three of his eight wives died young – the second just a fortnight after the wedding day, the third wife, Martha, before the marriage was even properly consummated. (Her death, according to one account, was brought on by Ivan's excessively enthusiastic foreplay.) The fourth wife, Anna, was married to Ivan by proxy, but "died of fright" at the prospect of meeting him. The fifth czarina, also named Anna, ran away, but was soon replaced with a sixth, Vasilissa. When she took a lover,

Ivan had the boyfriend impaled on a stake beneath her bedroom window and had her packed off to a convent. When he found out that his seventh wife, Maria, had lied to him about her virginity, he had her drowned the following day. His eighth and final wife, another Maria, survived him. He died playing chess.

10 Ethnic Funerals

1. The Berawan tribe of Borneo pot their recently deceased relatives in large earthenware jars. Then, as the corpse rots, they drain off the bodily fluids through a hole in the bottom of the jar and down a bamboo tube. Later, the dried remains are removed and interred in a smaller receptacle. The big jars are considered much too valuable to waste on a body because they can also be used in the kitchen to make rice wine.
2. In some cultures funerals are an opportunity to celebrate the life of the deceased, rather than to mourn death. The most extreme example of this is practised by the Nyakyusa people of Africa, where younger tribesmen and women often copulate at the graveside.
3. The Jivaro people of South America bury their women and children under their floorboards. The men are placed in a sitting position in a hut; corpse and hut are then set ablaze.
4. Whenever an Indonesian Mambai tribesman died, it was customary for the corpse to be seated in the family house, while relatives sat around and watched it rot for as long as they could tolerate the stench. In some parts of Indonesia, the widow of the deceased was obliged to rub fluids from his decomposing corpse onto her own body.
5. In Irian Jaya, Indonesia, deceased leaders and persons of great power were slowly smoked over a fire for several months, then hung from the eaves of their houses. From this position they could keep a permanent benevolent eye on the family home.
6. In Fiji it was once traditional for bereaved wives to be strangled or

buried alive with their deceased husbands. A similar custom prevailed in New Guinea: the widow would request strangulation so that she could accompany her husband on his trip to the next world.

7. Some Australian aborigine tribesmen traditionally lacerated themselves at funerals as a mark of respect for the dead, while widows would burn their breasts, arms and legs with firebrands. Now and then things got out of hand and the mourning would add to the death toll.
8. Masai tribesmen leave their deceased relatives out in the open for the hyenas to eat.
9. The Biami head-hunters of New Guinea never bury their dead. The corpses are left to rot on platforms in the open, and female mourners smear themselves with excrement from the bodies as a sign of respect for the deceased.
10. Funeral-goers in the US tend to be a lot more squeamish than their British counterparts. Americans seek to avoid what they consider to be the unnecessarily distressing aspects of death. This process has been taken to its logical conclusion in California, where it is increasingly common for the corpse itself to be excluded from the funeral.

10

All-Time Least Romantic Honeymoons

1. George Albert Crossman and his wife Ellen Sampson, a nurse, were married in January 1903. The morning after their wedding night they had an argument which resulted in Crossman killing his bride by smashing her skull in with a hammer. He hid the body in a tin box in an upstairs room at their home in Kensal Rise, London, where it remained for the next 15 months. For most of this time he was living with another woman, Edith Thompson. Eventually, a lodger named William Dell complained about the smell seeping into his digs. When the police closed in, Crossman slit his own throat with a razor.
2. In August 1994 Minnesota newly-wed Gregory McCloud broke his back while carrying his 20-stone bride Helen over the threshold. Doctors described the 10-stone groom's injuries as being consistent with those of someone who had been crushed by a car.
3. Cesare Borgia, the son of the early sixteenth-century Pope Alexander V, had his wedding night wrecked when a practical joker switched his regular medication for a bottle of laxative pills.
4. German-born Amy Weltz went to her wedding in Brisbane in September 1993 unaware of the Australian tradition of smearing wedding cake in your spouse's face. When her new husband Chas rubbed a slice of wedding cake in her face during the reception she

quickly responded by smashing a bottle over his head, killing him almost instantly.

5. On his wedding night the Victorian author and critic John Ruskin found the sight of his wife's pubic hair so shocking that he vowed never to sleep with her again.
6. King George IV nearly fainted when he first clapped eyes on his obese, ugly and sweaty wife Caroline of Brunswick-Wolfenbüttel the day before they were due to be married. On their wedding night he got himself blind drunk so that he could tolerate her "personal nastiness" long enough to sleep with her once – after which the couple went their separate ways, never once attempting to disguise their mutual loathing. When Napoleon Bonaparte died in 1821, a messenger rushed to inform the king: "Your Majesty, your greatest enemy is dead." George replied, "Is she, by God?"
7. A young Japanese couple, Sachi and Tomio Hidaki, were married in 1978, but they were so shy that they didn't get around to consummating their marriage for another 14 years. Sadly, the excitement of enjoying normal marital relations for the first time was too much for them and they both died of heart attacks.
8. On 11 June 1983, Moses Alexander, aged 93, was married to Frances Tompkins, aged 105, in New York. The next morning the newly-weds were removed, both of them dead, from their marital bed.
9. John Harvey Kellogg was the inventor of the cereal flake. On his wedding night with Ella Eaton he spent all evening writing *Plain Facts for Old and Young*, a 644-page treatise on the evils of sexual intercourse. This included a 97-page essay, "Secret Vice (Solitary Vice or Self-Abuse): its Symptoms and Results". Kellogg listed

39 tell-tale signs indicating that someone was masturbating, including sleeplessness, love of solitude, unnatural boldness, confusion of ideas, use of tobacco and acne. The marriage was never consummated.

10. According to royal biographer Andrew Morton, as a special honeymoon treat, Prince Charles allowed Diana to lie in the Balmoral heather while he read her passages from the works of Carl Jung and Laurens van der Post.

10 Failed Suicides

1. King Mithridates VI, who ruled in Asia Minor in the first century BC, deliberately took small doses of poison in the hope that he could build up enough resistance to survive a possible assassination by poisoning. He finally got an opportunity to test his theory in 63 BC. In an attempt to take his own life rather than fall into the hands of the invading Romans, he tried to poison himself. His body was so full of toxins that the poison had no effect at all, and the king had to order a slave to finish him off with his sword: hence the term "mithridate", meaning antidote.
2. In 1814 the defeated Napoleon abdicated and swallowed a phial of opium he had carried about him for two years. It left him alive but screaming with stomach cramps. He had planned to blow his brains out, but his valet had emptied the powder from the brace of pistols he always kept by his bed. Napoleon's attempted suicide was kept secret until 1933.
3. In March 1996 a Taiwanese couple, Huang Pin-jen, 27, and Chang Shu-mei, 26, of Kaohsiung, opted for a suicide pact when their parents refused to bless their recent marriage. The couple survived three suicide attempts, including driving their car off a cliff and a double hanging. Finally, after they survived a leap (from the top of a 12-storey building with multiple fractures (they landed on a roof), the in-laws promised to reconsider.
4. In 1994 financial problems caused seven members of a family from Council Bluffs, Iowa, aged between 10 and 71, to climb into the family car intent upon suicide. The driver engineered a deliberate crash, which injured the three occupants of the other car, but left him and his seven suicidal passengers completely unhurt.
5. In Manila in 1994, depressed Rogelio Aparicio, 46, pulled out a gun

on the steps of his local police station and fired two shots at his own head, missing completely both times.

6. Robert, Lord Clive "of India" (1725–74) twice failed to shoot himself in 1744. After the second attempt he declared: "It appears I am destined for something. I will live."
7. In 1993 *The Lancet* reported that an Englishman attempting suicide had been rescued after spending more than an hour inhaling automobile exhaust fumes. The medical journal explained that the man's bid to end his life had been thwarted by the relatively low carbon monoxide content of the exhaust, due to new European Community catalytic converter standards.
8. Empress Eugenie, wife of the French emperor Louis Napoleon III, attempted suicide by breaking off the heads of phosphorous matchsticks and then dissolving them in milk.
9. Classical composer Hugo Wolf (1860–1903) was institutionalized after attempting to drown himself.
10. In 1995 in Iola, Kansas, a 51-year-old prison inmate, Richard Barber, tried to kill himself by secretly hoarding enough dental floss to wrap around his neck and then leaping off a ledge. He succeeded only in badly cutting his neck. Barber was serving time for murdering a dentist.

8 WIDOWED FIRST LADIES

1. Anna Tuthill Symmes Harrison. In 1841, after she had borne his tenth child, her husband, William Henry Harrison, became the first US president to die in office, from pneumonia.
2. Margaret Mackall Smith Taylor, pipe-smoking wife of Zachary "Old Rough and Ready" Taylor. Her husband fell ill while taking part in a ceremony in blistering heat at the Washington Monument in July 1850, and died five days later.
3. Mary Todd Lincoln. Her husband, Abraham, was assassinated at Ford's Theatre, Washington on Good Friday, 14 April 1865 by an actor, John Wilkes Booth.
4. Lucretia Rudolph Garfield, wife of James Garfield, the second president shot in office. His assassin was an embittered lawyer who had been passed over for an important government job.
5. Ida Saxton McKinley, an epileptic who suffered a seizure during her husband William's second inaugural ball. President McKinley was standing in line at the Buffalo Pan-American Exposition in 1901 when he was shot twice by a Polish anarchist. He died eight days later.
6. Florence Harding, wife of the 29th US president, Warren G. Harding, who died of a heart attack in San Francisco in 1923 in his third year of office.
7. Anna Eleanor Roosevelt. Her husband, Franklin D. Roosevelt, died of a cerebral haemorrhage in April 1945 while at Warm Springs, Georgia.
8. Jacqueline Lee Bouvier Kennedy Onassis, wife of John Fitzgerald Kennedy, the youngest man elected president and the youngest to die in office. On 22 November 1963 he was shot dead as his motorcade passed through Dallas, Texas.

10 Ethnic Suicides

1. In some Eskimo cultures if an elderly or infirm person tells his family he is ready to die they oblige either by killing him on the spot or by abandoning him in the cold and letting nature take its course.
2. The ancient Britons practised euthanasia by throwing themselves off overhanging rocks. If they were too old to jump someone would give them a helpful shove.
3. In ancient Athens the local magistrate would keep a supply of poison handy for any elderly, depressed or terminally ill person who wanted to commit suicide. All you had to do was to ask.
4. In nineteenth-century Britain, failed suicides were hanged.
5. Scandinavians practised euthanasia by putting their old people in big earthenware jars and leaving them to die.
6. The Hottentot tribe of Africa used to give their senior citizens a huge farewell party before abandoning them to die in a hut in the wilderness.
7. In Ceos, in ancient Greece, it was obligatory for people over the age of 60 to commit suicide.
8. Old Ethiopians who wanted to die allowed themselves to be tied to wild bulls.
9. Congolese natives used to jump up and down on their elderly or terminally ill relatives until they had finished them off.
10. The suicide method most commonly used by Western men is carbon monoxide poisoning in cars. Among women the most common method is overdose. Britain's suicide rate has fallen by about one-fifth since 1960. One theory for the decrease is that less toxic North Sea gas has made sticking the head in the oven less attractive to potential

suicides. More American veterans of the Vietnamese war have died by suicide after their return than were actually killed in battle. The greatest mass suicide in history was committed by the seventeenth-century Orthodox cult, "the Old Believers", in protest against certain liturgical reforms in their religion. It was estimated that about 20,000 cult members burned themselves alive. Beachy Head, the East Sussex spot, is now the world's most popular suicide destination, overtaking San Francisco's Golden Gate Bridge. Beachy Head has been a lure for suicides since the seventh century, when St Wilfrid noted that people were jumping off the cliff in despair after a three-year drought.

10 USES FOR A DEAD PERSON

1. When D.H. Lawrence died, his lover Frieda had his ashes tipped into a concrete mixer and incorporated into her new mantelpiece.
2. In 1891 French surgeon Dr Varlot developed a method of preserving corpses by covering them with a thin layer of metal (in effect, he was electroplating the dead). Dr Varlot's technique involved making the body conductive by exposing it to silver nitrate, then immersing it in a galvanic bath of copper sulphate, producing a millimetre-thick coating of copper: "a brilliant red copper finish of exceptional strength and durability".
3. In ancient Rome, where human blood was prescribed as a cure for epilepsy, epileptics hung around near the exit gates of public arenas so that they could drink the blood of slain gladiators as they were dragged out.
4. In medieval Europe it was fashionable to eat and rub into the body bits of ancient Egyptian mummy for medicinal purposes. The body parts of decomposing Egyptians were widely touted as a cure for abscesses, fractures, contusions, paralysis, migraine, epilepsy, sore throats, nausea, disorders of the liver and spleen and internal ulcers. In the early part of this century some Arab tribes were still using mummies to prevent haemorrhaging. Mummy-trafficking became a lucrative and highly organized

business, starting in the Egyptian tombs and following a well-planned route to Europe. The bottom finally fell out of the mummy market in the late seventeenth century, when people found out that dealers were selling "fake" mummy made from recently murdered slaves.

5. Elizabethan medical text books recommended an alternative cure-all: powdered human skull dissolved in red wine.
6. British farmers were "processing" human corpses to create raw materials long before the Nazis thought of it. On 18 November 1822 the *Observer* reported that the Napoleonic battlefields of Leipzig, Austerlitz and Waterloo had been "swept alike of the bones of the hero and of the horse which he rode", and that hundreds of tons of the bones had been shipped to Yorkshire bone-grinders to make fertilizers for farmers. After the siege of Plevna in 1877 a local newspaper farming column casually reported that "30 tons of human bones, comprising 30,000 skeletons, have just landed at Bristol from Plevna".
7. German scientists involved in car safety research at the University of Heidelberg routinely use human crash dummies, including the corpses of children. Researchers in other countries have condemned the practice of smashing human cadavers into brick walls as abhorrent, but it hasn't prevented many from paying to see the results.
8. When the mistress of the nineteenth-century French novelist Eugène Sue died, she willed him her skin, with instructions that he should bind a book with it. He did.
9. The philosopher and reformer Jeremy Bentham lamented the wasteful business of burying dead people, and suggested that every man, if properly embalmed, could be used as his own commemorative bust or statue: he called them "auto-icons". The possibilities, Bentham posited, were endless: portraits of ancestors could be replaced with

actual heads, ". . . many generations being deposited on a few shelves or in a modest sized cupboard". When Bentham died he put his money where his mouth was by leaving instructions that his own body be dissected for the benefit of medical science, then embalmed, dressed in his own clothes, and placed in a glass case. His head had to be replaced with a wax version, however, because he had taken on an unfortunately grim expression during the embalming process. Bentham's physician, Dr Southwood Smith, kept the body until his own death in 1850, when it was presented to University College, London.

10. The size of a regulation soccer ball, roughly the same as a man's head, was arrived at by design: the first football ever used in England was the head of a dead Danish brigand.

7 Alleged Famous Sex Offenders

1. Pope Sixtus III (432–40 AD). Tried for raping a nun in 440, but acquitted as there were no eye-witnesses.
2. Geoffrey Chaucer. In 1380 the English poet stood accused of rape by Cecile Champaigne, a baker's daughter. Chaucer paid her off and the charges against him were dropped.
3. Ernest, Duke of Cumberland, younger brother of King George IV, denied raping and impregnating one of his younger sisters.
4. Lord Palmerston, the British prime minister, attempted to rape one of Queen Victoria's ladies-in-waiting while a house guest at Windsor.
5. Fatty Arbuckle, US actor. The silent-screen star's career ended sensationally in 1921 when he was tried for and subsequently acquitted of rape and manslaughter, after the death of a starlet in a San Francisco hotel room.
6. Errol Flynn. Charged with statutory rape of two under age fans in 1942, and acquitted.
7. Chuck Berry. In 1989 police found hidden cameras used to video-tape female customers using the toilets of his restaurant.

10
All-Time Most Stressful Funeral Experiences

1. In June 1988 a funeral wake was held in the Ukrainian village of Zabolotye for a man who had died of poisoning after drinking black market industrial spirit. Unwisely, the very same drink was served at the wake, resulting in 10 more deaths.
2. When William the Conqueror died in 1087 his marble coffin was found to be considerably too small for the late king. Two soldiers were required to stand on the body to squeeze it in, which they did with considerable enthusiasm, jumping up and down on it until they broke the king's back. The broken spine tore a hole in his stomach and caused it to explode with a loud bang: the stench was so overpowering that everyone present had to flee the building.
3. In 1994 a Croatian, Stanislav Kovac, was knocked down and killed by a car on a business trip to Botrop, Germany. Local undertaker Rudolf Dauer subsequently completed a 560-mile trip from Botrop to his funeral in Zagreb, only to have to explain to bereaved relatives that he had forgotten to bring the corpse with him.
4. When Josef Stalin died in March 1953 thousands of people were trampled to death in the struggle to see his embalmed corpse lying in the state mausoleum.
5. King George IV was very badly embalmed and his body became so swollen that it almost burst through the lead lining in his coffin. The danger of explosion was averted by drilling a hole in his cask to let out some of the putrid air.

6. In 1927, when George V's wife Queen Mary attended the funeral of her brother Adolphus, the funeral procession was interrupted by the sound of her brother's body exploding noisily inside his coffin.
7. The 10th Duke of Hamilton, Alexander Douglas, outbid the British Museum when he paid £11,000 for a magnificent ancient tomb which had originally been made for an Egyptian princess. Douglas housed it in a fabulous mausoleum at his ancestral home, Hamilton Palace, where it awaited his death. It wasn't until his death in 1852 that he was discovered to be much too tall to fit inside it. The only way they could get him in was by sawing his feet off.
8. In 1994 in Baton Rouge, US, a funeral service for a 25-year-old man was disrupted when his corpse caught fire inside the closed coffin, causing smoke to pour out of the cracks. An investigation found that the embalming fluids had spontaneously combusted.
9. In June the crematorium at the Meadow Lawn Memorial Park in San Antonio, Texas, was partially destroyed by fire. It broke out when staff began cremating a body that weighed over 300 pounds. The owner of the crematorium explained that the regular crematorium fire had raged out of control because of the fat in the body, which had caused an unusually high temperature.
10. Frederick Armstrong was convicted in 1993 of stabbing an 81-year-old preacher to death and cutting off his head before stunned onlookers, including a few police officers, at a funeral home in Baton Rouge, US. Armstrong's defence attorney appealed against the verdict on the grounds that their client was obviously insane at the time: "A rational man," reasoned Armstrong's lawyer, "does not decapitate a man in the presence of a police officer."

10 All-Time most Sexually Incontinent Monarchs

1. King Augustus II of Poland. The eighteenth-century Saxon-born monarch was known as Augustus the Strong for his exceptional physical size and strength, and for his unquestionable virility. Over a period of 50 years he fathered 365 bastards and one legitimate heir. The king maintained an enormous warren of concubines, some of whom enjoyed official status. He found it so difficult to keep track of his bastards that he "accidentally" had at least one incestuous relationship with a daughter. Some of his progeny went on to become famous in their own right, including George Sand and Maurice de Saxe.
2. King Ibn-Saud of Saudi Arabia. The first Saudi king allegedly slept with three different women every night from the age of 11 until his death in 1953, aged 72.
3. Czar Peter the Great of Russia was a huge man blessed with boundless energy, most of which he directed into carnal pursuits. His wife's ladies-in-waiting were usually his mainstay for sexual gratification. When the czar and his wife visited Prussia in 1717 they took with them about 400 ladies-in-waiting, who acted as cooks, chambermaids and washerwomen for the party. About one in every four women was carrying a very well-dressed child. When pressed about the whereabouts of the fathers, each replied with a smile, "the czar did me the honour". He was unapologetic that he was the father of countless bastards and even consid-

ered it his patriotic duty to boost Russia's population. He regularly took prostitutes as well, but always excused himself by explaining that he spent less money on his mistresses than any other monarch in Europe.

4. King Louis XV of France. Most of the Bourbon monarchs were known for their unnaturally large sexual appetites, but the sex life of Louis XV was the most astonishing of all. He began his reign known as "Louis the well-beloved", but soon even the relatively small amount of sexual congress that his subjects got to hear about (in fact only the tip of the iceberg) led to false accusations that he had to bathe daily in children's blood to renew his exhausted body. His personal brothel, the Parc du Cerfs, was probably the grandest ever to service the needs of one man. The king's procurers were expected to make available a constant supply of healthy girls aged between nine and 18 years. Only from the age of 14 were they obliged to be in "active service". When the girls reached the ripe old age of 19 they were either married off or dispatched to a convent. Over a period of 34 years, several thousand girls may have passed through the Parc du Cerfs; most of them had no idea at all who they were sleeping with.
5. King John V of Portugal. The inappropriately self-styled "Most Faithful King" successfully combined his twin passions for Catholicism and sex by sleeping with nuns. The king enjoyed open sexual relationships with members of the Odivelas Convent which resulted in the birth of at least three illegitimate sons, known as "the children of Palhava" after the palace in Lisbon where they grew up.
6. King Philip IV of Spain. Although evidently insane for most of his reign, he fathered about 30 bastards.

7. King Frederick William II of Prussia. Unlike the other main figures in his dynasty, who were known for military, rather than sexual prowess, the eighteenth-century nephew of Frederick the Great, Known as "the Fat", dedicated his entire adult life to maintaining his personal harem, siring hordes of bastards by countless mistresses. His most enduring mistress, Wilhelmina Encke, began her acquaintance with him as a 14-year-old prostitute. Miss Encke was eventually married to someone else, but she was to remain the king's mistress for another 20 years. She introduced the king to an Italian drug called Diavolini, which was taken to stimulate the libido. The king subsequently entered into bigamous marriages with Julia von Voss and Sophia Dönhoff. Bizarrely, these marriages received the approval of the Prussian court priests, who claimed they had found a precedent for such arrangements in Martin Luther's blessing of a similar marriage contracted by Prince Philip of Hesse.
8. King Charles I fathered about 20 illegitimate children, of whom 14 were acknowledged by him.
9. King Edward VII slept with about three different women a week for nearly half a century.
10. King William IV. Over a 10-year period Queen Victoria's uncle fathered 10 illegitimate children – five sons and five daughters – by the Irish actress Dorothea Jordan, plus another one by an unknown woman. His bastards were known as the little Fitzclarences.

15 Notable Suicides

1. Zeno (336–264 BC) was the Greek who founded Stoicism, a school of philosophy characterized by impassivity and an indifference to pleasure or pain. He hanged himself at the age of 98 after falling down and wrenching his finger.
2. Socrates, Greek philosopher (470–399 BC), took the poison hemlock when he was condemned to death by his enemies.
3. Cato the Younger (95–46 BC), statesman and general, threw himself on his sword at Utica in North Africa after losing the last battle to save Rome's democracy.
4. Cleopatra VII (69–30 BC), Greek Queen of Egypt, took her own life with the help of an asp after she was militarily defeated and then rejected by Octavius.
5. Nero (AD 37–68), Emperor of Rome, cheated a Roman lynch mob by slitting his own throat.
6. Giralomo Cardano, sixteenth-century Italian mathematician and astrologer, became hugely successful after drawing up horoscopes for the crowned heads of Europe, including English king Edward VI. Cardano once boasted that he could predict his own death, down to the very hour. When the hour arrived and Cardano found himself in embarrassingly robust good health he took his own life rather than be proved wrong.
7. Robert Clive (1725–74), the man chiefly responsible for establishing British rule in India, killed himself when he was criticized for mis-government.
8. Lord Castlereagh (1769–1822) was the British foreign

secretary after the Napoleonic Wars and one of the most famous statesmen in Europe. He became mentally ill and, although innocent of any wrongdoing, convinced himself that he was about to be blackmailed about a homosexual scandal. He retired to a closet at his home and stabbed himself in the throat with a penknife.

9. Sultan Abdul Aziz of Turkey was deposed by a palace coup. Five days after his arrest he asked for a pair of scissors to trim his beard, and slashed the main arteries in both wrists.
10. Vincent van Gogh (1853–90), Dutch painter, took his own life while painting *Wheat Field with Crows*. He was depressed at having sold only one painting during his lifetime.
11. Adolf Hitler (1889–1945), former Austrian painter, took his own life. He was depressed at having been defeated by the Allies.
12. Sylvia Plath (1932–63), famous American poet, killed herself at the age of 31 by putting her head in a gas oven.
13. Peg Entwistle, Hollywood actress, depressed at being unable to get a decent film role, threw herself off the 13th letter of the Beverley Hills HOLLYWOOD-LAND sign.
14. Albert Dekker, Hollywood actor, hanged himself in his home in 1968. He was discovered wearing women's silk underwear, with his farewell note written on his anatomy in red lipstick.
15. Christine Chubbock, US TV news reader, shot herself on live TV in the middle of presenting the news. It later became apparent that she had scripted her death so as not to disrupt the schedules.

10 Sporting Deaths

1. Emil Kijek of Massachusetts achieved his first-ever hole in one at the age of 79 at the Sun Valley Golf Club in December 1994. The shock killed him.
2. Frenchman Jean Potevan threw his golf bag into a lake in disgust in May 1995 after a poor game at a course near Lyon. Realizing that his car keys were still in the bag, Potevan dived in after it, but drowned when he became entangled in weeds. His golf partner Henri Levereau revealed that his last words were: "I'm going for the keys, but the clubs stay down there."
3. Jim Fixx, the American who started the jogging craze, died of a heart attack while jogging.
4. Golfer Whitney McIntosh from Edinburgh drowned in 1994 while attempting to retrieve his ball from a water hazard.
5. Colombian soccer player Andres Escobar was gunned down by an irate wine waiter for scoring the own goal which helped eliminate his country from the 1994 World Cup finals. Twenty-four hours later the BBC issued an apology, after their World Cup commentator Alan Hansen noted: "The Argentine defender wants shooting for a mistake like that."
6. Golf widow Diana Nagy filed a lawsuit in Charleston, West

Virginia, against the manufacturer of the golf cart from which her husband fell to his death during a tournament at the Berry Hills Country Club. She admitted that her husband had been drinking heavily but complained that the cart should have been fitted with seat belts and doors.

7. The only deceased jockey ever to win a steeplechase was the American Frank Hayes. In 1925 Hayes rode a 20–1 outsider, Sweet Kiss, to victory at Belmont Park. When the horse's owner and trainer went to congratulate him they found him still firmly attached to the saddle but slumped forward, very dead. Doctors confirmed that he was already an ex-jockey when he crossed the finishing line.
8. Japanese golfer Takeo Niyama was arrested in January 1995 after beating his playing partner to death with a five-iron. Niyama, 43, lost his temper when Aioa Sakajiri laughed at his slice into the Tokyo course lake. Niyama had only two previous convictions for golf course assaults, including a six-month prison sentence in 1994 for a links assault.
9. The only English cricketer convicted of manslaughter on the field of play was William Waterfall, at Derby Assizes in 1775.
10. The US sports personality Phil Rizzuto was broadcasting a live commentary on a baseball game when he was informed that Pope Paul VI had just died. "Well now," Rizutto told millions of baseball fans, "that kind of puts the damper on even a Yankee win."

10 Royal Deaths

1. Emperor Menelik II of Ethiopia became convinced that he could cure illness by eating pages from the Bible. In 1913 he had a stroke and died while attempting to eat the entire Book of Kings.
2. Robert the Bruce, King of Scotland, died of leprosy aged 55.
3. Charles VIII of France died when, entering a tennis court in 1498, he fatally cracked his head on a low wooden beam.
4. Queen Eleanor, wife of Edward I, died of blood poisoning after sucking the pus out of her husband's septic wound.
5. King James II of Scotland died in battle in 1460 when one of his own cannons exploded and a piece of shrapnel sliced the top of his head off.
6. George II's heir Frederick, the Prince of Wales, caught a chill and died suddenly a few weeks later on 20 March 1751, aged 44. It was said that his premature death was "aggravated by an old cricketing injury".
7. Queen Caroline, wife of George IV, died of constipation, in spite of being force-fed so much castor oil that it "would have turned the stomach of a horse".
8. King Alexander I of Greece died of blood poisoning after being bitten by his pet monkey.
9. Princess Sophie of Bavaria strayed too near an unguarded gas lamp at a charity bazaar in Paris and became a human

fireball, identifiable later only by her dental chart.

10. Archduke Franz Ferdinand, nephew of Emperor Franz Josef and heir to the Austrian throne, was insanely fussy about his appearance. In order to present a perfectly crease-free appearance at all times he was sewn into his suits; buttons were sewn on later for decoration only. When he was felled by an assassin's bullet in Sarajevo on 28 June 1914 he bled to death while his aides struggled to cut him out of his clothes.

Love Hurts

1. Following the Lorena and Wayne Bobbitt trial in 1993, US newspapers reported a spate of copycat assaults on male genitalia. A Toronto woman snipped off her husband's penis with a pair of scissors during a domestic squabble, while in Los Angeles a woman was charged with cutting off her husband's testicles during a marital tiff, although the couple were reunited a month later. In Jefferson a 35-year-old woman was charged with tearing off her ex-boyfriend's scrotum with her bare hands. In a domestic dispute in Hong Kong the wife of Wong Cheong-do, 43, sliced his penis off, but doctors were able to sew it back after Wong had dashed with it to the local hospital. During a brawl in Davenport, Iowa, Jaime Johnson bit off a testicle belonging to one James Liske. In May 1994 a 35-year-old man in Saginaw, Michegan, required 65 stitches to his penis after his girlfriend bit him. In Thailand penis amputation has become such a standard form of retribution by angry women that there is even a name for the crime: penicide. Thai police estimate that more than 100 penises have been removed by angry spouses since 1992.
2. The punishment for male adulterers in ancient Athens was to thrust a radish up the offender's fundament.
3. In September 1992 a homeless couple, Darryl Washington and Maria Ramos, were injured when a train hit them as they were copulating on a mattress on the tracks at a New York City subway station. The couple subsequently filed a lawsuit against the Transit Authority for "carelessness, recklessness and negligence". The couple's lawyer told

the *New York Daily News*: "Homeless people are allowed to have sex, too."

4. The *Bangkok Post* reported in October 1993 that charlatan physicians had performed at least 100 bogus penis-enlargement operations in Thailand. The operations involved injections of a mixture of olive oil, chalk, and various other substances. A Chiang Mai hospital official noted that he had even seen victims' penises containing portions of the Bangkok telephone directory.
5. The Ibo tribe of Nigeria excels in a variety of punishments for adulterous couples. One involves tying the couple up, putting a stake through them and carrying them off to a pool filled with crocodiles.
6. In January 1993 the wife of Zhang Jingui cut off her spouse's penis with a pair of scissors, acting on the advice of a Beijing fortune-teller on how to improve their marital relations. The fortune-teller had concluded that the problem in the relationship was Zhang's inadequate organ and that their only hope of saving the marriage was to remove it, so that a new one could grow.
7. In 1993 a 55-year-old man in Wooster, Ohio removed his own penis with a knife because he was dissatisfied with it. For apparently similar reasons a 23-year-old from Arcadia, Florida, removed his genitalia with an electric saw. In the same year 34-year-old prisoner Clifford Roby sliced off his manhood with a Bic razor in Keene, New Hampshire and flushed it down the toilet, explaining that it was "God's will".
8. The US Patents Office currently holds plans for five anti-rape devices. In 1977 Charles Barlow of Arizona patented a device designed to be inserted into a woman, containing three spears with harpoon-like barbs which would mutilate

the penis of a would-be rapist. Anna Pennystone's anti-rape device, patented in 1983, also involved a rigid sheath inserted into the woman: the inside of the device was coated with adhesive and contained chemicals which would burn the flesh. Others included Alston Levasque's "Penis Locking and Lacerating Vaginal Insert", and George Vogel's "Female Protective Device" – a large lump of metal with a solid spear in the centre. A creation devised by Joel Rumph and Lynda Warren promises to inject the assailant's penis with a fast-working sedative, rendering him unconscious. None of these or similar devices have ever got off the drawing board because of a basic design flaw: each device would have to be large enough to house an erect penis and would make wearing it uncomfortable, not to mention dangerous if any of them accidentally "went off".

9. According to medical research, every year up to 200 men break their penises during intercourse. The break is accompanied by a distinct cracking sound, and the patient requires 30–40 stitches, a splint and complete bed rest for six weeks.
10. "Lovestone" is a potion commercially available in the US and sold as an aphrodisiac. When an un-named 23-year-old man was reported to have died in New York in 1995 after swallowing some of it, the manufacturers were swift to point out that the potion was only ever intended to be rubbed into the genitalia.

The Earth Moved for Them: 10 Post-Mortem Experiences

1. The uncertainties of medieval medical science regularly produced premature burials – embarrassing for the undertaker and a pain in the arse for the victim – so it became normal to observe a three-day waiting period before the funeral took place, just to be on the safe side. It was not unknown for corpses to revive within three days but, as a Canterbury monk observed, recoveries after more than a week were a bit special. Anyone lucky enough to survive Extreme Unction, however, soon discovered that life for an ex-corpse wasn't all bier and skittles, and that there were certain strings attached. People who carried on living after receiving the final sacrament were not allowed to eat meat, to walk barefoot, or to have sex.
2. The sixteenth-century anatomist Vesalius was dissecting the body of a Spanish nobleman when the victim suddenly came round. The Don subsequently complained to the Inquisition, and Vesalius was sentenced to death.
3. A woman freshly hanged in 1724 in Musselburgh, Scotland, became the centre of a grisly dispute between her family and a bunch of enthusiastic anatomists. Her relatives were determined to give her a decent Christian burial; a party of medical students had other plans for the corpse, and were equally determined to get their hands on it. A bloody fight broke out over the body, which settled the argument by suddenly sitting up. The woman lived on for an-

other 30 years with a new nickname – "Half Hangit Maggie Dickson".

4. In London in 1752 a 19-year-old traitor sat up on the dissecting table only minutes after his execution. A quick-thinking surgeon responded by clubbing him to death with a mallet.
5. The guillotine held a morbid fascination for the French medical profession, who marvelled at the speed of execution and speculated whether or not the brain would continue to function after decapitation. Some people believed that the razor-sharp blade struck the victim so cleanly that they lost their heads before knowing anything about it, a theory fuelled by dozens of stories about victims who continued to protest after they had lost their heads. Eye-witnesses recorded that when the head of Jean Paul Marat's assassin Charlotte Corday was held up and slapped by the executioner, it showed unmistakable signs of anger. French doctors were allowed to carry out various macabre experiments on severed heads, including pinching the cheeks, sticking things up the nostrils, holding lighted candles near the eyeballs and even shouting the victim's name very loudly in the ear of the severed head. In 1880 the murderer Menesclou had the blood of a living dog pumped into his head. It was recorded that the head responded with a look of "shocked amazement". Much more recent research by Russian doctors actually gives some substance to these stories: they have found that if, for any reason, the brain is suddenly cut off from its oxygen supply, it uses an emergency system which keeps the victim conscious for several minutes.
6. The operatic composer Giacomo Mayerbeer, who lived with a constant fear of premature burial, arranged to have bells tied to his extremities so that any movement in his coffin would

make a noise. To date, however, Mayerbeer has continued to decompose quietly without any outward sign of life.

7. A nineteenth-century German missionary, Reverend Schwartz, was revived by the sound of his favourite hymn being played at his funeral. Mourners were amazed to hear the voice of the prematurely buried priest from within the coffin, joining in the singing.
8. During a freak August heatwave in Romania in 1994, which brought two consecutive days of temperatures in the 100s, mortuary attendants reported incidents of recently deceased persons exploding.
9. In 1994 a Brooklyn undertaker named Harold Plinburg was taken aback when the corpse he was embalming suddenly emerged from a deep coma and gave him a severe beating. "None of my friends in the funeral business has ever had anything like this happen," Harold observed later from his hospital bed.
10. A Spanish woman, Micaela Velasco, was being prepared for burial in her home town of Zamora in September 1996 when her lips suddenly moved. "We all had this sensation of total shock," said undertaker Francisco Heredero, "then we found she really was alive." She was subsequently examined by a doctor who declared her "as fit as a lady of her age can be". Mrs Velasco was 101 years old.

History's 50 most Famous Syphilitics

1. Pope Alexander VI.
2. Ludwig van Beethoven.
3. Emil von Behring.
4. Queen Cleopatra.
5. Christopher Columbus.
6. Al Capone.
7. King Charles VIII of France.
8. King Christian VII of Denmark.
9. Randolph Churchill.
10. Emperor Commodus.
11. Captain James Cook.
12. Frederick Delius.
13. Albrecht Dürer.
14. Queen Elizabeth I.
15. Desiderius Erasmus.
16. King François I of France.
17. King Frederick II the Great of Prussia.
18. King Frederick V of Denmark.
19. Paul Gauguin.
20. King George I.
21. Johann Wolfgang von Goethe.
22. Francisco Goya.
23. Heinrich Heine.
24. King Henry VIII.
25. King Herod of Judaea.
26. Adolf Hitler.
27. Czar Ivan the Terrible.
28. King James II.
29. Pope Julius II.
30. Julius Caesar.
31. John Keats.
32. Pope Leo X.
33. Ferdinand Magellan.
34. Emperor Marcus Aurelius.
35. Mary Queen of Scots.
36. Guy de Maupassant.
37. John Milton.
38. Edouard Monet.
39. Benito Mussolini.
40. Friedrich Nietzsche.
41. Czar Paul I.
42. Czar Peter the Great.
43. Cardinal Richelieu.
44. Marquis de Sade.
45. Franz Schubert.
46. Arthur Schopenhauer.
47. Jonathan Swift.
48. Emperor Tiberius.
49. Henri Toulouse-Lautrec.
50. Oscar Wilde.

10 It's Your Funeral: Reasons why you May Wish you'd Died in Ignorance

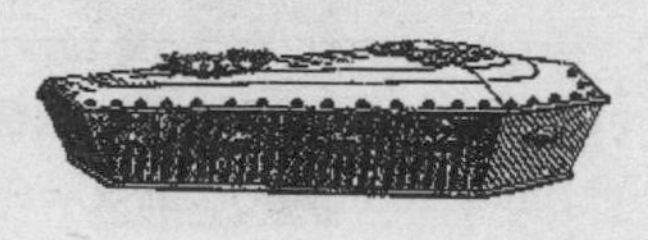

1. The most reliable methods of diagnosing death are: (a) pouring freezing water in your ear (should provoke an eye movement in the living); (b) poking something in your eye ("testing the corneal reflex"); (c) poking something down your throat ("testing the gag reflex"); (d) grinding knuckles into your sternum ("testing the pain reflex"); and (e) squeezing your testicles (see (d)). If none of these techniques elicits a response, you are probably deceased.
2. A corpse left above ground in warm weather will be reduced to a skeleton in about nine days. The rate of decay varies, because fat people decompose more quickly than thin people: the extra flab retains body heat, which speeds up the bacterial process that breaks down body tissue.
3. As your corpse dissolves, your skin colour may change from green to purple to black. Rigor mortis starts in your feet, then travels towards your head.
4. Your mouth will be either sutured or glued shut. Modern-day embalmers often superglue a corpse's lips together to prevent the mouth from falling open. A coating of softened wax is also applied to both the upper and lower lip to prevent cracking and flaking.
5. The cremated remains of most adults weigh between 2.5 and 8 pounds. The difference is to do with your bone size, not your live weight.
6. To avoid any possibility of insects entering your body via your nose, your nostrils are deep-packed with cotton wool saturated with a liquid insecticide.

7. The putrefaction process releases gases which can make the body swell to two or three times its normal size in 12 to 18 hours, and the pressure of accumulating methane can cause internal organs to be forced out of the lower orifices. Embalmers always check your abdominal and thoracic regions for any signs of distention or bloating caused by gaseous build-up, then relieve pressure by opening an anal vent.
8. Fingernails and hair do not continue to grow after death. This myth arose from the illusion created by skin retracting around the hair and nails, which makes them stand up and stick out more prominently.
9. Until the 1950s, coffins were hardly ever made to measure. If your body didn't fit your coffin the undertaker would normally break your ankles and bend your feet back.
10. Because of the high water content of the average human adult, cremation is tricky even with modern furnaces. Modern crematoria are equipped with electrically operated crushing machines designed to pulverize unburned bones. In some Third World countries, bodies are first wrapped in layers of animal fat to aid combustion. In India many families can't afford enough fuel to do the job properly, and half-burned bodies are often thrown into the river.

2
FOOD & DRINK

10

Historical Figures you would Least Want to Share a Dinner Table with

1. Mary Mallon, better known as "Typhoid Mary", was the world's most notorious disease carrier. In her capacity as a New York cook before World War I, she was personally responsible for 53 separate outbreaks of typhoid involving 1,300 people, resulting in at least three deaths. She often changed her name to avoid health officials. Mary spent the last 23 years of her life detained in quarantine in a state hospital, protesting her innocence to the end.
2. Emperor Vitellius perfected the Roman art of disgorging food by sticking a feather down his throat between courses, so that he could binge all over again. He was also known for bizarre culinary creations, the most famous of which was "Minerva's shield", an enormous dish assembled on a vast silver platter. Vitellius deployed the Roman navy to scour the four corners of the known world to find ingredients for his dish, which included peacock brains, pike livers and flamingo tongues. Vitellius eventually handed over the government of Rome to a freed slave so that he could concentrate on eating.
3. Anne Boleyn had a distressing habit, first observed during her coronation banquet, of vomiting between courses. She employed a lady-in-waiting, whose job it was to hold up a sheet when the queen looked likely to throw up.

4. The inquisitive Holy Roman Emperor Frederick II studied the human digestive system by butchering his dinner guests.
5. Benito Mussolini, who liked to break bread with his guests, was treated for giant roundworm infestation of his gut. The lifecycle of the roundworm begins with open-air defecation: the worm eggs develop in the soil and are usually carried into the mouth of the victims by contaminated fingers. According to Mussolini's doctor, exotic disease specialist Sir Aldo Castellani, the roundworm which eventually emerged from an unspecified orifice of Il Duce was enormous: "a real hypertrophic fascist ascaris".
6. Banquets in the Imperial court of the Chinese Emperor Shih Hu (AD 334–49) were a trial for his guests but particularly bad news for the ladies in his harem. The emperor would select a girl from his harem, have her beheaded, then have the torso cooked and served to his visitors. Shih Hu would then impress his guests by passing the uncooked head around on a platter for inspection before they ate it, to prove that he hadn't sacrificed his ugliest mistress.
7. The Russian Czar Peter the Great was said to have the table manners of "a baptized bear", and regularly trampled across the banquet table, treading on dishes and cutlery with his unwashed feet.
8. Dr Johnson had a voracious appetite coupled with unfortunate table manners. According to Samuel Boswell, he swilled, gorged and stuffed himself until sweat ran down his cheeks and the veins stood out on his forehead. Johnson's favourite dish, which he took at the Cheshire Cheese inn, off Fleet Street, was a vast pudding contain-

ing beefsteaks, kidneys, oysters, larks and mushrooms.

9. The Roman Emperor Heliogabalus liked to surprise his guests with the rarity of the dishes he provided. His menu included flamingo brains, camel brains, parrot heads and sows' udders. Occasionally, he would amuse himself by serving his guests exact replicas of the food he was eating, but made of wood, ivory, pottery or stone. The guests were not allowed to spoil his joke and were expected to continue eating as though nothing had happened.
10. All French kings from Louis XIV onwards were insatiable gluttons, identifiable by their "Bourbon Waddle" and their terrible table manners. Although the best known portraits of Louis XIV portray him as a dapper little man, he was seriously obese. Even in his late 80s his diet continued to astound onlookers and frighten his doctors; it even fuelled a rumour that the king was inhabited by a giant tapeworm. In his final years, however, he struggled to force food into his mouth because his doctors, while removing several of the king's bad teeth, had accidentally broken his upper jaw and smashed his palate. From that moment on Louis always had difficulty chewing, and bits of food often came down his nose. Louis XVI's father, the Dauphin Louis, was so enormously fat at the age of 16 that it is thought he may have suffered from some sort of glandular affliction. When the naturalist Buffon saw the king dining he said the spectacle reminded him of a large monkey at feeding time at the zoo. The reign of "Louis the Fat" was not to be: he died of tuberculosis, aged 34. His son was slightly taller than the average at that time, but was severely overweight. His official title was His Most Christian Majesty King Louis XVI, but to his courtiers he was generally known as "the fat pig". He got through so

much chocolate that he appointed an official courtier at Versailles known as Chocolatier to the King. In later years he grew alarmingly fat and lethargic and would often fall asleep in cabinet meetings. The epicurean King Louis XVIII was the most hideously obese of all the Bourbons. Swollen with gout and vastly overweight, he made desperate attempts to deflect attention from his size by overdressing in extravagant, diamond-studded clothes. In 1814, when the Prince Regent invested the new French king with the Order of the Garter, he discovered that Louis had an elephantine knee. "Prinny" remarked that it was like "fastening a sash round a young man's waist". Louis XVIII suffered from a variety of illnesses which transformed him in old age to a living skeleton. By 1823 he was in such a state of physical decay that when his valets were removing his sock one evening, they discovered a loose toe.

10 Surprise Fillings

1. An Italian stripper, Gina Lalapola, was found dead inside a cake she was supposed to leap from at a bachelor party in Cosenza in 1995. She had lain suffocated inside the sealed wooden cake for more than an hour before her death was discovered.
2. The Sex Pistols guitarist Steve Jones once admitted ejaculating into a French bread roll and feeding it to fellow band member Glen Matlock as elevenses.
3. In August 1983 *The Times* reported that a man living in West Germany had found a human finger in his bread finger-roll.
4. Ursula Beckley of Long Island, USA, filed a $3.6 million suit for damages against a local supermarket in 1989 after the three-egg omelette she was making suddenly yielded an unexpected protein bonus in the form of a healthy, six-inch black snake. Her lawyers said she was so deeply traumatized that it was unlikely that she would ever be able to look at another egg again.
5. In 1997 a couple from Carlisle, Craig Wilde and Simone Rooney, found a a six-inch bloodstained hypodermic needle inside a half-eaten loaf purchased from a local supermarket.
6. In March 1992 an American bread company was taken to court after a woman in Los Angeles found a used condom in a large loaf. In 1997 Dalvin Stokes sued the Morrison's cafeteria in Winter Haven, Florida, when he discovered a condom in his sweet potato pie. In 1997 Jeff Bolling of Hoover, Alabama,

sued a McDonald's drive-in restaurant after biting into what he thought was a pickle, but which was in fact a rolled-up condom.

7. In 1991 Wang Guang, owner of the White Temple Restaurant in China, built up a huge following for his heavily spiced Sichuan-style dumplings, which were stuffed with human flesh. Over a four-year period the exotic fillings were supplied by Guang's brother, who worked as an assistant in the local crematorium. The grim secret ingredient of the White Temple Restaurant's menu was exposed after police were tipped off by the parents of a young girl who had died in a road accident. When they came to cremate her body they discovered that parts of it were missing.
8. Although it is widely held that modern food is "less natural" than it used to be, meal-times in the nineteenth century were a far riskier activity. Business morals in the British catering industry were never lower than in Queen Victoria's day. Deliberate food adulteration, with no laws to prevent it, grew to horrific proportions as food suppliers cheerfully ripped off and poisoned their customers at the same time. Some of the most common frauds included the use of ground Derbyshire stone instead of flour, fake Gloucester cheese coloured with red lead, baked horse offal from the knacker's yard in coffee, lead chromate in mustard and even iron bars baked in loaves to make weight. People died after eating green blancmange coloured with copper sulphate and yellow Bath buns coloured with arsenic. Fifteen people died after buying sweets from a Bradford market which were found to be laced with white arsenic. Beer-drinking was possibly the most dangerous activity of all: in one year there were over 100 breweries convicted for contaminating beer with poisonous substances, including sulphuric acid, which was added to

"harden" new beer, and iron sulphate, added to give it a good frothy head.

9. A recipe once favoured by Indian princes involved the following: take one sparrow and stuff it inside a quail. Stuff the quail into a sand grouse, and the sand grouse inside a chicken. Stuff the chicken inside a peacock, the peacock inside a goat, and the goat inside a whole camel. Place the camel in a hole in the ground, then steam.
10. A unique case of food contamination occurred in October 1992, when nine people complained that Linda McCartney's famous brand of vegetarian pies had been spiked with steak and kidney.

The Dog's Bollocks and other Hors d'Oeuvres: 10 National Delicacies

1
Cena Molida – contains roasted mashed cockroaches (Belize).

2
Fried, roasted or boiled guinea pig (Ecuador).

3
Rat meat sausages (Philippines).

4
Crispy fried rat with lemon/boiled bamboo rat/desiccated petrified deer's penis (China).

5
Boodog – goat broiled inside a bag made from the carefully cut and tied goatskin. The goat is either barbecued over an open fire or cooked with a blow torch (Mongolia).

6
Fruit bat soup (Thailand).

7
Pickled puffin (North Wales, nineteenth century).

8
Larks' tongues (England, sixteenth century).

9
Lumbuli – small roast animal testicles (Ancient Rome).

10
Khachapuri – traditional cheese pie of the former Soviet Republic of Georgia. In 1995 authorities closed down a bakery whose speciality was khachapuri when it emerged that the pies were being baked in the Tbilisi morgue.

10 People who Choked to Death

1. Roman Emperor Claudius choked to death on the feather he used to tickle his gullet and induce vomiting at a banquet.
2. Pope Adrian IV, a.k.a. Nicholas Breakspear, the only English pope, choked to death when he accidentally swallowed a fly.
3. Janis Joplin, US rock singer, choked on her own vomit.
4. Sherwood Anderson, US novelist, choked to death on a toothpick.
5. Jimi Hendrix, rock guitarist, choked on his own vomit.
6. Mama Cass Elliott, obese lead singer with 1960s US band The Mamas and the Papas, choked on a chicken sandwich.
7. Jim Morrison, lead singer of The Doors, choked on his own vomit.
8. Roman Novarro, Hollywood actor, choked to death on a lead Art Deco dildo, which was thrust down his throat by two burglars. The dildo had been a present from Rudolph Valentino.
9. John "Bonzo" Bonham, Led Zeppelin drummer, choked on his own vomit.
10. Robert Pueblo, a 32-year-old from St Louis, US, stole a hot dog from a convenience store in October 1994 and crammed it in to his mouth before running off. Police found him lying dead a block away with a six-inch piece of hot dog lodged in his throat.

10 Acts of

CANNIBALISM

1. Fritz Haarmann, a meat dealer in post-World War I Germany, was the most prolific homicidal cannibal of all time. In the 1920s the "Vampire of Hanover" picked up young male refugees at the local railway station and lured them back to his ghetto apartment, where he sexually assaulted them and killed them by biting their throats. After selling their clothes and valuables he disposed of his victims by throwing the bones into the River Leine. He sold their flesh as horse meat in an open market to Hanover's mostly starving population, eating what he couldn't sell. His activities came to an end in 1924 when some young boys fishing in the river discovered several human skulls. It was estimated that Haarmann averaged two victims per week. He was only ever charged and convicted with the murders of 27 young men, aged between 13 and 20, although police estimates of the actual death toll ranged as high as 600 in one year alone. Haarmann was beheaded in Hanover prison on 15 April 1925.

2. Ed Gein, a middle-aged man from Wisconsin, was the inspiration for the film *Psycho* and later *Silence of the Lambs*. Gein was both cannibal and necrophiliac. He began by digging up female corpses to satisfy his perversions, then graduated to murder as a means of obtaining bodies. A police raid on Gein's well-stocked fridge in 1957 helped account for 15 bodies. There they discovered human skin bracelets, a human drumskin, two lips on a string, four noses in a cup and dozens of human organs. Gein later admitted that he enjoyed draping himself in the skin of his dead victims.
3. During the third crusade King Richard I dined on curried head of Saracen.
4. Lewis Keseberg was one of 87 men, women and children who set out in 1846 on a disastrous 2,000-mile trek west to California. The expedition, led by Illinois farmer George Donner and his family, was badly planned, without even enough food to survive the harsh winter. Of the original party only 47 made it to the end of the trail – and they had survived only by eating their dead companions. Some of the survivors struck a less than penitent attitude about their terrible dilemma. Lewis Keseberg cheerfully confessed to a preference for human liver, lights and brain soup, and paid this emotional tribute to George Donner's wife Tamsen: "She was the healthiest woman I ever ate." Years later Keseberg became wealthy by opening a steakhouse.
5. American grandfather Albert Fish went to the electric chair at Sing Sing prison in 1936 after killing and eating at least 15 children. Fish wrote to the mother of his final victim, a 10-year-old girl, six years after she had vanished: "Grace sat on my lap and kissed me. I made up my mind to eat her."
6. The Milwaukee cannibal Jeffrey Dahmer admitted at his

trial in February 1992 to killing and eating 17 people. Police raiding his apartment found severed heads in the fridge, skulls in his filing cabinet and body parts in a kettle. When they discovered a human heart in the deep freeze, Dahmer explained, "I was saving it for later."

7. In 1989 the American killer/cannibal John Weber was convicted for the murder of a 17-year-old Wisconsin schoolgirl. During his trial Weber confessed that he made a pâté from the girl's leg.
8. Uganda's former President Idi Amin was a member of the Kakua tribe, who believed that if you killed a man and then ate a part of him, he would not return to haunt the murderer. In 1973 Amin ordered the assassination of his foreign minister, Michael Ondanga. Before Ondanga's body was dumped in the river, in accordance with tribal ritual, Amin removed and ate part of his liver.
9. During China's cultural revolution in the sixties and seventies, members of Mao Tse-Tung's Red Guard ate the flesh of their enemies to prove to their venerable leader that they were fully class-conscious.
10. In 1977 US government officials staged a grand opening ceremony of their brand new Department of Agriculture staff canteen, attended by Robert Bergland, US agriculture secretary. Mr Bergland unveiled a brass plaque naming it the "Alfred Packer Memorial Dining Facility", after one of America's most famous nineteenth-century frontiersmen. A few months later the plaque was hurriedly removed when someone remembered what the late Mr Packer had been chiefly famous for: he was a cannibal, convicted of killing and eating five Colorado gold prospectors in the 1870s.

15 Strange Diets

1. The mad Victorian artist Richard Dadd (1817–86) lived for several years exclusively on hard boiled eggs and ale.
2. In order to demonstrate the cultural inferiority of the United States, ex-Pogues lead singer Shane MacGowan once ate a Beach Boys album.
3. During the Crimean War, British soldiers were supplied with a daily ration of caviar.
4. The Danish author Theodore Reinking was forced to eat his own words. In 1644 he wrote a book entitled *Dania ad exteros de perfidia Suecorum*, which lamented the diminished fortunes of the Danes after their defeat by their neighbours, Sweden, in the 30 Years' War. It offended the Swedes so much that he was imprisoned for life. After several years in gaol, he was given a straight choice: eat your book or lose your head. He chose the former.
5. In 1994 fisherman Renato Arganza spent several days at sea clinging to a buoy after his boat capsized off the Philippines. On being rescued he remarked that he had survived by eating his underpants.
6. Henry Ford I took to eating weed sandwiches every day when he heard that the American scientist George Washington Grover did the same.
7. During widespread food shortages in Cuba in 1994 the cat population fell by 400,000.

8. For the last 15 years of his life Howard Hughes lived almost exclusively on ice-cream. He generally stuck to the same flavour until every supplier in the district had run out.
9. Even at a time in Roman history known for culinary decadence, the Emperor Heliogabalus was renowned for his adventurous diet, dining on such delicacies as heads of parrot, flamingo brains, thrush brains and camel heels. At one feast he astonished his guests by serving up 600 flamingo heads, from which guests were expected to scoop out and eat the brains with gold spoons.
10. Ernest Hemingway wrote all his works on a diet of peanut butter sandwiches.
11. The ancient sailors of Spain and Portugal regularly ate rat meat on long voyages. The crew on board Magellan's ship during his ill-fated attempt to circumnavigate the world sold rats to each other for one ducal each.
12. In the eleventh century a group of monks called the Cathars, who weren't terribly keen on procreation, practised frequent and savage flagellation and sodomy (which they didn't consider sinful because it didn't involve the risk of procreation). The Cathars were vegetarians on the grounds that animals were produced by sexual intercourse, and that their flesh was therefore sinful. They did, however, eat plenty of fish in the mistaken belief that fish do not copulate.
13. The eccentric nineteenth-century geologist William Buckland dedicated a lifetime to perverse gastronomic experiences. Buckland dined on crocodile, hedgehog, mole, roast joint of bear and puppy. He bragged that he was prepared to eat anything that moved, but admitted that he wouldn't be tempted to revisit stewed

mole or bluebottle. His son Francis not only inherited but pushed to new limits his father's deviant eating habits. After serving mice on toast to his fellow students at Oxford, Buckland Jnr went on to form the Society for the Acclimatization of Animals in the United Kingdom, ostensibly to teach the British public how they could ease food shortages by eating new types of meat, but mainly an excuse for Buckland and his friends to get stuck into boiled and fried slices of porpoise head, boiled elephant's trunk, rhinoceros pie, grilled panther, garden snails, slug soup and earwigs. At a Society formal dinner in 1862 they sat down to Japanese trepang sea slug, steamed and boiled kangaroo, wild boar, roasted parrot and leperine.

14. Sylvester Graham (1794–1851), famous in the US as the inventor of the sugared brown crackers used in pie crust, spent a lifetime crusading against masturbation and poor eating habits. Graham believed that most health problems could be traced to sex or diet. His ideas were greatly influenced by an English clergyman, William Metcalfe, a pioneer of vegetarianism and a firm believer in the future of asparagus seed as a coffee substitute. Graham was mainly concerned with the carnal passions provoked by meat-eating. He rejected established medical science, theorizing that, as the stomach was the major organ of the body, it was also the seat of all illness. Hunger or sexual desire were a drain on the immune system and increased the chance of disease and death. Graham's cure for virtually every human sickness was simple: exercise, to help prevent "nocturnal emissions", a proper diet to facilitate regular bowel movements, and sexual moderation – more than once a month for married couples was definitely not adviz-

able. His "Lecture to Young Men", written in 1834, was the first of a whole genre of medical tracts on the subject of masturbation, which he preferred to call "self-pollution". According to Graham, a masturbator grows up "with a body full of disease, and with a mind in ruins, the loathsome habit still tyrannizing over him, with the inexorable imperiousness of a fiend of darkness." It was primarily the chief cause of teenage acne: ". . . ulcerous sores, in some cases, break out upon the head, breast, back and thighs; and these sometimes enlarge into permanent fistulas, of a cancerous character, and continue, perhaps for years, to discharge great quantities of foetid, loathsome pus; and not unfrequently terminate in death." By 1840 Graham's public career was over, but not without having first influenced a generation of diet experts, including John Harvey Kellogg, inventor of the cereal flake (see below).

15. Dr John Harvey Kellogg probably performed more enemas than any other human in history. Dr Kellogg ran the Battle Creek Sanitarium, Michigan, known as the Kellogg Sanitarium, or more popularly, "the San". Originally it had been the world headquarters of the Seventh Day Adventists, a fundamentalist sect who are also committed vegetarians. Kellogg, a fellow fundamentalist, was highly regarded in Adventist circles for his no-nonsense medical journalism and his unwavering belief in the power of roughage. Kellogg made an issue of personally abstaining from all sexual relations to prove that sex was an impairment to good health: "An erection," he announced, "is a flagstone on the grave." The chief target for Kellogg's invective were "chronic masturbators". He imposed a ban on masturbators from the

San, commenting: "A remedy which is almost always successful in small boys is circumcision . . . the operation should be performed by a surgeon without administering an anaesthetic, as the brief pain attending the operation will have a salutary effect upon the mind . . . in females, the author has found the application of pure carbolic acid to the clitoris an excellent means of allaying the abnormal excitement." Dr Kellogg designed a variety of house specialities for his patients, including Caramel Cereal Coffee, Bulgarian yogurt and meat substitutes called Protose and Nuttose, the latter a veal substitute made entirely from nuts. This was Kellogg's "nut period": he wrote a medical paper, "Nuts May Save the Race", and also invented peanut butter. After a couple of years at the San, Kellogg had a minor breakthrough when he came up with a mixture of oatmeal and corn meal, baked into biscuits which he named Granula – a controversial decision, given that the only other cereal in existence at the time was also called Granula. Once sued, Kellogg wisely renamed his product Granola. After more trial and error Kellogg discovered a new treat for his patients called Granose, the first flaked wheat cereal. He set up production in a barn behind the Sanitarium, and soon the whole town of Battle Creek was gripped with "flake fever", as cereal and health food manufacturers appeared overnight. Dr Kellogg's brother William had no interest in crusading against masturbation or bad eating habits, but he had some business sense and saw a potential fortune in the Doctor's invention. William eventually persuaded his eccentric brother that they should form a new company to manufacture corn flakes, and the Battle Creek Toasted Corn Flake Company was born in 1906. Dr Kellogg was the majority shareholder, but he distributed part of his stock among the Sanitarium doctors. Later, while Dr Kellogg was away, William quietly bought up a majority of the shares and became the new president.

Death Row Cuisine: 10 Last Meals of Condemned Murderers

1. Ham, eggs, toast and coffee – Gee Jon, Chinese murderer, the first man ever to be executed in the US by lethal gas, at Carson City State Prison in 1924.
2. Hot fudge sundae – Barbara Graham, convicted murderess, executed by lethal gas at San Quintin, California in 1955.
3. Steak and chips followed by peach cobbler dessert – murderer Charlie Brooks, executed by lethal injection at Huntsville, Texas in 1982.
4. Cheez Doodles and Coca-Cola – mass poisoner Margaret Velma Barfield, a 52-year-old grandmother and the first woman ever to die by lethal injection, at Central Prison, North Carolina in 1962.
5. Hamburger, eggs and potatoes – British killer Gary Gilmore, who became the first man to be executed in the US for a decade when he was shot dead by firing squad at Utah in 1977.
6. Candy – Chauncey Millard, the youngest person ever executed in the state of Utah, killed by firing squad in 1869. The 18-year-old was still eating his candy bar as he was being shot.
7. A large steak salad, potato pancakes and two helpings of

jelly and ice-cream – Isadore Zimmerman, a 26-year-old convicted of murder, at Sing Sing in 1939. Zimmerman continued to protest his innocence to the last mouthful.

8. A US one dollar bill sandwich – Joshua Jones, hanged at Pennsylvania in 1839 for the murder of his wife. While Jones was awaiting execution he sold his body to the prison doctors for 10 dollars. He spent nine dollars on delicacies to vary his prison diet. Realizing that he still had a dollar bill in his pocket just minutes before his execution, he requested two slices of bread.
9. Two hamburgers and Coca-Cola – Leslie B. Gireth, executed at San Quintin in 1943 for the murder of his girlfriend. Gireth had lost his nerve halfway through a suicide pact with her. His last meal was an exact replica of what she had eaten just before he shot her.
10. Garlic bread, shrimp, French fries, ice-cream, strawberries and whipped cream – the heroic last order of Perry Smith and Richard Eugene Hickock, before their double hanging at Kansas in 1965. Sadly, they completely lost their appetites at the last minute and the meal was untouched.

15 Historical Dipsomaniacs

1. According to the Old Testament, Noah was the first person ever to get pissed.
2. Socrates could drink and think you under the table at the same time. His ability to hold his liquor was legendary and he would continue to philosophize when everyone else at the symposium had long since passed out or gone home.
3. Pope Benedict XII (1334–42) was such a hardened drinker that the expression "drunk as a pope" became popular in his lifetime.
4. Alexander the Great, the bisexual Macedonian king who ruled an empire stretching from Greece to India, was as famed for his marathon drinking sessions as for his military conquests. During one of Alexander's drinking contests 35 men died. During another bout he killed one of his closest friends with a spear. Alexander finally dropped dead during a drinking contest at the age of 32. His best friend Hephaestion expired while drinking half a gallon of wine for breakfast.
5. Selim II (Sultan of the Ottomans 1566–74) also known as "Selim the Sot". It was said that he could drink a bottle of Cyprus wine without drawing breath. When he ran out of his favourite tipple, one of his advisers suggested he capture Cyprus to replenish his stocks, and the mad Turkish leader eagerly agreed. His men massacred 30,000 Cypriot Christians in the process. Their leader, Bragadino, was flayed alive and his skin was stuffed with straw and displayed to the Turkish troops.
6. Ludwig van Beethoven died of hepatic cirrhosis of the liver as a result of alcoholism at the age of 57. Before he expired he cheerily

announced: "Wine is both necessary and good for me."

7. William Pitt the Younger (British prime minister 1783–1801, 1804–6) was advised as a young man to drink a bottle of port a day for his health. He took it to heart: at his peak he drank six bottles of port, two bottles of madeira and one and a half bottles of claret daily. He often made speeches in the House of Commons when drunk, and before making important interventions in debates was seen to duck behind the Speaker's Chair to throw up. He finally drank himself to death aged 46.
8. Lord Melbourne (British prime minister 1834, 1835–41), an habitually heavy drinker, was in a drunken stupor throughout Victoria's coronation. His excuse was that he was suffering from violent constipation, and tried to get through the ceremony by swigging large quantities of brandy and laudanum. He didn't attend Cabinet meetings after that for a week.
9. Franklin Pierce (US pres. 1853–7) spent most of his presidency drunk, a situation which gave rise to the popular slogan "Franklin Pierce, the hero of many a well-fought bottle". He was arrested while in office for running over an old woman with his horse, but the case was dropped for insufficient evidence. Pierce's wife Jane lost her mind after the death of a child; Pierce drank himself to death in 1869.
10. Andrew Johnson (US pres. 1865–9) was famously drunk when he was sworn in as vice-president to Lincoln and made a rambling, incoherent speech. When the US chief of justice was sent to inform him that Lincoln was dead and that he was now president they found him in a filthy, dishevelled state, apparently trying to shake off a terrible hangover. Johnson took the oath of office as required but then fell asleep. He had to be dressed and taken to the White House, where he was bathed and shaved before any visitors were allowed to see him.
11. Ulysses S. Grant (US pres. 1869–77) was prone to bouts of

drunkenness which were invariably passed off as migraine attacks. When Grant and President Andrew Johnson made a whistlestop tour of the US, Grant was generally too drunk even to put in an appearance. In 1854 he resigned his army commission rather than face a court-martial for public drunkenness.

12. Herbert Henry Asquith (British prime minister 1908–16) drank wine copiously, although he was incapable of holding his drink. In 1911 he was to be seen slumped on the front bench in the Commons during an important debate, too drunk to speak. During the war years his alcoholism became much worse, prompting the singer George Robey to mock:

    Mr Asquith says in a manner sweet and calm
    Another little drink won't do us any harm.

13. The Yorkshire CC slow left-arm bowler Bobby Peel (1857–1941) played cricket for England from 1884 to 1896. He was regularly inebriated during matches, and often drank himself into a state tactfully referred to in the cricketing bible *Wisden* as "unwell" or "gone away". During one county game the Yorkshire captain Lord Hawke was forced to suspend Peel from the side for "running the wrong way" and "bowling at the pavilion in the belief that it was the batsman". Peel was eventually sacked from the Yorkshire team after his performance against Warwickshire at Edgbaston in May 1896. During an unbeaten partnership of 367 with Lord Hawke, Peel relieved himself on the pitch.
14. During World War II Sir Winston Churchill had marathon drinking sessions which usually started late in the morning and went on until the early hours of the following day. Churchill once tried to persuade Saudi Arabia's strict Moslem King Ibn Saud that he drank alcohol because it was part of his religion. Although it wrecked his health, he liked to brag: "I have taken more out of alcohol than

alcohol has taken out of me". Eventually the pressure of work, old age, the excessive use of sedatives and prolonged alcohol abuse rendered Churchill, during his second term as prime minister, almost completely incapable of carrying out any of his duties. His continuing decline after 1951, exacerbated by a series of strokes, was so alarming that in spite of a cover-up by his inner cabinet circle even the British press began to comment on it. By 1953, although he was still prime minister, Churchill was virtually completely inactive.

15. Elliott Ness, head of the US Prohibition Bureau, died an alcoholic.

Cereal Killers: 10 Victims of Food Rage

1. Restaurant-owner Gilbert Menezes was sent for trial in 1996 for killing his wife's lover, then serving his liver, with fried onions, to his customers.
2. In 1984 Argentinian police found a set of bones belonging to a missing 19-year-old, Carlos Sanchez, beneath a Buenos Aires building which was used by devil worshippers. The occupants explained that they had phoned an order for pizzas, but after an interminable delay had decided to eat the delivery boy instead.
3. In Perth, Australia, in 1994 street trader Igor Roskny was beaten to death by an irate customer because he put mustard on his tuna sandwich by mistake. The murderer complained that he had clearly requested mayonnaise.
4. In January 1995 an Egyptian threw his wife from the window of their second-floor Cairo flat because his dinner wasn't ready. She suffered concussion and multiple fractures: he was freed on £8 bail.
5. Thirty-one-year-old Brenda Hunter, of Zion, Illinois, shot her brother in 1994 because she disliked the type of cheese he was putting on their chilli dinner.
6. Heinrich Gembach of Munich choked his wife to death in 1995 by force-feeding her wheat cereal. He told police that this was what she had given him for breakfast every morning for the last 10 years.
7. In 1994 Peter Weiller, a German film-goer, was beaten to death by ushers in a Bonn cinema because he had brought his own popcorn.
8. The Sioux Chief "Rain In The Face" admitted that after the Battle of Little Big Horn in 1877 he had cut out General

Custer's heart and eaten it. He said he didn't much like the taste of human flesh – he just wanted revenge.

9. A Frenchman, Noël Carriou, killed both of his wives because they were poor cooks. Fifty-four-year-old Carriou was sentenced to eight years in jail in 1978 after killing his second wife for cooking him an overdone roast. Seventeen years earlier he had broken his first wife's neck after she served him an undercooked meal. In passing sentence the judge sympathized with Carriou: good cooking, he agreed, was an important part of married life.
10. Ghengis Khan killed his own brother in an argument over a fish.

12 Gross World Eating Records

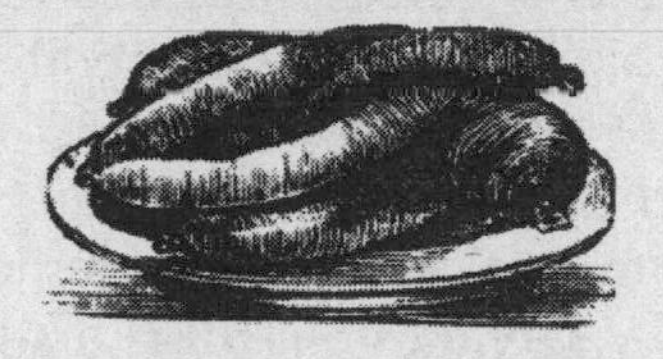

3.5 lb of cooked dog in 18 minutes, 10 seconds.

12 slugs in 2 minutes.

28 cockroaches in 4 minutes.

60 earthworms in 3 minutes, 6 seconds.

100 live maggots in 5 minutes, 29 seconds.

2 lb of eels in 32 seconds.

144 snails in 11 minutes, 30 seconds.

12 bananas, including skins, in 4 minutes, 14 seconds.

13 raw eggs in 1.4 seconds.

4 lb 13 oz of baked beans in 10 minutes.

24 hot dogs in 12 minutes.

15 bowls of noodle soup, 100 pieces of sushi, 5 plates of wheat noodles, 5 plates of beef with rice, and 5 plates of curry and rice in 2 hours (Japanese national eating championships).

8 Last Suppers

1. Buddha died at the age of 80 in 483 BC, from an intestinal haemorrhage after eating a hot curry.
2. Elvis Presley: fried banana and peanut butter sandwich.
3. King John: dropped dead at an abbey in East Anglia, England, after gorging on peaches and cider.
4. Robert Maxwell: drowned on two bananas.
5. King George I: melon.
6. King Henry I: "a surfeit of lampreys".
7. British prime minister William Pitt the Younger: his last words were "I think I could eat one of Bellamy's veal pies."
8. Robert Greene, sixteenth-century English dramatist and pamphleteer: expired after consuming too much Rhenish wine and pickled herring at an author's gala luncheon.

12 All-Time most Disgusting Beverages

1. China produces a Three Penis Wine, made from one part seal penis, one part dog penis and four parts deer penis. It is allegedly an effective cure for anaemia, shingles and memory loss, and is described as "robust and nutritious".
2. In Ireland, sheep droppings boiled in milk was once highly valued as a cure for whooping cough.
3. The world's most exclusive coffee is made from a bean which has already passed through the colon of a cat. The droppings of the Palm Civet wild-cat, indigenous to the coffee plantations of Sumatra, are sold at market at £150,000 per tonne. In Japan the coffee sells at about £10 a cup.
4. The Yukon Territory in Canada is home of the Sour Toe Cocktail, which has just two ingredients: an amputated human toe and the spirit of your choice. The only rule which has to be observed is: "You can drink it fast, you can drink it slow, but the lips have got to touch the toe." The original artefact was discovered in a disused log cabin by a Mountie in 1973. It was used in the drink more than 700 times before it was accidentally swallowed by a miner.
5. The Cocoma tribe of Peru drank the ground-up bones of deceased relatives in a fermented brew, believing that it was much better for the dead to be inside a warm friend than outside in the cold earth.
6. The Tomb of Mausalus, one of the Seven Wonders of the World (later destroyed by earthquake), was built in 353 BC in Turkey by Queen Artemisia on the death of her husband King Mausalus. The original idea was that the king's body was to be placed in the tomb, but there was a

last minute change of plan: the queen had him cremated, then poured his ashes into a goblet of wine and drank the lot.

7. Professional chariot-racers in ancient Rome were encouraged to promote muscle growth by drinking a solution of dried boar's dung.
8. Vietnam has a popular liqueur made from lizard's blood.
9. In 1885 the US army captain and part-time naturalist John Bourke published a detailed description of the Urine Dance of the Zuni Indians of New Mexico. Bourke related that he had been privileged to witness this unique ritual, which involved a dozen Zuni Indians dancing around a fire while drinking several gallons of fresh urine. When the Zuni invited their guests to participate in a similar ceremony, this time involving human excrement, Bourke made his excuses and left.
10. Elizabethan women drank the urine of puppy dogs to improve their complexions.
11. After the Great Fire of London in 1666 the remains of the deceased former dean of St Paul's, John Colet, were rescued from the cathedral where they had lain since 1509. Although they were protected by a lead-lined coffin, it was noted by two gentlemen named Wyld and Greatorex that the dean's remains had become cooked in his preserving fluids and had dissolved into a soupy substance like "boiled brawne". They tasted the "soup" and declared that it tasted "only of iron".
12. When Admiral Horatio Nelson died his corpse was placed in a keg of brandy to preserve it on the long journey home. Although the admiral's body had been bubbling away in it for days, this didn't prevent his crew from drinking the spirits later.

10 Food-Related Deaths

1. In 1994 15 mourners at a funeral in Nsukka, Nigeria, died after eating the deceased's dog.
2. Australian Paul Cook, a 21-year-old storeman from Sydney, died after injecting himself with his favourite spread, Vegemite.
3. An Italian, Paolo Ginelli, visited a Naples hotel restaurant in November 1994 to celebrate his 80th birthday. On his way out the restaurant sign fell on his head and killed him.
4. Abraham Lincoln's mother died after the family dairy cow ate poisonous mushrooms and Mrs Lincoln drank the milk.
5. In 1994 a 47-year-old Japanese bakery worker, depressed because his wifc had lcft him, took his own lifc by throwing himsclf into a giant dough mixer.
6. King Henry I died from eating "a surfeit of lampreys".
7. The English statesman Francis Bacon died inventing frozen food. He was travelling in a coach one winter's day when it occurred to him that food could be preserved by freezing. While stuffing a dead chicken with snow he caught a chill and died.
8. Tadoa Tanak was chef to the Japanese Emperor Hirohito – a high-profile job, as the meals he prepared were always subject to the royal ritual of food-tasting, a practice which continued until 1989. Every scrap of Hirohito's food had to be pre-tested under laboratory conditions for signs of contamination, then served on sterilized plates. Even the royal faeces and urine had to be chemically analyzed afterwards

for signs of food poisoning. Although Tadoa Tanak's record was unblemished, as Hirohito never once had cause for complaint about his food, when the emperor died his chef was also obliged to commit ritual suicide.

9. Reinaldo de Carvalho, the "Fat King" of Rio de Janeiro's Carnaval celebration, died trying to lose weight. He entered a weight-loss clinic in Rio and dropped dead after losing 66 pounds in 30 days.
10. The biggest ever case of food poisoning from one source occurred in Spain in 1981. Ramon and Elias Ferroro and 36 other company executives were jailed for a combined total of 6,000 years when 600 of their customers died after eating contaminated cooking oil.

16 Human Recipes

1. In 1996 the victim of a Japanese gangland killing, Shoichi Murakami, was hacked to pieces and his hands were used to make soup of the day in a local restaurant. The starter was eaten by about 50 satisfied customers.
2. Captain James Cook, the great explorer who had often written in his journals about the cannibalistic habits of some of the natives he encountered, almost certainly ended his days as an Hawaiian buffet. All that Cook's men could find of him after he had been killed and dismembered at a heianu ceremony at Keala Kekua were a few bones and some salted flesh.
3. The nineteenth-century English eccentric William Buckland claimed he ate the heart of King Louis XIV of France. The organ was allegedly plundered from the Sun King's grave during the French Revolution and had found its way onto Buckland's plate via his friend, the Archbishop of York.
4. When Thomas Hardy died it was the author's wish that his final resting place should be his birthplace, Stinsford, in Dorset, England. The authorities knew better, however, and decreed that he was far too important for such a humble interment. A compromise was reached: it was decided that most of his remains should be sent to Westminster Abbey, but Hardy's heart could be buried at Stinsford. On the morning of the ceremony, his sister inadvertently left the open casket on the kitchen table and the heart was consumed by the Hardy family cat.
5. Father Jean de Brébeuf, a seventeenth-century French

missionary, found himself on the receiving end of one of the worst documented torture sessions. In 1649 the Jesuit priest was part of an expedition to Canada when he and his fellow missionaries were captured by Iroquois Indians. Brébeuf tried to convert his captors to Christianity, who reciprocated by chopping his hands off then stabbing him repeatedly with various iron instruments. Red-hot tomahawks were suspended around his neck, and a belt made of bark and smeared with pitch was tied around his torso and set alight. The tortures were carefully designed to produce a slow, agonizing death, but the still-conscious priest continued to irritate them with a constant flow of preaching. They pushed burning sticks from the fire down his throat, but when even this failed to silence him they cut off his lips and doused him with boiling water. Finally the Indians cut chunks of flesh from his legs, arms and torso, roasted them in a fire and ate them. Finally they amputated his feet and scalped him for good measure.

6. The anthropologist Paul Shankman compiled a world-wide cannibal cook book which listed the various ways mankind has chosen to cook and eat his fellow man. Methods include pot-boiling, spit-roasting, steam-baking, cookery on pre-heated rocks, in earth ovens, smoking, drying, powdering, stuffing, and eating raw. The most creative preparation in Shankman's list involved burying the body, then exhuming it and eating the putrefying flesh. The maggots were scraped off, wrapped in banana leaves, and eaten separately as an entrée.
7. During World War II the British Minister of Food, Lord Woolton, carefully considered but finally rejected a plan, proposed by his government scientists, to feed the country on black pudding made from surplus human blood bank donations.
8. According to West Indian cannibals, the tastiest bits on a

human being are the palms of the hands, the fingers and toes.

9. One of Chicago's master butchers of the 1870s was the German Adolph Luetgert, whose driving ambition was to make his sausages famous all over America. Luetgert's dream came true. He was arrested and tried for the murder of his wife Louisa after disposing of her corpse by melting it down in one of his giant vats and incorporating her into his sausage production line. For two years after Leutgert's conviction, sausage sales in Illinois and neighbouring Michigan hit an all-time low.
10. The Carib Indians of the West Indies, first discovered by Columbus, were the cannibal world connoisseurs of human haute cuisine: the local word for "Carib" is Caniba – the origin of the word cannibal. Caribs even bred children expressly for consumption: the children were first castrated because it improved the flavour. Columbus noted that the Caribs considered the French to be the very tastiest people in the world.
11. Marco Polo noted in 1275 that the people of south east Asia ate the feet of their captives, believing them to be "the most savoury food in the world".
12. When the Chinese famine of 206 BC killed half the population, human flesh became the staple diet. The taste for human flesh lingered on long after famine conditions had gone. During the T'ang dynasty in the late ninth and tenth centuries cannibalism was permitted by law and human flesh was sold publicly in street markets.
13. The Tartar hordes who swept over Europe in 1242 were particularly fond of girls. Appetizing young maidens were issued as rations to army officers, while common soldiers chewed on the tough flesh of older women. Breast meat was regarded as the finest titbit, and was reserved for the prince's table.

14. Fijian cannibals acquired a taste for hanks of salted human flesh – a variation on European or American chewing tobacco.
15. The African Bafum-Bansaw tribe forced boiling palm oil into their victims' bowels to give them an enema before they ate them, because it made the flesh more tender.
16. Sir John Franklin, one of the greatest British Arctic explorers, was probably eaten by Eskimos or by his fellow adventurers. Sir John and his crew of 129 men perished attempting to walk across 1,000 miles of the Arctic Circle in 1847 after abandoning their ice-bound ship.

3
ART & ENTERTAINMENT

10 HARD ACTS TO FOLLOW:

Part 1

1. A Beatles tribute band lost its "George Harrison" in a tragic motorway accident in 1994. The "quiet Beatle", a.k.a. 27-year-old Duncan Bloomfield, fell out of the back of their transit van on the M40 while the band was travelling home from a performance in London. The rest of the band had driven for 25 miles before they realized that he was missing.
2. Richard Versalle, a tenor performing at the New York Metropolitan Opera House in 1995, suffered a heart attack and fell 10 feet from a ladder to the stage after singing the line "You can only live so long" from the opening scene of *The Makropulos Case*, a Czech opera about an elixir that confers eternal youth.
3. The US actor Lorne Greene had one of his nipples bitten off by an alligator while filming *Lorne Greene's Wild Kingdom*.
4. The American stage actress Annie von Behein was performing in the Coliseum Theatre, Cincinatti in a drama called *Si Slocum*, in which her real-life fiancé, Frank Frayne, was required to shoot an apple from her head, *à la* William Tell, with a musket. Frayne shot too low and the 2,300-strong audience watched as the musket ball hit her neatly in the forehead. She died 15 minutes later, while the audience was still leaving the theatre.

5. In October 1980 an Indian mystic, Khadeshwari Baba, attempted to show off his incredible powers of meditation by remaining buried alive in a 10-foot-deep pit for 10 days. In a carnival-like atmosphere a crowd of over 1,000 people, including several local officials from the town of Gorakhpur, watched as Baba was ceremoniously lowered into the pit, and the hole was filled in behind him. Ten days later the pit was re-opened. From the accompanying stench it was estimated that the mystic had been dead for at least a week.
6. American Orville Stamm entertained by lying on his back with a piano on his chest. While Orville sang, the pianist would bounce up and down on his thighs, belting out the tune to "Ireland Must Be Heaven Because Mother Comes From There".
7. One of the world's most tasteless stage acts was performed by the American Tommy Minnock, a variety artiste who plied his trade in Trenton, New Jersey, in the 1890s. Minnock allowed himself to be literally crucified onstage: while the nails were being driven into his hands and feet, he would entertain his audience by signing "After The Ball Is Over".
8. The 1954 film epic about Genghis Khan, *The Conqueror* starring John Wayne, was made near a nuclear testing site in Utah's Escalante Desert within months of an atomic explosion. Over the next few decades cancer claimed the lives of several members of the cast and crew, including Wayne, the director/producer Dick Powell, co-stars Susan Hayward and Agnes Moorehead, and Pedro Armendariz, who shot himself when he learned he had the disease.
9. In 1994 health department workers fumigated the San Francisco Opera House after musicians complained of

itching, caused by scabies. It was reported that some violinists had to drop their bows during performances in order to scratch.

10. The original cast of the US sitcom *Friends* had a seventh regular member, Marcel the monkey. He was fired because of his habit of vomiting live worms on the set.

10 Worst Ever Published Poets in the English Language

1. William McGonagall (1825–1902).

Oh! It was a most gorgeous sight to be seen
Numerous foreign magnates were there for to see the Queen
And to the vast multitude there of women and men
Her Majesty for two hours showed herself to them.

The Queen's Diamond Jubilee Celebration

McGonagall was the son of an Irish handloom worker who settled in Scotland. After a brief and spectacularly unsuccessful career as an actor he discovered his muse in 1877, and dedicated the next 24 years of his life to composing unredeemingly diabolical verse. His choice of subject matter was eclectic, including three memorable poems about the Tay Bridge, and was often inspired by contemporary news events. His output was immense, but these few lines from his *Calamity in London: Family of Ten Burned To Death* are a good example of his deftness of touch:

Oh, Heaven! it was a frightful and pitiful sight to see
Seven bodies charred of the Jarvis family;
And Mrs Jarvis was found with her child, and both carbonized,
And as the searchers gazed thereon they were surprised.

And these were lying beside the fragments of the bed,
And in a chair the tenth victim was sitting dead;
Oh Horrible! Oh Horrible! What a sight to behold
The charred and burnt bodies of young and old.

Some of McGonagall's most famous work was dedicated to Queen Victoria. Whenever she visited the Highlands he would present himself at Balmoral in the hope of giving his sovereign a recitation of his latest work, although he never succeeded in getting beyond the palace gates. McGonagall carried a visiting card which ran:

W.M. McGONAGALL
LYRIC INDITER AND RECITER
POETRY PROMPTLY EXECUTED

One day he received a letter from the queen's private secretary, Lord Biddulph, which stated somewhat evasively that Her Majesty was unable to accept a couple of his verses. This near-brush with royalty went to McGonagall's head and he quickly restyled himself "Poet To Her Majesty". His regular public readings in public houses were occasionally halted by the police on the grounds that his poems constituted a breach of the peace, because the locals invariably pelted him with rotten vegetables. He became an intellectual cult figure in Dundee, however, where his readings drew large audiences; he was serenely unaffected by the laughter which invariably greeted his performances. His works include the seminal collection *Poetic Gems*, which was followed by the imaginatively titled *More Poetic Gems*, *Still More Poetic Gems*, *Yet More Poetic Gems*, *Further Poetic Gems*, *Yet Further Poetic Gems*, and *Last Poetic Gems*. Although he once managed to sell just one copy of his poems to a policeman on the gates of Balmoral for twopence, the only work that he was ever commissioned to write, and for which he received two guineas, was a rhyme to promote Sunlight Soap:

You can use it with great pleasure and ease
Without wasting any elbow grease
And when washing the most dirty clothes
The sweat won't be dripping from your nose.

His subsequent attempts to sell more poems, including his sole attempt to crack the American market, were fruitless, but his contribution to poetry is legendary.

2. King Ludwig I of Bavaria (1786–1868).

The second man to hold the title King of Bavaria was Ludwig I, a member of the extraordinary Wittelsbach family. Ludwig was a stone-deaf, shabby, parsimonious little man, generally considered by his subjects to have been harmlessly eccentric, unlike his famous castle-building grandson Ludwig II, who was certifiably insane. King Ludwig I was often seen wandering the streets of Munich late at night wearing tatty, threadbare clothes, and carrying a battered umbrella – considered a great novelty at the time. Ludwig's main eccentricity, however, was his life-long hobby of composing outstandingly bad poetry. His muse compelled him to put every experience he ever had, no matter how trivial or mundane, down in rhyme. When the king was badly gored by a bull in Italy, he sat down and recorded the event in rhyming couplets. The string of actresses he bedded throughout his reign were all to discover in time that the only gifts likely to be lavished on them by the tight-fisted old king were reams of execrable poetry. King Ludwig achieved international notoriety by falling in love with a courtesan who was young enough to be his grand-daughter. Ludwig was 61 years old when he met the 28-year-old Irish dancer Lola Montez: it was said that Lola introduced herself to the old king by ripping open her bodice and revealing her breasts. She was acknowledged as one of the most beautiful women in Europe; her elderly lover, on the other hand, had few teeth, less hair and a disproportionately large head which drew attention to a large cyst in the middle of his forehead.

Ludwig pledged his undying love to Lola in verse, but was eventually forced by pressure from the mob and his ministers to banish her from the country. Some suggested she went willingly to escape another burst of the king's poetry. Ludwig never met his Lola again, but continued to harass her with his love poems by mail. He outlived her and died in 1868, aged 82.

3. Alfred Austin (1835–1913).

> Along the wires the electric message came
> He is no better, he is much the same
>
> *Ode to the dying Alfred, Lord Tennyson*

The post of Poet Laureate has been held by three greats – Dryden, Wordsworth and Tennyson, many mediocre poets, and several truly bad poets. Of these, Alfred Austin was the most outstandingly awful. His appointment was blatantly political: Austin was a conservative leader-writer in *The Standard*, and had twice failed to be elected to parliament when he was awarded the laureateship by the prime minister, Lord Salisbury, who saw no reason why a failed politician with no track record as a poet shouldn't make a success of it, provided he supported the right party. Although only 5 feet tall, Austin had an enormous ego, and was sublimely ignorant of his limitations. He took his appointment as proof that he was officially England's greatest writer – in his own words, "at the head of English literature". Austin quickly became known for his overblown epics and his insensitive right-wing politics. His efforts were universally panned by the critics, who followed his career with mounting disbelief, but Austin struck a pose of lofty indifference, continuing to churn out rubbish and to lecture his public about the literary deficiencies of his contemporaries and the idiocy of all critics. One of his best known works, a poem about the infamous South African expedition, the Jameson Raid, in which Austin acclaimed Jameson as a hero, was greeted with hilarity and derision and even earned a rebuke from Queen Victoria. He interpreted the scathing attacks on his efforts as jealousy. When someone dared point out to him that his poems were full of basic grammatical errors, Austin replied: "I dare not alter these things. They come to me from above."

4. Joseph Gwyer (1835–90?).

I wish you Alfred now a good night;
You gives your mother great delight;
Don't you wake and ask for baa
Or you'll offend your dad-dad-a.
Lines to his son, Alfred Gwyer

Queen Victoria had the misfortune of reigning during the careers of two talentless but patriotic poets who bombarded her with excruciating verse. Joseph Gwyer, the "McGonagall of Penge", pursued his two great obsessions, poetry and potato-growing, with roughly equal enthusiasm, and often combined the two with devastating effect, as evidenced by his 1875 volume *Sketches Of The Life of Joseph Gwyer (Potato Salesman) With His Poems (Commended By Royalty)*. It should be pointed out that at no time in his career was any of his work ever commended by anyone, least of all royalty. A good example of his genre was his *Love and Matrimony*, in which he points out that the most important thing a man should look for in his choice of bride is an ability to cook and roast POTATOES (in Gwyer's work, the word "potatoes" was always underlined or written in capitals). The importance of Gwyer's potato theme in contemporary literature often baffled his public but was not lost on all of his critics. A *Punch* review of his work *The Alexandra Palace, Muswell Hill, Destroyed By Fire* began: "We consider this work no small potatoes."

5. Julia A. Moore (1847–1920).

> Lord Byron was an Englishman
> A poet, I believe
> His first works in old England
> Was poorly received
> Perhaps it was Lord Byron's fault
> And perhaps it was not.
>
> *Byron: A Critical Survey*

> My parents moved to Algoma
> Near twenty-five years ago
> And bought one hundred acres of land
> That's a good sized farm, you know.

Generally acknowledged as the worst ever American poet, Moore had her first collection of poems, *The Sweet Singer of Michegan Salutes The Public*, published in 1876. It was immediately hailed as a millstone in contemporary literature. Mark Twain later claimed it had kept him laughing for the best part of 20 years. She had "the touch that makes an intentionally humorous episode pathetic," Twain noted, "and an intentionally pathetic one funny". Twain even satirized her in *Huckleberry Finn* as Emmeline Grangerford. Moore had a penchant in her poetry for violent death, which caused one critic to note that she rattled off poems "like a Gatling Gun". The public recitations of Mrs Moore were greeted with laughter wherever she went, but like McGonagall and Austin, she was impervious to embarrassment or even the most stinging of personal attacks. It is likely that she would have enjoyed even this assessment in *The Oxford Book of American Light Verse*: "A writer so transcendentally, surpassingly, superlatively bad that she belongs in a special genre in which normal rules and habits of judgment were magically suspended."

6. J. Gordon Coogler (1865–1901).

> Alas for the South, her books have grown fewer –
> She never was much given to literature.
>
> *Purely Original Verse*

The prolific American had a sign in the window of his Columbia printing works which read: "Poems Written While You Wait". Coogler began writing romantic poetry when he was a schoolboy: his first effort was for a girl called Minnie, who apparently went to Galveston and died in a hurricane. Coogler was a complete innocent, who would occasionally preface his works with selections of the critical comments he encountered, even though they were always less than flattering. During his all-too-brief career (he died aged 36) he had a number of fan clubs across America. "An excellent young man," noted the obituary-writer of the *Charleston News and Courier*, "who unfortunately thought he was a poet."

7. Amanda McKittrick Ros (1860–1939).

Dear Lord, the day of Eggs is here . . .
Ode To Easter

The reclusive Ulster poet developed a unique style which she attributed to never having read any books. "My chief object of writing is and always has been to write if possible a strain all of my own," she explained, adding: "This I find is why my writings are so much sought after." Her works were, in fact, much sought after by connoisseurs of bad taste, for she had her very own appreciation society, established at Oxford in 1907. From her home in remote Co. Antrim she issued a torrent of mostly abusive verse on her pet subjects, which were lawyers, fashion, the Kaiser, the abandonment of moral standards, clerics and, inevitably, critics. Her two best known collections of verse were *Poems of Puncture* (1932) and *Fumes of Formation* (1933), although she was equally famous for a series of remarkably bad and quite unfathomable romantic novels. For the most part she was blissfully impervious to criticism, although she never quite recovered from what she took to be the massive snub of failing to secure a nomination for the Nobel Prize for Literature in 1930.

8. The Reverend Cornelius Whur (1782–1853).

Thou pretty little jumping thing
What e'er may be thine age
Thou hast a most amusing swing
While turning in thy cage.
On A Domesticated Squirrel

Whur was a Wesleyan minister from East Anglia, easily the worst of many of nineteenth-century clerics with too much time on their hands. He put to verse his pious observations and homespun pontifications, mostly on the state of the Victorian poor. Whur's fame rests on two epic collections, *Village Musings on Moral and Religious Subjects* (1837) and *Gratitude's Offering – Being Original Productions On A Variety of Subjects* (1845). Nicholas T. Parsons, author of *The Joy of Bad Verse*, says of this literary phenomenon: "The Reverend Whur possesses the most pedestrian mind in English Literature, yet he makes compulsive reading."

9. Henry James Pye (1745–1813).

> Of Pig-economy exalt the praise
> Oh flatter Sheep and Bullocks in thy lays

As shown in the lines above, Henry Pye, a bookish and slightly eccentric country squire, specialized in rambling verse on largely agricultural themes, including his extraordinary treatise *The Effect Of Music On Animals.* Unfortunately, he was also Poet Laureate, a job handed to him by William Pitt, evidently as compensation for losing his parliamentary seat. Blessed as he was with a dull prose style and a complete lack of imagination, Pye's position was made even more difficult by the fact that his patron, George III, went completely and irretrievably mad during his laureateship. Pye did his best to avoid the subject – a tricky business at the best of times, but especially when it came to the obligatory annual King's Birthday Ode.

10. Carmen Sylva (1843–1916).

Rumania's first Queen Consort, Elisabeth of Wied, a member of a minor German royal house, once entertained the Austrian Emperor Franz Josef, who went away declaring that she was "stark mad". There was certainly plenty of evidence of mental instability in her family. Elisabeth had been a difficult child, and to teach her self-control her parents took her daily to the local insane asylum to observe the inmates. Elisabeth's mother also fancied herself as a psychic healer, and the young princess spent her childhood surrounded by variously afflicted people hoping for a miracle cure. Unable to have children, Queen Elisabeth dedicated her life to the arts. Composing under the pen name of Carmen Sylva, she established a reputation as a Rumanian McGonagall. Anyone unfortunate enough to pass her rooms was likely to be dragged in and treated to an impromptu reading. Over the years Elisabeth acquired a cult lesbian following, and surrounded herself with a posse of young females who would lie at her feet looking suitably impressed while the queen, with her long white hair and flowing robes, recited poetry, worked on immense paintings or played the piano. In 1890 Elisabeth visited Queen Victoria at Balmoral, and the assembled British royal family were obliged to sit through one of Elisabeth's readings. Queen Victoria's diary entry noted: "Many of course could not understand, but all were interested." Elisabeth's husband, King Carol, kept a safe distance from his spouse, especially when he suspected that she had been visited by her muse. He hired a lady-in-waiting and part-time private detective named Olga, whose job it was to follow the queen and make sure she didn't do anything too embarrassing. When she wasn't reciting poetry to her disciples while consuming piles of ham sandwiches, Elisabeth would stand, at all hours of the day and night, on the terrace of her house overlooking the entrance to Constanze harbour, calling out poetic blessings to departing ships on a megaphone. She would often fling open a window of the palace and pose semi-naked in her flimsy nightgown, while a crowd gathered below. When her nephew, the Crown Prince Ferdinand, was struck down with typhoid fever in May 1897, she passed news of his condition to the larger-than-usual gathering beneath her bedroom window by miming medical bulletins to them as though it was a game of charades. Elisabeth's habit of hanging around on her balcony in her nightie finally caught up with her in 1916 when she died of pneumonia.

In the Best Possible Bad Taste: 10 Conceptual Artists

1. Piero Manzoni, sixties artist, and the sole exponent of the art movement *arte povera*, exhibited cans of his own excrement.
2. Louise Bourgeois, a Canadian feminist sculptor, creates work featuring severed penises and huge testicles hanging singly or in pairs or bunches, including a piece called *No Exit* – a stairway with two huge testicles restricting egress at the bottom – and *Untitled (with Foot)*, in which a baby is crushed by a large testicle.
3. Richard Gibson, another Canadian sculptor, exhibits pieces made from freeze-dried human body parts, especially limbs and ears. In 1986 he advertized for spare parts and was arrested and fined £500 for conduct likely to cause a breach of the peace.
4. In 1994 Ronnie Nicolino, the Californian artist, created a two-mile-long sand sculpture comprising 21,000 size 34C breasts. Nicolino said that his next project would be a giant chain of bras long enough to span the Grand Canyon, adding that in no way was he obsessed with breasts.
5. Gilbert and George, British artists, once staged a show at the South London Art Gallery which they called *Naked Shit Pictures*, comprising 16 large glossy photos of themselves surrounded by a series of "defecation motifs", including turd circles and turd sculptures. One critic described the work as "almost biblical".
6. Catherine Gregory's 1992 exhibition in Scarborough featured a dismembered dog chopped into nine pieces and suspended from the ceiling, 63 squashed mice mounted in plastic and the butchered remains of three rabbits. She said she did it for the animal rights movement.

7. In 1996 Brigid Berlin, the New York artist, showcased her collection of 500 photographs of penises, contributed by people she had met in the early 1970s during her acquaintance with Andy Warhol. She was previously known for her Tit Prints drawings, using her nipples instead of brushes, and her Penis Pillows – photo-montages of penises, photocopied and stuffed into plastic pillows.
8. Newton Harrison, an American artist, staged an art exhibition called *Portable Fish Farm* in 1971 at the Hayward Gallery, London, at which he planned to publicly electrocute 60 live catfish. The electrocution was finally called off after a protest by Spike Milligan, who made his feelings known by lobbing a brick through the Hayward Gallery window.
9. Hermann Nitsch, an Austrian artist, staged a performance in 1975 using a dead bull and 11 deceased sheep.
10. In 1994 Christian Lemmerz, a Danish artist, put six dead pigs in a glass case so that visitors to the Ezbjerg gallery could watch them change colour from a piggy-pink to black, via various shades of blue and grey. The artist declared it a triumph for people who value reality in art. The gallery owners said it was a triumph over their old ventilation system, which was unable to cope with the stench.

10 Literary Substance Abusers

1. Charles Baudelaire: hashish and opium addiction.
2. W. B. Yeats: mescaline addiction (hallucinogenic drug derived from a Mexican cactus).
3. Charles Dickens: opium user.
4. Samuel Coleridge: opium addiction.
5. Thomas de Quincy: opium and laudanum addiction. The author of *Confessions of an Opium Eater* degenerated into a physical wreck thanks to his habit of quaffing up to 8,000 drops of opium and six or seven glasses of laudanum a day.
6. Arthur Conan Doyle: cocaine user. His most famous character, Sherlock Holmes, used it in *The Sign of Four.*
7. Robert Louis Stevenson: cocaine addiction. *Dr Jekyll and Mr Hyde* was entirely cocaine-induced. He took vast quantities while working on it, which was why he was able to write and twice revise the 60,000-word manuscript in six days.
8. Tennessee Williams: amphetamine addiction.
9. Dante Gabriel Rossetti: morphine addiction and alcoholism.
10. Edgar Allan Poe: laudanum addiction and alcoholism.

10 Classical Composers who didn't make it to their 40th Birthday

1. Vincenzo Bellini (died at 33).
2. Georges Bizet (36).
3. Frédéric Chopin (39).
4. George Gershwin (38).
5. Felix Mendelssohn (38).
6. Wolfgang Amadeus Mozart (35).
7. Giovanni Battista Pergolesi (26).
8. Henry Purcell (36).
9. Franz Schubert (31).
10. Carl Maria von Weber (39).

10 Authors of Banned Works

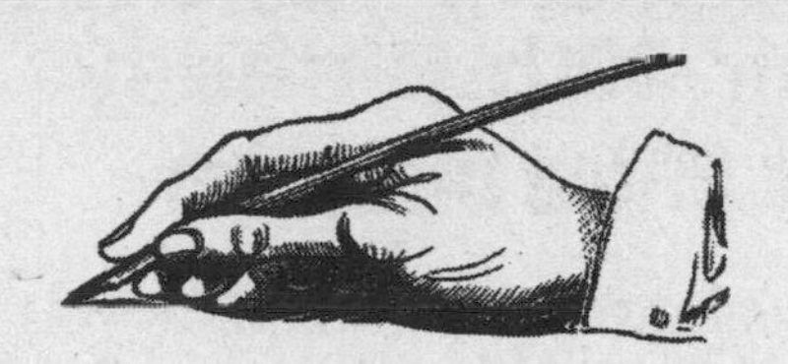

1. William Shakespeare. *King Lear* was banned in Britain from 1788 to 1820. The government considered the play inappropriate in the light of King George III's insanity.
2. Marquis de Sade. *Justine and Juliette* was banned by the French government in 1791 for obscenity.
3. Casanova. His *Mémoires* were banned by the Pope (1834) and by Mussolini (1935) on moral grounds.
4. Thomas Hardy. *Tess of the D'Urbervilles* (1891) and *Jude the Obscure* (1896) were banned from all British libraries.
5. Rudyard Kipling. In 1898 *A Fleet in Being* was banned by the British government on the grounds of national security.
6. Charles Darwin. From 1926 to 1937, *On the Origin of Species* was banned in the Soviet Union, Yugoslavia, Greece and the US state of Tennessee on moral grounds.
7. Arthur Conan Doyle. In 1929 the Soviet Union banned *The Adventures of Sherlock Holmes* on the grounds of "occultism".
8. D.H. Lawrence. *The Rainbow* and *Lady Chatterley's Lover* were banned in Brtain in 1929 for obscenity.
9. Adolf Hitler. *Mein Kampf* was banned in Czeckoslovakia (1932) and Palestine (1937) for being politically subversive.
10. Ernest Hemingway. In 1939 *A Farewell to Arms* was banned in Ireland for being immoral and irreligious.

HOLLYWOOD's 10 Biggest Box Office Disasters

1. *The Adventures of Baron Münchhausen* (directed by Terry Gilliam in 1988) lost $48.1 million.
2. *Ishtar* (1987) lost $47.3 million.
3. *Hudson Hawk* (1991) lost $47 million.
4. *Inchon* (1981) lost $44 million.
5. *The Cotton Club* (1984) lost $38 million.
6. *Santa Claus – The Movie* (1985) lost $37 million.
7. *Heaven's Gate* (1980) lost $34.2 million.
8. *Billy Bathgate* (1991) lost $33 million.
9. *Pirates* (1986) lost $30.3 million.
10. *Rambo III* (1988) lost £30 million.

12 Musical Bans

1. In the fourth century BC, Plato called for a ban on certain types of contemporary music from the Greek republic because he believed that pop music led to low morals.
2. In 1936, Adolf Hitler banned music by Mendelssohn because the composer was Jewish.
3. In 1963, *Dominique*, by The Singing Nun, was banned by Springfield, Massachusetts, station WHYN, because it was "degrading to Catholics".
4. In 1969, *Je T'Aime . . . Moi Non Plus* by Jane Birkin and Serge Gainsbourg was banned by US and European radio stations for content of an explicit sexual nature.
5. In 1962, *Speedy Gonzales*, an innocuous novelty single by the bland US crooner Pat Boone, was considered offensive to Mexicans and banned in the US.
6. In 1966, The Beatles accidentally snubbed Imelda Marcos at Manila airport and were banned in the Philippines.
7. In 1966, The Beatles' *A Day In The Life* was widely banned because of alleged drug references.
8. In 1968, Communist party leader Chairman Mao Tse-Tung banned *The Sound of Music* in China because it was a blatant example of capitalist pornography.
9. In 1970, The Rolling Stones released their new single *Cocksucker Blues*, a ploy to get them out of a contractual obligation. It worked.

10. In 1977, the queen's Silver Jubilee year, the Sex Pistols caused offence with *God Save The Queen*. Despite a

BBC radio ban, the single climbed to No. 2.

11. In 1984, the year's best-selling UK record, *Relax*, by Frankie Goes to Hollywood, was played by BBC Radio 1 for several weeks before D.J. Mike Read discovered that the lyrics were about gay sex.
12. In 1994, Dudley and District Hospital Radio banned the Frank Sinatra standard *My Way* from their airwaves because the lines "And now the end is near/And so I face the final curtain" were considered too depressing for terminally ill patients. Other suggested NHS record bans include Tony Bennett's *I Left My Heart In San Francisco* – too distressing for coronary patients – and Andy Fairweather-Low's *Wide Eyed and Legless* – unsuitable for amputees.

10 Literary Deaths

1. Pietro Aretino (1492–1556), Italian satirist, poet and critic, laughed so hard at a scene in a play which involved one of his sisters that he fell off his chair, struck his head on the floor and died.
2. Christopher Marlowe (1564–93), Renaissance English poet and playwright, died after dining in a rooming house in Deptford: he was stabbed to death by a friend in a drunken argument over the bill.
3. Lord George Gordon Byron (1788–1824) fell ill in 1824 with a fever – probably a virulent form of malaria, allegedly brought on by rowing an open boat across a lagoon in a thunderstorm – and then lapsed into a fatal coma. Byron was also epileptic – he had a major fit three months earlier in Greece when he collapsed in agony clutching his stomach, and treated himself with huge quantities of cider with brandy chasers. His death caused such a sensation that his body was brought home for burial in a Royal Navy warship.
4. Edgar Allan Poe (1809–49), US author and poet, was discovered lying in a Baltimore street gutter suffering from delirium tremens. He died a few days later.
5. Honoré de Balzac (1799–1850), French novelist, died of caffeine poisoning. He regularly drank about 50 cups of black coffee per day.
6. Charles Baudelaire (1821–67), French poet, died insane, paralyzed and speechless in 1867 at the age of 46 from the combined effects of syphilis and addiction to alcohol, hashish and opium.
7. Charles Dickens (1812–70) died of a stroke while writing *The Mystery of Edwin Drood.*
8. Oscar Wilde (1854–1900) died in France, where he had taken the name of Sebastian Melmoth. He had an abscess on the brain, which had spread from an infected middle ear, despite an

operation by an ear specialist. When Wilde was informed how much the failed operation had cost he replied: "Oh well, then, I suppose I shall have to die beyond my means." The even wittier but sadly apocryphal version of Wilde's last words were: "Either that wallpaper goes or I do."

9. Rupert Brooke (1887–1915), the poet, wrote: "If I should die, think this only of me:/That there's some corner of a foreign field/That is for ever England," but he died in a French hospital ship of blood poisoning, the result of an infected mosquito bite aggravated by sunstroke, on his way to fight in the Dardanelles campaign.
10. Arnold Bennett (1867–1931) died of typhoid, after cheerfully drinking a glass of tap water in a Paris hotel to demonstrate how completely safe it was.

10 Hollywood Greats who spent time in Mental Institutions

1. Wally Reid.
2. Alma Rubens.
3. Clara Bow.
4. Buster Keaton.
5. Margaret Sullavan.
6. George Zucco.
7. Frances Farmer.
8. Busby Berkeley.
9. Marilyn Monroe.
10. Gene Tierney.

Hollywood's

Biggest Gas Bills

1. Robert Ames: gassed himself to death 1931.
2. Jack Dougherty: gassed himself to death 1938.
3. Claire Maynard: gassed herself 1941.
4. Tyler Brooke: gassed himself 1943.
5. Spencer Charters: comic actor: gassed himself 1943.
6. Charles Butterworth: gassed himself 1946.
7. Barbara Bates: gassed herself 1969.
8. Bella Darvi: gassed herself 1971.

Courting the Muse:

20 Artistic Eccentricities

1. In 1863 the authoress Louisa May Alcott fell ill, and noted in her journal that she suffered from terrible hallucinations, in which she was repeatedly molested by a big Spaniard with soft hands. She recovered and went on to write *Little Women*.
2. The mad nineteenth-century French poet Gérard de Nerval could occasionally be seen taking a lobster for a walk on the end of a length of ribbon. After being institutionalized eight times he was discovered dead, hanging from a Paris lamp post in 1855.
3. The schizophrenic German composer Robert Schumann had two imaginary friends called Florestan and Eusebius, who gave him ideas for his scores. Schumann died in an insane asylum.
4. The nineteenth-century French writer Honoré de Balzac believed that sex was a drain on his creativity. After several months of abstinence he was once tempted into a Paris brothel, but moaned later: "I lost a novel this morning."
5. Michelangelo was partial to underage sex with boys. He had numerous gay lovers throughout his long life, especially the male models for his work. One of these models, Gherardo Perini, lived with the artist for over 10 years. Another, Cecchino dei Bracci, was 13 when the

66-year-old Michelangelo became infatuated with him. When Bracci died just two years later Michelangelo was devastated and spent a year writing passionate epitaphs for Bracci's tomb. Michelangelo's diaries, letters and poetry contain many references to his passion for boys, but the writings were suppressed for centuries after his death. His love poems, written to Cavalieri, were published with the gender changed from male to female. Michelangelo's 18-foot-high sculpture David has been described as the ultimate expression of homoeroticism.

6. Samuel Johnson wrote *Rasselas* in seven days flat to pay for his mother's funeral.
7. Arnold Bennett's novels were renowned for attention to detail. Once he was complimented on his description of the death of Darius Clayhanger in the Clayhanger series, a death scene acclaimed as the most realistic of its kind in the history of English literature. Bennett explained later how this had been possible: "All the time my father was dying I was at the bedside making copious notes."
8. The eighteenth-century artist Benjamin West had an executed criminal exhumed and crucified to see how he hung.
9. Gustav Mahler, famous for his funeral marches, suffered from depression and had a morbid fixation about death. He wrote his first funeral march when he was six.
10. In 1733, after completing *Gulliver's Travels*, Jonathan Swift wrote a treatise on excrement entitled *Human Ordure*, under the pen-name Dr Shit.
11. Friedrich von Schiller, eighteenth-century German poet and dramatist, couldn't work without placing his feet on a block of ice and inhaling the fumes of rotting apples.

12. Percy Bysshe Shelley loathed cats: he once tied one to a kite in a thunderstorm, hoping to see it electrocuted.
13. John Ruskin, celebrated Victorian art critic and essayist, suffered intermittently with bouts of mental illness for the last 20 years of his life. He finally went mad while lecturing at Oxford and had to be dragged screaming from the podium.
14. Algernon Charles Swinburne's Victorian public schooling left him with an addiction to flagellation. He was an avid reader of the Marquis de Sade and regularly visited a London flogging house. His tribute to the joy of whipping, *The Flogging Block*, now resides in the British Museum.
15. Poet Laureate Sir John Betjeman once wrote an obscene but unpublished poem about choirboys.
16. From childhood the Victorian nonsense poet and artist Edward Lear suffered from what he called "the Demon" – epilepsy – and "the Morbids" – manic depression – both of which he always maintained were the result of excessive masturbation.
17. Although the nineteenth-century writer Edgar Allan Poe never actually spent time in an asylum, he was said to have been certifiably insane. Poe was an alcoholic and laudanum addict but it didn't stop him joining the local Temperance Society and giving lectures on the evils of drink.
18. James Whistler, the American-born painter and graphic artist, once dyed a rice pudding green so that it wouldn't clash with the walls of his dining room.
19. Richard Wagner was a rabid anti-Semite. He refused to conduct the music of Jewish composer Mendelssohn unless he wore gloves. Because of his views Wagner

was subsequently "adopted" by the Third Reich. Wagner, a notorious womanizer, always composed in a stiflingly hot room perfumed with roses, while wearing a silk dressing gown. He was also touchy about critics: he often invited friends around, treated them to a sneak preview of his work then asked them for a frank opinion. Anyone who didn't offer a positive review would be threatened with physical violence.

20. The best known and most remarkable works of the Victorian artist Richard Dadd were completed in Bedlam, where he was serving a life sentence for the murder of his father Robert. In 1842 Dadd accompanied his patron, Sir Thomas Phillips, on a Grand Tour of Europe and the Middle East. During the trip Dadd began to experience headaches and "sun stroke". In Rome, he experienced an uncontrollable urge to attack the pope during one of his public appearances. It appeared that Dadd had become convinced that he was being called upon by God to do battle with the Devil, who could assume any shape he desired, including the Pontiff. In spite of this fixation, Dadd continued working in Newman Street, London, living on hard-boiled eggs and beer. Dadd's father had Alexander Sutherland of St Luke's Hospital examine his son, and Sutherland concluded that the artist was clinically insane. Dadd's brother, George, was at this time also showing signs of mental illness. In 1843 Robert Dadd accompanied Richard on a trip to Cobham, and during this trip Dadd attacked and killed his father with a knife and a razor. He fled to Dover and boarded a ship for Calais, then set off in the direction of Paris, but on the way drew attention to himself by attempting to cut the throat of a fellow

traveller. He was finally detained in Montereau, where he confessed to the murder of his father. In July 1844, shortly after Dadd's 27th birthday, he was sent to the Hospital of St Mary of Bethlehem (Bedlam), in London, where he remained for almost 20 years, during which period he completed his famous works *The Fairy Feller's Master-Stroke, Contradiction, Oberon and Titania* and *Portrait of a Young Man.* In 1864 Dadd was moved to the brand new asylum at Broadmoor, near London, where he died two years later of lung disease.

10 Writers who Died of Tuberculosis

1. John Keats (1795–1821).
2. Emily Brontë (1818–48).
3. Anne Brontë (1820–49).
4. Charlotte Brontë (1816–55).
5. Robert Louis Stevenson (1850–94).
6. Anton Chekhov (1860–1904).
7. Franz Kafka (1883–1924).
8. D.H. Lawrence (1885–1930).
9. George Orwell (1903–50).
10. William Somerset Maugham (1874–1965).

12 Fatal Hollywood Drug Overdoses

1. Jeanne Eagels: heroin, 1930.
2. Tom Forman (film director): sleeping pills, 1938.
3. Carole Landis: sleeping pills, 1948.
4. Marilyn Monroe: sleeping pills, 1962.
5. Clara Blandick (Judy Garland's "Aunt Em" in *The Wizard of Oz*): sleeping pills, 1962.
6. Bobby Driscoll (former Disney child star and heroin addict): methadrine, 1968.
7. Alan Ladd: cocktail of drugs and alcohol, 1964.
8. Judy Garland: sleeping pills, 1969.
9. George Sanders: sleeping pills, 1972.
10. Charles Boyer: sleeping pills, 1978.
11. Jean Seberg: barbiturates, 1979.
12. Margaux Hemingway: the barbiturate phenobarbital, 1996.

10 Items of Trivia unlikely to be of any use to you in a Pop Quiz

1. A report called *The Effect of Country Music on Suicide*, published in 1996 by two American sociologists, Steven Stack and Jim Gundlach, was the first known academic study of the link between country music and suicide rates. It concludes that wherever country music is played, the white suicide rate is higher than average, "independent of divorce, southernness, poverty, and gun availability".
2. In 1995 in Wanganui, New Zealand, a 21-year-old man who said he had a bomb took over the local STAR FM radio station, demanding to hear the song *Rainbow Connection* by Kermit the Frog.
3. The eccentric pop producer Phil Spector was a perfectionist in the recording studio. Once when he was working with Leonard Cohen, he held a gun to the singer's head in order to achieve the vocal performance he was looking for.
4. In 1995 mourners at a funeral service at All Saints, Gravesend were startled when the church PA system inadvertently relayed Rod Stewart's song *Do Ya Think I'm Sexy*, including the line "If you want my body . . ."
5. Funeral music requests played at West Hertfordshire Crematorium include *Wish You Luck As You Wave Me Goodbye*, *I'd Like To Get You On A Slow Boat To China*, and *Happy Days Are Here Again.*

6. During the recording sessions for *Sgt Pepper's Lonely Hearts Club Band*, Beatle George Harrison complained to EMI about the studio's hard, scratchy toilet paper. According to producer George Martin, an executive decision was taken at boardroom level to replace it with the softer variety.
7. A Christian radio station in Vevay, Indiana was burgled and set ablaze in 1994. Police said their prime suspect was a caller who had become irate when a D.J. refused to play *Don't Take the Girl* by Tim McGraw.
8. The most requested tune at British funerals is *I Will Always Love You* by Whitney Houston from the film *The Bodyguard*.
9. In 1993 five prison guards at the Boise, Idaho Maximum Security Institution were accused of taunting death row inmates by playing the 1971 Neil Young song *The Needle and the Damage Done* during an execution by lethal injection.
10. In September 1996 Sidney Ambrose of Clacton had to have medical treatment after clapping too hard at a Beverley Sisters concert.

10 Rock & Roll Suicides

1. In April 1994 27-year-old singer Kurt Cobain, who wrote a song called *I Hate Myself And I Want To Die*, escaped from a detoxification centre in Los Angeles, then shot his own face off. At the funeral service his wife, Courtney Love, lead singer of the punk band Hole, read extracts from his suicide note. Days later a 16-year-old girl in Turkey shot herself in a "tribute" to Cobain.
2. Paul Williams, Temptations singer, shot himself a short walk away from the Tamla Motown offices.
3. Dennis Hughes, member of the seventies punk band The Deviants, jumped off Caernarvon Castle.
4. Ian Curtis, 23-year-old singer with Manchester band Joy Division, killed himself on the eve of their first US tour.
5. Sister Luc-Gabrielle, the Belgian Singing Nun, and her acoustic guitar provided the unexpected smash hit of 1963, *Dominique*. She left her convent to find fame and fortune, but took her own life when her new career flopped.
6. John Ritchie, a.k.a. Sid Vicious, the Sex Pistols bassist, failed in two suicide bids while he was in police detention for allegedly stabbing to death his girlfriend Nancy Spungen, but successfully overdosed on heroin as soon as he was released on bail in February 1979.
7. Richard Manuel, member of The Band, hanged himself during their reunion tour.
8. Joe Meek, legendary record producer, shot himself in the head on the eighth anniversary of Buddy Holly's death.

9. Bobby Bloom, American one-hit wonder, who made No. 3 in the British charts in 1970 with *Montego Bay*, shot himself.
10. Tommy Boyce, the songwriter who wrote *Under The Moon Of Love*, *She*, *Words*, and who co-invented The Monkees, blew his brains out with a shotgun.

10 HARD ACTS TO FOLLOW:

Part 2

1. One of Ronald Reagan's finest moments on the silver screen, *Bedtime For Bonzo*, in 1951, was marred by the accidental death of his co-star chimpanzee the day before the film's premiere.
2. Mexican entertainer Ramon Barrero played "the world's smallest harmonica". In mid-performance in Iguala in January 1994 he inhaled and accidentally choked to death on his mouth organ.
3. In May 1870 the travelling James Robinson & Co. Circus and Animal Show elected to spice up its advance publicity for the lucky inhabitants of Middletown, Missouri, by having the band perform on the roof of a cage full of performing Numidian lions as the circus paraded through the streets. The show's management ignored repeated warnings that the cage roof was insecure and the trick was highly dangerous, and ordered the band to sit on it anyway. Sure enough, the roof gave way, and the musicians were thrown into the pit of hungry lions below. The crowds watched, paralyzed with fear, as the lions tore legs and arms from sockets and half-devoured, dismembered parts of the band were strewn across the cage floor. Of the 10 band members, three were killed outright and four more were fatally mutilated.
4. Dora Oberling, a stripper from Tampa, Florida, cheated

death in May 1996 when a dissatisfied member of the audience tried to shoot her. The bullet bounced off one of her silicone breast implants.

5. Signora Girardelli, a nineteenth-century cross between Fanny Craddock and the Marquis de Sade, spiced up her cookery "act" by running a red-hot poker over her limbs, frying eggs in boiling cooking oil in her cupped hands, and by climbing inside a huge, blazing oven to keep an eye on her baking.
6. Matthew Buchinger, a German who lived in the late seventeenth century, was probably the first ever all-round entertainer. He mastered a dozen musical instruments, was a fine dancer and a brilliant magician. He was also an excellent marksman, a superb bowler and an accomplished calligrapher. His chief claim to fame, however, was that he was only 2 feet 4 inches tall, and possessed neither arms nor legs.
7. In September 1996 Francis Mortell, an Italian club-owner in Foggia, was convicted and fined £300 for deliberately pumping laughing gas into the audience to get laughs for his comedy acts.
8. In 1994 Copenhagen Zoo blamed the sudden and mysterious death of its prized okapi on the music from a Wagnerian opera which was being played very loudly at a nearby outdoor concert. Officials decided to make the most of their loss by saving the carcass of the extremely rare antelope for dissection. The scientific endeavour was thwarted, however, by zoology students, who stole and barbecued it to celebrate the end of term.
9. In September 1994 a glass eye worn by Armando Botelli shattered when a soprano hit a high note during an opera in Milan.

10. The virtuoso of the anal accordion was the French baker Joseph Pujol, who earned fame and fortune at the turn of the twentieth century as Le Pétomane or, roughly translated, "the manic farter". At an early age Pujol made two remarkable discoveries while lying in his bath-tub: the second was that he could control the intake of water into his body by contracting his abdominal muscles. At first Pujol put his supernatural sphincter to good use by demonstrating a unique water spouting act. Having discovered that he could also control air, modulating the sound with completely odourless farting, he never looked back. Pujol took his act to Paris, where he became an overnight sensation, outselling even France's favourite actress Sarah Bernhardt. His act included a series of imitations, including the sound of calico being torn, a cannon, an eight-day-old pup, a creaking door, an owl hooting, a duck, a swarm of bees, a bullfrog and a pig. He could play, by placing a small flute in his rectum, *By The Light Of The Silvery Moon*, and could anally extinguish a candle at a distance of one foot. For an encore Pujol would insert a yard of rubber hosing with a cigarette in one end into his rectum, then draw on the cigarette and exhale smoke. The highlight of Pujol's spectacular career was a continental tour, which attracted many of the crowned heads of Europe (although King Leopold II of Belgium felt obliged to see his show in disguise). His career ended with World War I, and he went back to baking. Pujol died in 1945, aged 88.

The only legitimate European female *pétomane* (i.e. one who performed without mechanical aids, such as bellows concealed beneath their skirts) was a lady known as La Mère Alexandre, whose act was proudly billed as "without trickery or odor". Mme Alexandre's anal dexterity was such that she could imitate the farts of the famous, and perform a series of entertaining "occupational farts", including nuns and freemasons. Her *magnum opus* was her impression of the bombardment of Port Arthur.

A 1980s American *pétomane* and part-time stripper known as Honeysuckle Divine could extinguish a candle flame at two paces and could fart *Jingle Bells*.

Japan's answer to Le Pétomane appeared on television in 1980, claiming he could break wind 3,000 times in succession. He took off his pants and lay on the studio floor while the compère held the microphone in a suitable position. He could also apply a blowgun to his rectum and, accompanied by a studio orchestra, accurately fire darts into a target.

10 Essential Elvis Facts

1. Before discovering Elvis, Colonel Tom Parker's most notable success was "Colonel Parker's Dancing Chickens", an act which involved persuading chickens to perform by sticking them on an electric hotplate.
2. There are an estimated 48,000 Elvis impersonators worldwide. In the Islamic state of Mogadishu in Somalia, it is illegal to impersonate Elvis without a beard.
3. The ghost of Elvis has possessed the TV remote control in a woman's house in Memphis, Tennessee. According to Phyllis Callas, whenever she watches television the channel starts changing to football games by itself, toilets rattle and doors slam. There is also a stain on the patio door in the image of the King. The house was originally owned by Elvis at the beginning of the 1960s, and backs onto his Graceland estate. A local School for Psychics performed an energy scan over the property and confirmed that Elvis's spirit does visit occasionally.
4. Death was Elvis's best ever career move: had he lived he would almost certainly have been bankrupt within six months.
5. Elvis would also have had a problem with political correctness: just about the only thing that would prevent him from seducing a woman was knowing that she had been with a black man.
6. The First Presleyterian Church of Elvis the Divine was formed in the US in 1988. Among the King's 31 Commandments: Eat six meals a day.
7. The King's favourite snacks included fried peanut butter and banana sandwiches, burnt bacon, lemon meringue pie, and cornbread in buttermilk. He also had a fridge in his bedroom stocked with his favourite confectionery, Eskimo Pies and Nutty Buddys. In the 1970s his kitchen was manned 24 hours a day. The busiest time was around 4.30AM, when he liked to binge on three double-

decker cheeseburgers and six or seven banana splits. As Elvis was usually heavily sedated with his regular nightly cocktail of barbiturates and tranquillizers, his aides frequently had to save him from choking to death by reaching down his throat to remove food lodged in his windpipe.

8. During the last two and a half years of the King's life, his personal physician George Nichopoulos gave him about 20,000 doses of narcotics, stimulants, sedatives and anti-depressants, but Elvis had many other sources for his drugs, too. The pathologist who compiled the toxicology report after his death in 1977 testified that he had never before seen so many drugs in one body.
9. Next to sex and gluttony, his favourite nocturnal pastime was visiting the Memphis morgue to look at the corpses.
10. In July 1993 retired Texan US Air Force Major Bill Smith filed a lawsuit in Fort Worth against the estate of Elvis Presley. Major Smith charged that Presley's estate had perpetrated a fraud by keeping up the pretence that the King had died in 1977. The major complained that this had interfered with his attempts to sell his new book on Elvis's current whereabouts.

12 Esoteric Works in the British Library

1. *The Romance of Leprosy*, E. Mackerchar, 1949.
2. *Why Bring That Up? A Guide to Seasickness*, J.F. Montague, 1936.
3. *Penetrating Wagner's Ring*, John L. Di Gaetanao, 1978.
4. *Jews At A Glance*, Mac Davis, 1956.
5. *Constipation and Our Civilization*, J.C. Thomson, 1943.
6. *A Pictorial Book of Tongue Coating*, Anon., 1981.
7. *A Government Committee of Enquiry on the Light Metal Artificial Leg*, Captain Henry Hulme and Chisholm Baird, 1923.
8. *Daddy Was An Undertaker*, McDill, McGown and Gassman, 1952.
9. *A Short Account of the Origin, Progress and Present State of the New Rupture Society*, Anon., 1816.
10. *Amputation Stumps: Their Care and After-treatment*, Sir Godfrey Martin Huggins, 1918.
11. *A Study of Masturbation and its Reputed Sequelae*, J.F.W. Meagher, 1924.
12. *Sex After Death*, B.J. Ferrell and D.E. Frey, 1983.

9 Causes of Death of Classical Composers

1. Carl Philipp Emanuel Bach (1714–88): a stroke, following an unsuccessful eye operation.
2. Alban Berg (1885–1935): blood poisoning from an infected insect bite.
3. Johannes Brahms (1833–97): cancer of the liver.
4. Claude Debussy (1862–1920): cancer of the rectum.
5. Franz Liszt (1811–86): pneumonia.
6. Wolfgang Amadeus Mozart (1756–91): Bright's Disease.
7. Sergei Rachmaninov (1873–1943): malignant melanoma.
8. Franz Schubert (1797–1821): typhoid.
9. Peter Ilyich Tchaikovsky (1840–93): cholera.

10 Hollywood Suicide Shootings

1. Bobby Harron, actor 1920.
2. Karl Dane, actor 1932.
3. George Hill (director), through the head with a hunting rifle in 1934.
4. Aleta Freel, actor 1935.
5. Herman Bing (comic actor), 1948.
6. James Cardwell, actor 1954.
7. George Reeves (the original TV "Superman" actor), 1959.
8. Pedro Armendariz, shot himself while working on *From Russia With Love*, 1963.
9. Gig Young, in 1971, two years after receiving an Oscar for his supporting role in *They Shoot Horses Don't They*, shot himself and his wife in a suicide pact three weeks after their wedding day.
10. Donald "Red" Berry, actor 1980.

10 Pop Deaths by *Heroin*

1. Frankie Lymon: overdosed on 28 February 1968, aged 26.
2. Janis Joplin: 4 October 1970, aged 27.
3. Vinnie Taylor: 17 April 1974, aged 36.
4. Tim Buckley: 29 June 1975, aged 28.
5. Brian Cole: 2 August 1975, aged 28.
6. Tommy Bolin: 4 December 1976, aged 25.
7. Tim Hardin: 29 December 1980, aged 39.
8. James Honeyman-Scott: 16 June 1982, aged 25.
9. Will Shatter: 9 December 1987, aged 31.
10. Johnny Thunders: 23 April 1991, aged 38.

10 Musicians who Died from Gunshot Wounds

1. Tupac Shakur, the 25-year-old rap star whose lyrics were famous for glorifying violence, was hit by four bullets in a drive-by shooting on his way to a party after the Mike Tyson–Bruce Seldon title fight in Las Vegas in September 1996. He was on bail, pending appeal, after serving eight months in a New York prison for sex abuse. It was the second time Shakur had been shot in less than two years: in 1994 he was hit by five bullets during an apparent robbery.
2. Notorious B.I.G., New York rapper, was gunned down as he left a party in March 1997. A week earlier he had previewed a track on his new album which contained a track called *You're Nobody ('Til Somebody Kills You)*, which the rapper dedicated to the late Tupac Shakur (above).
3. John Lennon was murdered by Mark Chapman in December 1980, outside his New York apartment.
4. In 1984, the day before his 45th birthday, Marvin Gaye was shot dead by his father during a domestic row.
5. Sam Cooke, a 33-year-old singer, was shot dead during an argument at a Los Angeles motel after a woman alleged he had attacked her.
6. Peter Tosh, reggae musician and left-wing militant, for-

mer member of Bob Marley's band The Wailers, was shot dead in his Jamaica home in September 1987. The official police version was that he was killed by burglars, although there was some evidence linking his death to political opponents.

7. Carlton Barrett, also a member of The Wailers, was murdered five months earlier in Jamaica.
8. Terry Kath, guitarist with US band Chicago, was entertaining party guests in 1978 when he pointed what he believed to be an empty gun at his head.
9. Larry Williams, the 1950s US rock & roller, was found dead with gunshot wounds.
10. Scott la Rock, New York rapper, was killed in a gangland shooting.

10 Least Successful Countries in the Eurovision Song Contest*

1. Lithuania.
2. Romania.
3. Slovakia.
4.= Bosnia and Herzegovina.
4.= Morocco.
6. Slovenia.
7. Turkey.
8. Æstonia.
9. Iceland.
10. Finland.

*Since 1993 the bottom end of the Eurovision score board has been almost exclusively dominated by the plucky new participant nations from Eastern Europe and the Balkans. Lithuania's 1994 debut in Eurovision (their only entry in the competition to date), *Lopsine Mylima*, by Ovidijus Vysniauskas, finished last with a perfect "nul" score. In the same year, Romania's sole entry finished in 21st position out of 25 countries. Slovakia's 1994 debut, *Nekonecna Piesen*, by Martin Durinda and Martin Sirvas, finished 19th, a position which they improved upon by just one placing with their second entry in 1996. In one of the more creative interpretations of European geography, Morocco participated in Eurovision in 1980, and finished 18th out of 19 entries with a song called *Bitaket hob (Message d'amour)*, performed by Samira Bensaid. Since Finland first entered the Eurovision fray in 1961 they have appeared in the competition 34 times, finishing last on an unequalled nine occasions with songs which sounded as though they were originally designed to frighten elks. Finland's finest moment to date was in 1973, when Marion Rung's *Tom Tom Tom* achieved sixth place.

Paradies, Wo Bist Du?: 30 songs that scored "Nul Points" in the Eurovision Song Contest*

1. *Llámame* performed by Victor Balaguer of Spain, 1962.
2. *Ton nom*, by Fud Leclerc, Belgium, 1962.
3. *Nur in der wiener luft*, by Eleonore Schwarz, Austria, 1962.
4. *Katinka*, by De Spelbrakers, Netherlands, 1962.
5. *Een speeldoos*, by Annie Palmen, Netherlands, 1963.
6. *Solhverv*, by Anita Thallaug, Norway, 1963.
7. *Muistojeni Laulo*, by Laila Halme, Finland, 1963.
8. *En gång i Stockholm*, by Monica Zetterlund, Sweden, 1963.
9. *Mann gewöht sich so schell an das schone*, by Nora Nova, Germany, 1964.
10. *Oraçào*, by Antonio Calvario, Portugal, 1964.
11. *Zivot je sklopio krug*, by Sabahudin Kurt, Yugoslavia, 1964.
12. *I mile pensieri*, by Anita Traversi, Switzerland, 1964.
13. *Que bueno, que bueno*, by Conchita Bautista, Spain, 1965.
14. *Paradies, wo bist du?*, by Ulla Wiesner, Germany, 1965.
15. *Als het weer lente is*, by Lize Marke, Belgium, 1965.
16. *Aurinko laskee länteen*, by Viktor Klimenko, Finland, 1965.

17. *Bien plus fort*, by Tereza, Monaco, 1966.
18. *Dio, come ti amo*, by Domenico Madugno, Italy, 1966.
19. *Quel couer vas-tu briser?*, by Géraldine, Switzerland, 1967.
20. *Je suis tombé du ciel*, by David Alexander Winter, Luxembourg, 1970.
21. *Mil etter mil*, by Jahn Teigen, Norway, 1978.
22. *Aldri i livet*, by Finn Kalvik, Norway, 1981.
23. *Nuku Pommiin*, by Kojo, Finland, 1982.
24. *Opera*, by Cetin and The Shortwave, Turkey, 1983.
25. *Quién manéja mi barca*, by Remedios Amaya, Spain, 1983.
26. *Sarkim sevgi Ustüme*, by Seyyal Taner and Locomotif, Turkey, 1987.
27. *Lisa, Mona Lisa*, by Wilfried, Austria, 1988.
28. *Pao sem enginn sér*, by Daniel, Iceland, 1989.
29. *Venedig im regen*, by Thomas Forstner, Austria, 1991.
30. *Lopsine Mylima*, by Ovidijus Vysniauskas, Lithuania, 1994.

*Thanks to a peculiarity of a voting system which has changed many times, there were no "ducks" until the seventh Eurovision Song Contest in 1962. The Netherlands are the only country ever to register two nil scores in consecutive competitions (1962 and 1963).

Austria, Norway, Finland and Spain have each failed to register a single vote in the scoring system on three occasions.

Rock Bottom:*

The UK's 10 Greatest Eurovision Song Contest Flops

1. *Only The Night,* by Rikki – 13th in Brussels, 1987.
2. *The Bad Old Days,* by Co-co – 11th in Paris, 1978.
3. *A Message To Your Heart,* by Samantha Janus – 10th in Rome, 1991.
4. *We Will Be Free,* by Frances Rufelle – 10th in Dublin, 1994.
5. *Love City Groove,* by Love City Groove – 10th in Mill Street, Ireland, 1995.
6. *A Man Without Love,* by Kenneth McKellar – ninth in Luxembourg, 1966.
7. *One Step Further,* by Bardo – seventh in Harrogate, 1982.
8. *All,* by Patricia Bredin – seventh in Lugano, 1957.
9. *Mary Ann,* by Black Lace – seventh in Jerusalem, 1979.
10. *Love Games,* by Belle and The Devotions – seventh in Luxembourg, 1982.

Taking into account home advantage, Bardo's effort in 1982 represents arguably the UK's greatest song contest failure of all. This disaster was eclipsed, however, by Norway's Jahn Teigen, the first person to score "nul points" in the competition for eight years.

*Lyndsey de Paul and Mike Moran, 2nd in 1977.

40 Most Awful US and UK Chart Hits of All Time

As voted for by nearly 300 people in the music business, mostly local and national D.J.s and writers in the UK and the US, who were invited to disclose their own personal most hated Top Ten singles. For the purpose of this list a "hit" single is defined as anything which made the charts of both of the two biggest English-speaking singles markets – America and the UK – and entered the Top 40 of at least one of them. Sadly not included, therefore, is the 1967 classic *Sing Along With Mao,* which featured a live recording of the Chinese leader chanting some of his favourite thoughts, plus excerpts of discussions with Defence Minister Lin Piao and Premier Chou En-Lai. Apparently it sold a million copies, a remarkable fact made even more remarkable when you consider that China didn't have a million record-players in 1967. Not included either are the UK-only classics *There's No One Quite Like Grandma* (St Winifred's School Choir), *Agadoo* (Black Lace) or *Grandad* (Clive Dunn). Nor is there room for the author's personal favourite, *I Remember Elvis Presley (The King Is Dead)*, by Danny Mirror (1977).

1. *Long-Haired Lover From Liverpool,* Little Jimmy Osmond, 1972. For music-lovers, the prospect of yet another singing Mormon in the original "boy band" – the toothy and omnipresent Osmond family – was not regarded with much enthusiasm. What pop fans were really looking forward to was news of Pa Osmond's vasectomy. Here, the angry young man of bubblegum refers back to Beatlemania, which gave rife to a multitude of similar efforts in the sixties, including Rolf Harris's *Ringo For President* and Dora Bryan's *All I Want For Christmas Is A Beatle.*

2. *Dominique*, The Singing Nun, 1963. Proof, if you needed it, that the devil really does have all the best tunes. The unexpected smash-hit of 1963 came from a Belgian nun with an acoustic guitar. Her single topped the US charts for a whole month until the American market capitulated before Beatlemania. There was a million-selling album too, featuring such classics as *Mets Ton Joli Jupon* (*Put On Your Pretty Skirt*) and *J'ai Trouvé Le Seigneur* (*I Have Found The Lord*). The single prompted a similarly dreadful film about a singing nun some three years later, starring Debbie Reynolds. Sister Luc-Gabrielle's newly acquired Hollywood fame led her to kick the habit and revert to plain Jeanine Dekers, whereupon she signed a deal with Phillips records. She wasn't heard of again until she committed suicide a few years later. Apart from the obligatory religious Yuletide releases, the Almighty has had a fairly thin time in terms of chart success. One notable exception was the 1979 UK chart-topper co-written by Kris Kristofferson, called *One Day At A Time*, in which singer Lena Martell asked the Lord to help her through another day while you, the listener, prayed for the strength to get you through the next three and a half minutes.
3. *Teddy Bear*, Red Sovine, 1981.
   Standard tasteful country and western fare: a little crippled boy with a recently deceased pa (the poor trucker died in a terrible crash in blinding snow) and a poverty-stricken ma who works her fingers to the bone by day and cries herself to sleep at night, is rescued by golden-hearted CB enthusiasts. Sadly, Red was unable to enjoy all his success as he had already been dead for 12 months by the time the song reached the UK charts.
4. *Deck of Cards*, Wink Martindale, 1959.
   The infamous religious monologue about a soldier who used a pack of playing cards as a Bible. *Deck of Cards* got its first airing back in 1948, when it was a hit for a country and western outfit

called Four Stars. The song was written by one T. Texas Tyler, who died in 1972. Wink, real name Winston Conrad Martindale, only ever recorded one hit single, then returned to an acting career which eventually led him to become a popular quiz show host on American TV. Between 1959 and 1963 the original *Deck of Cards* charted several times on both sides of the Atlantic and sold over a million copies, peaking at No. 5 and No. 7 in the UK and US charts respectively. British music-lovers are also familiar with an equally unlovable 1973 version by Max Bygraves. With *Deck of Cards*, Max's run of 20 UK Top 40 hits ground mercifully to a halt.

5. *Disco Duck (Part 1)*, Rick Dees and his Cast of Idiots, 1976.
   US D.J. Rick Dees correctly surmised that in the mid-1970s anything with "disco" in the title was bound to be a big earner. This record was an intentional parody, but at the time the charts were so full of banal disco records that parody became indistinguishable from the real thing. Dees was banned from playing his single on his own show and was subsequently sacked when his radio station caught him plugging it.
6. *The Streak*, Ray Stevens, 1974.
   Ray Stevens first came to the attention of the British public in 1970 when he sang *Everything is Beautiful* – a sentiment which some found hard to swallow. Evidently no one had yet told him about syphilis, cat litter trays or the carp gill tapeworm, which isn't even very attractive to members of its own species. This "comedy" single had to compete with a plague of streaking singles, but it showed them all a clean pair of cheeks into the shops and gave him a No. 1 hit on both sides of the Atlantic.
7. *Tie A Yellow Ribbon Round The Old Oak Tree*, Dawn (featuring Tony Orlando), 1973.
   This huge trans-Atlantic hit, a UK No. 1 for four weeks, was originally inspired by a TV news item involving an American ex-convict. Irwin Levine and L. Russell Brown wrote a song about it,

one of the world's all-time worst dressed men backed by a couple of Motown session girls sang it, and before long strong men were ready to tear off their own ears rather than listen to it again.

8. *Convoy*, C.W. McCall, 1976.

The US trucker folklore single was helped into the charts by a sudden explosion in numbers of CB radio freaks, a craze which was soon to go the same way as Lord Lucan and Shergar. C.W. McCall was a character dreamed up by an American advertising agency to sell bread. Sam Peckinpah was so moved by *Convoy* that in 1978 he made a whole film about it.

9. *Sugar, Sugar*, The Archies, 1969.

Wombles, Smurfs and Muppets were all kiddies' TV favourites who went on to become major chart phenomena. Wombles were furry collectors of litter and had hits with *Banana Rock*, *Remember You're A Womble* and *We Wish You a Wombling Merry Christmas*. Smurfs looked as though they were in advanced stages of cardiac arrest and were originally fronted by a Dutchman with a limited grasp of English on *The Smurf Song*, *Dippety Day* and *Christmas in Smurfland*. Muppets hit the big time with *Ma-Na-Ma-Na* and *Halfway Down The Stairs*. The daddy of them all was an American newspaper cartoon strip called The Archies, which found new life as a cheaply animated TV series starring Archie Andrews, Jughead Jones, Veronica Lodge, Reggie Mantle, Betty Cooper and Mr Weatherbee. It led to the ultimate "bubblegum" anthem and one of the biggest-selling singles of 1969 via a bunch of session musicians fronted by lead vocalist Ron Dante. *Sugar, Sugar* followed the Stones' *Honky Tonk Women* to the top of the American charts and then duplicated the feat in Britain, where it hogged the No. 1 spot for a staggering eight weeks.

10. *My Ding-A-Ling*, Chuck Berry, 1972.
This did wonders for Chuck Berry's bank balance but not much for his reputation as one of rock & roll's founding fathers. In the UK it also upset anti-porn crusader Mary Whitehouse, who tried to get it banned. Berry had little to do with the decision to record this embarrassing novelty hit. He had been using *My Ding-A-Ling* in his live act for several years (he originally recorded it in 1958 as *My Tambourine*), but no one bothered to tell him that he was being taped live in a Coventry ballroom on 3 February 1972 before 35,000 students. Afterwards he complained bitterly that his record company should have been courteous enough to let him and his backing band in on the secret so that they might have made a better job of it. Berry stopped complaining when he heard that it had sold over a million copies and topped the charts on both sides of the Atlantic. It all came as a big surprise to the old rocker, who hadn't had a hit for seven years and had resigned himself to never being anywhere near the top of the charts again.
11. *Coward of the County*, Kenny Rogers, 1980.
Kenny Rogers became the first country singer to top the British charts since J.J. Barrie's slimy *No Charge*, some four years earlier. Rogers demonstrated with the likes of *Coward of the County* and *Lucille* that he had more or less cornered the market in maudlin barfly ballads about domestic problems. *Coward of the County* became one of the year's 10 best-selling records in the UK, peaking at No. 3 in America in February 1980. It was also the title of a film which Roger appeared in, released in 1981.
12. *Tell Laura I Love Her*, Ray Peterson, 1960.
In 1960 Billboard reported that Decca had scrapped 25,000 copies of this single because it was "too tasteless and vulgar for the English sensibility". Nevertheless, a subsequent cover version became a UK chart-topper for one-hit Welsh wonder Ricky Valance, the only artist ever to get his inspiration for a stage

name from bed linen (not to be confused with Ritchie Valens of *La Bamba* fame). The big single of 1960 told the tragic tale of Laura and Tommy: Tommy enters a stock car race because he needs to win enough loot to buy Laura a wedding ring. Needless to say he crashes and his car overturns in flames, but as they pull him from the twisted wreck "With his dying breath they heard him say:/ 'Tell Laura I love her / Tell Laura I need her / Tell Laura not to cry / My love for her will never die'." The fact that Tommy was written off in spite of his lucid and quite lengthy "dying breath" suggests that he may have been carrying an organ donor card at the time.

13. *Mandy*, Barry Manilow, 1975.

When he wasn't knocking out radio and TV jingles for toilet cleaners, Band-Aids and Pepsi Cola, Manilow concentrated on his awesome ability to churn out vacuous hit singles, inspiring amongst his legion of adoring female fans the sort of blind devotion only normally associated with World War II Japanese fighter pilots. Manilow got his first smell of success by working on a couple of album projects with Bette Midler, after which he was invited to support her on a tour and performed some of his own material. *Mandy*, which started life as a single by one Scott English and was released in 1972 as *Brandy*, was an American No. 1 and the first of Manilow's 16 US hit singles in the 1970s. Disturbingly, in 1980 a North American syndicated radio show called The Weekly Top 30 polled over 20,000 listers who voted *Mandy* the second-best track of all time.

14. *Je T'Aime . . . Moi Non Plus*, Jane Birkin and Serge Gainsbourg, 1969.

Brigitte Bardot was the first person to have a crack at this, but insisted it was shelved once she heard it because her version was much too naughty for human ears. Jane Birkin and Serge Gainsbourg were two of France's top film and recording stars of the era. Although Jane was English, the short trip across the channel made her a French sex symbol almost overnight. Gainsbourg wrote this heavy breathing number, and in spite of the fact that most radio stations immediately banned it, the single became a massive hit throughout Europe – No. 1 in six countries – and eventually in America, when it was released there a few months later. The BBC maintains that it never bans a single as such: it simply won't play it if the song is likely to offend, or if no one is likely to want to listen to it. Even if it's No. 1. *Je T'Aime . . . Moi Non Plus* charted in the UK again when it was re-released in 1974.

15. *I Think I Love You*, The Partridge Family, 1970.

Children's TV was awash with half-hour series starring frolicking teenybop groups in the early seventies: The Partridge Family (who were not a real band at all), The Jacksons and The Osmonds (who were), The Monkees (who were not) and the Bay City Rollers (who were a real group although we all prayed that they weren't). The Partridge Family featured actress Shirley Jones and her four children – just your typical, average, all-American family. When mom wasn't in the kitchen baking apple pie or doing a spot of needlepoint, she liked nothing better than to slip into an impromptu garage jam session and belt out the occasional mega hit single with her four unctuous offspring. The joke became ingrowing when demand from genuine record-buyers who couldn't tell the difference between TV fiction and the real thing made *I Think I Love You* a US chart-topper for three whole weeks. More hits followed for the Patridges, including *Breaking Up is Hard to Do, Looking Through the Eyes of Love* and *Walking in the Rain.* The eldest son of this remarkable TV family was one David Cassidy – the real life step-son of Shirley Jones. Between 1972 and 1975 Cassidy vied with Donny Osmond for his place on bedroom walls with a string of releases including the No.

1 hits *How Can I Be Sure* and *Daydreamer/The Puppy Song*, then suddenly "retired" from the pop business. The Partridge dynasty wasn't entirely finished. David resurfaced in 1985 on *Top Of The Pops* with *The Last Kiss*, apparently unscathed by his sabbatical, but wearing so much hair lacquer that Greenpeace began to take notice.

16. *Honey*, Bobby Goldsboro, 1968.

    In terms of wrist-slashing, stomach-churning sentiment, this saga about the death of a young bride ranks right up there on the depressometer with the very worst of country and western. Goldsboro lays on the sentiment with an earthmover. He was Roy Orbison's guitarist before he came across *Honey*, written by one Bobby Russell (also responsible for *He Ain't Heavy, He's My Brother*). It was America's best-seller for five weeks when it was first released in 1968, ahead of Gary Puckett's *Young Girl*. In Britain the situation was reversed, with *Honey* at No. 2. The record was re-released in the UK in 1974 and again got to No. 2 in the charts.

17. *Annie's Song*, John Denver, 1974.

    John Denver's real name was John Henry Deutschendorf. The Annie immortalized here, and whose name never actually gets mentioned other than in the song title, was, of course, Mrs Deutschendorf. All this soul-baring and troth-pledging didn't do their marriage much good in the long run – the couple were divorced in 1983. Surprisingly, "mental cruelty caused by her husband's singing career" didn't even get a mention. The British never quite took Denver to their bosoms in the way that his fellow countrymen did. In the UK this was his sole Top 10 hit, yet millions of Americans were sufficiently impressed by his simple melodies to give him three more No. 1 hits with *Sunshine on my Shoulders*, *Thank God I'm a Country Boy* and *I'm Sorry*. *Annie's Song* resurfaced as an instrumental performed by James Galway in 1978, and reached No. 3 in the UK charts. The only version really worth listening to appeared in 1980 on Monty Python's *Contractual Obligation* Album. A brief and fitting tribute entitled *Farewell To John Denver* featured Python Eric Idle singing "You came on my pillow . . ." to the opening bars of *Annie's Song* and ended with the sound of John Denver being strangled. Mr Denver didn't get the joke and the track was withdrawn from later copies.

18. *Release Me*, Engelbert Humperdinck, 1967.

Flying in the teeth of drugs, peace and psychedelia, the biggest chart name of 1967 belonged to a crooner with matinée idol looks and several yards of sideburn. He was born Gerry Dorsey in Madras, India, and a singing career which had trundled along without event for several years took a sharp turn when he found himself sharing the same management as Tom Jones and the same name as a dead German composer. His swaggering vocal style and low regard for taking big fashion risks quickly established him as the darling of the more mature audience. His version of the aged country ballad *Release Me* topped the UK charts for six weeks and paved the way for a dozen big hits from 1967 to 1976.

19. *Macarthur Park*, Richard Harris, 1968.

In which a famous actor finds himself in a traumatic ongoing damp cake situation. Harris had already demonstrated in the lead role of the movie musical *Camelot* (1967) that he couldn't sustain a note if his life depended on it. "An appaling movie" wrote one critic, "with only sporadically good acting to recommend it." *Macarthur Park* gave Haris a huge hit all over the world, which was only kept off the No. 1 spot in America by Herb Alpert. It wasn't that Harris couldn't sing (he couldn't, but that wasn't it), or that it went on for at least four minutes longer than it ought to have done: it was just that it had a certain hammy quality which Donna Summer's version, 10 years later, couldn't quite match. Connoisseurs of bad taste should also note the completely over-the-top orchestral arrangement. Ms Summer chopped it down to under four minutes and gave it a disco back-beat for her US No. 1. A third version of *Macarthur Park*, by the Four Tops, also charted in America in 1971.

20. *Do The Clam*, Elvis Presley, 1965.
    On the evidence of which he should have stuck to driving trucks. Starting with his first film, *Love Me Tender* in 1956, Elvis showed his apparently limitless capacity for appearing in increasingly diabolical movies which, more often than not, resulted in increasingly diabolical soundtracks. This was one of five tracks recorded by Elvis on 5 June 1964 and featured in the 1965 film *Girl Happy*, his 20th film in nine years. Judged even by the dire standard of Elvis films, *Girl Happy* was a major mistake. This time the "plot" required him to act as chaperone for a group of college girls on a trip to Fort Lauderdale. As always, it was a thinly disguised vehicle for him to swivel his hips and rattle off the odd tune, and he had a song to match the occasion with *Do The Clam* – undisputedly the most uncollectable Elvis waxing of all time. It made the top 20s in both America and the UK.

21. *Mull of Kintyre*, Paul McCartney & Wings, 1977.
    In 1977 not owning a copy of *Mull of Kintyre* was seen in the UK as an act of subversion: every home should have at least three. After what seemed like a lifetime at No. 1 (but which was, in fact, only nine weeks) it became the nation's all-time biggest selling single, and is now a sound as familiar to most Britons as the speaking clock. Apparently, Paul McCartney wanted to write a modern national anthem for Scotland, and like all national anthems it had to be very boring. The promotional video saw

the performers strolling wistfully around a misty Kintyre landscape. Paul and Linda played guitar, while Denny Laine played gooseberry. After he'd written it McCartney wasn't at all convinced he had a hit single on his hands, even if his session bagpipe players from the local Campbeltown Pipe Band were. Doubts about the record's hit potential explain why it was released as a double "A" side with *Girls' School* – a song which most people would now be hard-pressed to recall. It peaked at only No. 33 in the American charts. The single's reign as the all-time UK best-seller was eventually ended by Bob Geldof and Midge Ure's epic Band Aid charity release *Do They Know It's Christmas* in 1984.

22. *Let's Get Together*, Hayley Mills, 1961.

This horror came from a forgettable Disney film called *The Parent Trap*, in which 15-year-old Hayley Mills (daughter of Sir John) played identical twin sisters who try to reunite their divorced parents. There isn't much of *Let's Get Together* – under two minutes – yet it ranks as one of the most truly formidable pop performances of all time. Hayley's singing abilities are matched by a lyric-writer who thought nothing of rhyming "twosome" with "gruesome" in a love song, and was capable of penning this remarkable middle eight:

Oh, I really think you're swell
Oh, we really ring the bell
Ooee and if you stick with me
Nothing could be greater
Say hey alligator.

The single made the Top 10 in America and peaked at No. 11 in the UK in November 1961. Hayley had even bigger success with her US follow-up, *Johnny Jingo*, which climbed to No. 6 in April 1962.

23. *Living Next Door To Alice*, Smokie, 1976.

Smokie's sixth single was provided by the seventies British songwriting phenomena Mike Chinn and Micky Chapman, who took a sadistic glee in churning out popular dross for the early teenies. Smokie looked like a cross between The Faces and The Wombles, and were aimed at your more-laid-back-than-average toddler, competing in the same arena as Mud, Sweet, The Rubettes, Suzi Quatro and Showaddywaddy. "Chinnichap", as they became known, penned five No. 1 UK hits during their brief but highly lucrative reign, although none of these pearls went Smokie's way. It is difficult to recall any of Smokie's singles with any degree of affection, but this was certainly the daftest: the moving tale of a chap's unrequited love for a next door neighbour who, after 24 years, has scarpered without leaving a forwarding address. And she never said anything about a tin of paint. In 1977 *Living Next Door To Alice* became Smokie's sole American chart success.

24. *Stand By Your Man*, Tammy Wynette, 1975.

Tammy, real name Virginia Pugh, is a former beautician, now known for her absurdly sentimental redneck country and western standards, but not for her extreme feminist views or for ozone-friendly hairstyles. *Stand By Your Man* had been in the American Hot Hundred in 1968, when it established her as the so-called Queen of Nashville, so it was already seven years old by the time it hit No. 1 in the UK. It was the only Tammy Wynette song ever to "cross over" into the American pop charts, and is the biggest-selling single by a female artist in the history of country music. Tammy is something of an authority in the standing by men department: she has been married five times.

25. *Puppy Love*, Donny Osmond, 1972.
The fifth eldest of the all-conquering Osmonds. While his nearest contemporary in the pre-pubescent pop market, David Cassidy, was busily wooing the early teenies, Donny went straight for the pram with *Puppy Love*, a song which had been a million-seller for Paul Anka 12 years earlier. Although this was Donny's fourth consecutive million-selling single in the US, his solo chart career in the UK was less spectacular – just half a dozen hits spanning two years, not counting his dire offerings with various permutations of the rest of the Osmond clan.

26. *Float On*, The Floaters, 1977.
Another single to have occupied the UK No. 1 spot, a coveted position previously held by such distinguished luminaries as Cilla Black, Jackie Trent, Joe Dolce and St Winifred's School Choir. This sub-Stylistics nonsense from four chaps with high-fibre diets was a chart-topper in the UK and a million-seller in America. It was the Detroit vocal quartet's first and only hit single to date.

27. *Save Your Kisses For Me*, Brotherhood of Man, 1976.
The Eurovision Song Contest, an annual meeting of the the mad, the brave and the hopeless, still manages to cause a bit of a panic on the Continent, even though most Britons watch it with the same degree of morbid curiosity that tempts you to slow down when you're driving past a road accident. Yet back in 1967, the UK's first-ever winning entry, Sandie Shaw's *Puppet On A String*, established it firmly as a national institution second only in importance to the Grand National. The whole point of entering Eurovision is to try to come last – a coveted position which the crafty Finns have more or less cornered for years (see page 161). Miss Shaw's victory changed all that, and the British started to take the competition seriously. *Puppet On A String* was the record which laid down the ground rules for Eurovision for the next seven years. It was the first winning entry to hit upon the "bing-a-

bong" formula. The bingness or bongness of all subsequent entries could be measured in terms of *Puppet On A String*. Cliff Richard's entry in the following year, for example, had plenty of bing, but was considered by the judges to be a little short on bong. Lulu's entry, *Boom Bang-A-Bang*, in 1969, was nearer the mark. Dutch band Teach-In took the theory to its logical conclusion in 1975 when they simply changed the "b" to a "d" and won hands down with *Ding-A-Dong*. Eurovision standards continued to plummet effortlessly, reaching an all-time low in 1976 when Brotherhood of Man – the group who made Abba look raunchy – secured the UK's second-ever winning entry with *Save Your Kisses For Me*, the runaway best-selling single in the UK of 1976, and No. 27 in the American charts.

28. *Wand'rin' Star*, Lee Marvin, 1970.

The film version of the Broadway musical *Paint Your Wagon* was widely held to have been the worst adaptation in movie history. The story of life in the Californian Gold Rush boom towns ran for three hours and was, according to one American critic, "stupefyingly boring". Lee Marvin and Clint Eastwood starred in it, and Marvin got to sing this, the title track. Even allowing for the fact that he was supposed to be playing the part of a drunk at the time, his singing was diabolical. In fact, this was a double treat: Marvin's painful grunting noises are more than matched by the flip side, as Clint Eastwood sings like a dying dog on *I Talk To The Trees*. Incredibly, this was the sixth-biggest seller of the year in the UK and even prevented the Beatles' swansong, *Let It Be*, from getting to No. 1.

29. *Teen Angel*, Mark Dinning, 1960.

The fad for grisly death discs took off after the plane crash which claimed the lives of Buddy Holly, Big Bopper and Ritchie Valens. This event helped to "inspire" such forays into necrophilia as Ruby Wright's *Three Stars* and this, an American No. 1 in 1960.

Teen Angel had all the usual ingredients: boy meets girl; girl stalls her car on railway tracks and picks this inopportune moment to search for her boyfriend's missing school ring; girl is crushed to death by a moving train. Dinning's chart career sank without trace but *Teen Angel* was given another airing in George Lucas's 1973 rock nostalgia movie *American Graffiti*, as part of the film's spirit of '62 soundtrack.

30. *Yummy, Yummy, Yummy*, Ohio Express, 1968.
Ohio Express were a six-piece American group who got their first break supporting The Beach Boys at a 1967 US concert. *Yummy, Yummy, Yummy* sold more than a million copies and was their sole British hit, climbing to No. 5 in the charts. It fared marginally better in the US, where they went on to score five Top 40 hits. The name of one of their subsequent American hits, *Chewy Chewy*, shows them to have been one of pop's finest exponents of songs about food.

31. *Rivers Of Babylon/Brown Girl In The Ring*, Boney M, 1978.
Boney M were originally assembled by writer/producer Frank Farian, who needed a group to mime to his own single *Baby Do The Bump* on a couple of TV shows. The band didn't actually get to sing on their own records until their second single, *Ma Baker*. UK sales of *Rivers Of Babylon*, their fifth of a dozen Top 40 hits in the late seventies, were phenomenal, outstripping sales of every other hit single in 1978. At one stage British record presses were unable to cope with demand and hundreds of thousands of copies had to be pressed abroad. The song was quite old – simply a traditional "hymn", which in the hands of Boney M became tedious Caribbean disco-pop. The single's chart form was equally mysterious: it was not originally released as a double "A" side, but when the real "A" side started slipping down the charts, for no good reason some radio stations suddenly started to play the "B" side, *Brown Girl In The Ring*, and it continued to sell in vast

quantities. Both sides were voted for by our Top 100 panellists, so they are credited here jointly. Experts now agree that Boney M singles were always a good thing because they made everything else in the charts sound so much better. American record-buyers showed considerably less enthusiasm for the group: *Rivers Of Babylon* was their sole US hit and only reached No. 30.

32. *No Charge*, J.J. Barrie, 1976.

In 1974 Canadian Barry Authors set up his own recording company and made a single under the name J.J. Barrie. This was his and the label's sole hit, and Power Exchange subsequently went bankrupt in 1977. *No Charge* was about a boy who hands his own mum a bill for providing sundry services around the home and generally being an all-round good egg. These chores include mowing the lawn, making his own bed, going to the store, playing with little sister, taking out the trash and raking the yard, and he throws in getting a good report card at school. Unfortunately, his mother is completely out of step with these Thatcherite principles and fobs him off with some wet excuse about being a caring parent. Scots comic Billy Connolly was swift to lampoon this a couple of months later in the UK with *No Charge (No Chance)*. Melba Montgomery topped the American country and western charts with her version. Tammy Wynette's version of *No Charge* was not a hit single, but is also well worth avoiding. In 1980 Barry Authors recorded another single, with Nottingham Forest's Brian Clough, called *You Can't Win 'Em All*.

33. *My Way*, Elvis Presley, 1977.

The definitive barfly anthem, *My Way* was written by three Frenchmen, Thibaut, François and Revaux, and in its original form was called *Comme d'habitude*. Paul Anka supplied the English lyric. This live recording gave Elvis his 106th consecutive Top 40 hit in the US and his 38th (and second posthumous) UK Top 10 hit, and went on to become a million-seller. The release of such an incredibly awful single soon after his death was either very good commercial sense or shameless exploitation, depending upon how you feel about these things. It had absolutely no redeeming features; by 1977 Elvis was not only looking but also sounding like several tons of mashed potato. Legend has it that Phil Spector was called in to edit out the burps.

34. *In The Navy*, Village People, 1979.
The Village People came direct from the New York gay club scene dressed as cowboys, red indians, bikers, GIs, cops and construction workers, and took disco dancefloors by storm in late 1978 with YMCA, a track from their triple-platinum album *Cruisin'*. YMCA was tongue-in-cheek, a poke in the eye for American manhood – the point emphasized by their stereotype macho stage gear. Most of the people who bought it probably didn't get the joke, but at least they could dance to it. By the time the next cut from *Cruisin'* hit the charts the joke was beginning to wear thin. The lyrics were banal – innuendo about sailors wasn't the world's most original idea – and the fad began to grate. Comic Billy Connolly laboured the point with his parody single *In The Brownies*, which became a UK hit a few weeks later.
35. *Gimme Dat Ding*, The Pipkins, 1970.
In the early seventies it was common practice to create a fictitious band to showcase a hit tune. If a writer thought he had chart material on his hands he would get a bunch of session people to record it and worry about finding a name for the band later. This was one such record, bubblegum chart fodder penned by Albert Hammond, who had also provided *Little Arrows* for Leapy Lee. The bloke who sang *Gimme Dat Ding*, when he wasn't being The

Pipkins, was busy supplying Edison Lighthouse with the lead vocal for their UK No. 1 hit *Love Grows. Gimme Dat Ding* climbed to No. 6 in the UK and No. 9 in America.

36. *The Laughing Gnome*, David Bowie, 1973.
Featuring Bowie in another of his famous guises, this time as The Man Who Made Crap Singles. The solo career of Tin Machine's former lead singer had very dodgy origins indeed. His 1967 debut album *Love You Till Tuesday*, out in the same year as the original release of *The Laughing Gnome*, was full of stuff in a similar vein. The album and single amounted to a curious collection of whimsy, none of which gave any clues about the sensational change of direction his career was about to take. Both album and single were sensibly ignored by the public and The *Laughing Gnome* gave him his 11th consecutive flop: it's a wonder he ever dared make another record again. Then, six years later, with Bowie's stock riding high, Deram re-issued it. *The Laughing Gnome* shot to No. 6 in the UK charts, selling over 250,000 copies. Not many diehard Bowie fans were prepared to admit that the record was embarrassing rubbish, and even today some of his more obsessive admirers try to explain it away as a very good children's record and yet another example of their hero's versatility.

37. *We Are The World*, USA for Africa, 1985.
A good cause, but a shocking record all the same. Harry Belafonte set the wheels in motion for this American famine relief effort, but the initial inspiration was provided by Bob Geldof, who showed them it could be done with Britain's Band Aid single *Do They Know It's Christmas.* Belafonte later told St Bob that he felt "ashamed" that a bunch of white British kids had been left to do a job that his fellow black Americans should have been doing already. Michael Jackson and Lionel Ritchie wrote it, and more or less everyone who was anyone, including Stevie Wonder, Dylan,

Diana Ross, Tina Turner and Paul Simon were persuaded to turn up – 45 of them in all. Even the presence of Smokey Robinson couldn't save it from being awful. Apparently, Stevie Wonder caused a bit of a panic when he suggested that they all sing the lyrics in Swahili, as he'd gone to the trouble of getting it translated.

38. *If*, Telly Savalas, 1975.
Beware of Greeks bearing discs. Undisputably the worst record of 1975 was this corny monologue provided by TV's flavour of the month baldy cop Kojak – a cover version of a song Bread had taken into the US charts some four years earlier, and which went on to sell catfood on British TV. If you thought *If* was iffy, listen to Kojak's version of *You've Lost That Lovin' Feeling*, a follow-up which surprised no one when it stiffed.

39. *Ringo*, Lorne Greene, 1964.
Times were hard on the Pondorosa in 1964. So hard that Ben Cartwright and his boys were forced to augment the ranch's meagre income by recording albums for RCA. Their second album, *Welcome To The Pondorosa*, included Pa's tale about how he saved the life of the infamous gun-toting dude Johnny Ringo. Soon Pa's dramatic monologues were the talk of the bunkhouse, and within a few weeks *Ringo* had topped the American charts. Imagine how surprised Hoss and the boys were when it sold over a million copies. Lorne Greene recorded seven more albums for RCA. He died in 1987, aged 82.

40. *Kung Fu Fighting*, Carl Douglas, 1974.
In 1974 Bruce Lee was very much the man of the moment. In fact he was very much dead, but 10th rate Kung Fu flicks like his preposterous *Enter The Dragon* and the interminable series of martial arts spin-offs kept the Bruce Lee cult alive. No less ludicrous was the scenario painted by Londoner Carl Douglas in his disco cash-in single, *Kung Fu Fighting*. The act of reducing

people to piles of catmeat at the slightest provocation, he assured us, was quite a "funky" pastime performed by "funky" Chinamen, so boogie-oogie-oogie on down to the dance floor with your rice flails and chop someone up to a disco beat. *Kung Fu Fighting*, a worldwide No. 1 with estimated sales of nine million, took 10 minutes to make. Apparently his follow-up, *Dance The Kung Fu*, took even longer.

4
HEALTH & BEAUTY

10 BAD HAIR Days

1. In 1993 a 22-year-old Dutchman went on a rampage causing £30,000 damage to a barber shop in Hengelo. He was upset because the barber had overdone his request for "a slight trim".
2. Californian hairdresser Joseph Middleton, 56, was sentenced to 60 days' community service in 1996. Middleton had masturbated with his free hand while doing his female customer's hair: at his trial the court heard that he had, in fact, been able to finish both jobs, because the customer was too frightened to object.
3. Mary, Queen of Scots was bald, a secret which she hid even from many of her closest acquaintances with a thick auburn wig. The first hint that Mary was follically challenged was on the day of her execution. After she had been beheaded the executioner picked her head up by the hair to show it to the crowd, and it came away in his hand.
4. In 1994 hundreds of Uruguayans sued a local shampoo manufacturer after using the patent dandruff treatment Dander-Ban. However, none of the victims, male or female, could argue with the company's advertizing claim that Dander-Ban was guaranteed to get rid of their dandruff: within hours of using the shampoo they had gone completely bald.
5. In March 1983 the Danish hair-fetishist Luigi Longhi was jailed for life after he was found guilty of kidnapping, then murdering a West German girl hitch-hiker. Longhi ad-

mitted he'd washed her hair four times before strangling her.

6. Hair from corpses was widely used in the manufacture of wigs for 300 years, although the quality of hair was nothing to write home about. The bottom fell out of the periwig business during the Great Plague of London in 1665. No one dared buy a new wig for fear that the hair had been cut off the heads of plague-infected cadavers. Samuel Pepys once recorded in his dairy that he had bought a brand new wig, but had quickly returned it to his barber in disgust because it was full of headlice. "It vexed me cruelly," Pepys wrote, "that he should put such a thing in my hands."
7. Michael Potkul, 33, won a $400,000 malpractice award against surgeon Dominic Brandy in Pittsburgh, US in 1996. Brandy had promised Potkul that he could give him a nearly full head of hair by grabbing the hairy scalp at the back of his head and stretching it over the bald bit on top. Potkul became so depressed after six unsuccessful operations that he attempted suicide.
8. According to Ronnie Spector, singer with the 1960s US girl band The Ronettes, her famous writer/producer husband Phil always switched the light off when they went to bed so that he could remove his toupée in private. He then applied so much solvent to get rid of the glue that held it in place that for the rest of the night he had a reek that would kill a horse.
9. In Denver, David Joseph Zaba, 32, pleaded guilty to assault for pouring varnish on his wife during sex, causing her hair to fall out. The court heard that the couple had been using food as part of their sex life for seven years: on this particular occasion Angela Zaba was

expecting honey and chocolate syrup.

10. In 1994 Ernestine and John Kujan sued the New York dog-grooming salon Pet Pavilion after watching their cocker spaniel Sandy accidentally bake to death in an automatic blow dryer.

12

Celebrity Fashion & Beauty Tips

1. The seventeenth-century Hungarian lesbian Countess Elizabeth de B'athory scorned traditional moisturisers and anti-wrinkle creams, preferring to bathe in warm virgins' blood. To help her look a little lovelier every day, she slaughtered more than 650 girls.
2. On the day of his execution, King Charles I wore two vests.
3. In his later years, composer Gioacchino Rossini suffered from alopecia, which made him completely bald, and he took to wearing a wig. In exceptionally cold weather he wore two or three wigs simultaneously.
4. Queen Isabeau, wife of King Charles VI of France, decreed that the waistlines of all her court ladies-in-waiting should not exceed a maximum of 13 inches. In the process of meeting this requirement, a few of them starved to death.
5. Queen Anne's cousin, Lord Cornbury, the 3rd Earl of Clarendon, was governor-general of New York and New Jersey from 1701 to 1708. Cornby was a veteran British parliamentarian and a transvestite. In 1702 this large, heavily built man opened the New York Assembly wearing a blue silk ball gown studded with diamonds, satin shoes and a fancy headdress. When Queen Anne's American subjects complained about their governor's dress code, Cornbury dismissed the locals as "stupid". It was perfectly obvious, he said, that as a representative of Her Majesty he had a duty to represent her as accurately as he could.

6. In an attempt to make himself more attractive to his girlfriend, Gala, Salvador Dali shaved his armpits until they bled and wore a perfume made of fish glue and cow dung.
7. When syphilis robbed the great sixteenth-century Danish astronomer Tycho Brahe of his nose he had an attractive artificial gold and silver version made.
8. The famous French racing driver Jean Behra (1921–59) wore a plastic right ear after losing one in a racing crash in 1955. He always carried a spare false ear in his pocket, just in case.
9. Queen Elizabeth I always carried a bag of sweets to mask her foul breath. Sugar was so expensive in Elizabethan England that black teeth were a sign of affluence. When she finally lost all her teeth, Elizabeth took to stuffing layers of cloth under her lips to fill out her face. The queen's breasts were always heavily powdered and covered in ceruse, the popular lead-based whitener which scarred and poisoned the women of northern Europe for centuries, and her veins were highlighted with blue dye. She also wore an attractive hair pomade made from a mixture of apples and puppy fat.
10. Mae West wore 10-inch heels and false nipples.
11. George Washington had at least four sets of false teeth, which he soaked in port overnight to make them taste better. He probably lost his teeth as a result of cracking Brazil nuts between his jaws. By the time he became president, he had only one tooth left. He wore a set of dentures fashioned from cow's teeth, and later contacted a leading dentist in Philadelphia, who produced a state-of-the-art set carved not from wood, but from hippopotamus tusk. The new dentures were thoughtfully drilled with a

hole to accommodate his one remaining tooth. Unfortunately, they were a very bad fit and caused constant pain, which the president tried to ease by taking laudanum. Washington is noted for not smiling very much for his portraits.

12. Following a visit to the US by Diana, Princess of Wales in 1996, the *New York Observer* reported that requests for colonic irrigation treatments had increased tenfold.

10 All-Time most Dangerous Doctors

1. The third-century Greek anatomist Galen, personal physician to the Roman Emperor Marcus Aurelius, helped kill more people than any other man in medical history. For more than 1,000 years Galen was acknowledged by the Church to be the world's only official authority on human anatomy. His word on the inner workings of the human body was inviolable: even to question Galen's authority on the subject was an act of heresy punishable by death. The Church was not in the least concerned by the minor complication that Galen had never actually seen the inside of the human body, and that his 100 or so medical text books were wild guesswork based on his observations of dead pigs and dogs. Although Galen was undoubtedly a man ahead of his time and managed to get a few things right, his numerous mistakes had terrible consequences for centuries. Thanks to Galen, generations of medical students learned that the brain was a large clot of phlegm, that the heart had two chambers, that the best way to cure a headache was to cut holes in the skull, that the quickest way to cure a cough was to amputate the uvula at the back of the patient's palate, and that post-operative wounds should be dressed with pigeon's blood. The ban on human anatomical dissection remained long after Galen's death; only a pope could grant permission for the odd criminal to exhumed and cut open, albeit under the severest of restrictions. The dissection had to be performed by a servant, while a doctor stood solemnly reading from the works of Galen and pointed to the parts described. When it became obvious, as it nearly always did, that

Galen was a fraud, his errors were always excused by the official line that the corpse was a criminal, and therefore abnormal.

2. The incompetent Dr Fagon, the eighteenth-century resident French court physician at Versailles, was known as "the killer of princes". Within a fortnight in 1715 he wiped out almost the entire French royal family, including Louis XIV, by treating a measles epidemic with a tough regime of purges, emetics and prolonged bleedings. The infant Louis XV only survived because his nurse hid him from the doctor.
3. The "production line lobotomy", performed with an ice pick under local anaesthetic, was the tour de force of Dr Walter Freeman, Professor of Neurology at the George Washington University. His first live patient was a manic depressive 63-year-old woman from Kansas, who chose surgery rather than face a lifetime in a mental institution. She had second thoughts on the operating table when she learned that her headful of curls would have to be completely shaved off. Freeman reassured her that she could keep her precious curls, quietly confident that after the operation she would no longer care. In the 1940s and 1950s the Freeman lobotomy was performed on more than 20,000 patients as he toured across the US in his specially equipped camper van, which he called his "Lobotomobile". Nurses and hospital officials who witnessed Freeman in action, wielding his hammer and ice pick on patient after patient, quite often fainted. His most famous patient was the rebellious Hollywood starlet Frances Farmer, who was subjected to the Freeman lobotomy at the age of just 34. Freeman had a photo taken of himself performing the lobotomy on her, which he would show off to friends. He performed his last lobotomy in 1967 when he was 72 years old.
4. John Richard Brinkley, "the Milford Messiah", was the world's

foremost practitioner of goat gland science. Brinkley was born in Tennessee in 1885, and set up a small town doctor's practice in Milford, Kansas. One day an elderly farmer entered his clinic complaining of a diminishing libido and asked Brinkley if anything could be done. Remembering a book he had once read about endocrinology, Brinkley theorized that by transplanting the sexual glands of a goat into the male scrotum he could renew the male sex drive. In spite of his limited experience as a surgeon he persuaded the farmer to allow him to test his theory – and a year after his transplant the farmer's wife gave birth to a baby boy named Billy. For a mere $750, Brinkley offered his services to anyone else willing to undergo his surgery, and found plenty of eager subjects. The first few transplants, using gonads from the odourless breed of Toggenberg goats, were performed without any major hitch. The next two recipients were fitted with testicles from the Angora breed, and according to the doctor they left the operating theatre smelling like a steamy barn in midsummer. From now on Brinkley would always use only Toggenberg gonads, even allowing his patients to select their own donor goat from a pen outside "The Brinkley Clinic". His goat gland therapy came to the attention of Harry Chandler, owner of the *Los Angeles Times*. Chandler also underwent Brinkley's surgery and, highly satisfied with the results, began to publicize the technique in his newspaper. The publicity made Brinkley famous, but also brought the unwanted attentions of the California state medical authorities, who quickly revoked his licence to practise and began criminal proceedings against him. Brinkley fled back to Kansas, where he found his surgery in ever-increasing demand, thanks to his radio station, KFKB, an eccentric mixture of medical lectures and country and western music. Hundreds of males from all over the US flocked to Kansas, and at one stage about 40 goats a week were being shipped to The Brinkley Clinic by rail. In the 1930s Brinkley hit on a new scam, which he thought would be even more financially rewarding than his goat gland operation. He began a programme on his radio station called *Doctor Brinkley's Medical Question Box.* Listeners were invited to write to him with their health problems, and he would prescribe his own treatments on air. These cures invariably involved his own product line of patent medicines, which for the most part were coloured water. The Kansas authorities finally had the excuse they needed to revoke his broadcasting licence: blatantly unethical practice. Brinkley simply moved his operation to Del Rio, Texas, and set up a huge new transmitter across the Mexican border. His new station, XER, could now be heard throughout North America, and continued to bring him patients. In the late 1930s Mexican officials, pressured by the US government, shut down Brinkley's transmitter and eventually he was forced to declare bankruptcy. In 1942, as the US fraud squad moved in, he evaded trial by dying in San Antonio, Texas. His amazing career prompted a complete overhaul of medical practice and telecommunications by the US government.

5. Minutes before going into surgery to have his gangrenous right foot amputated in February 1995, 51-year-old diabetic William King joked with staff at the University Community Hospital in Tampa, Florida: "Make sure you don't take the wrong one." King awoke to discover that surgeon Rolando Sanchez had inadvertently removed his left foot, leaving the gangrenous foot intact. He subsequently had both legs amputated below the knee and settled with the surgeon for $250,000. Later the hospital revealed that it had implemented a new system to ensure the ghastly accident could never be

repeated: in future the word "no" would be written in marker pen on all limbs that were not to be amputated.

6. In October 1788 King George III fell ill with violent stomach cramps and began foaming at the mouth, the first of a series of attacks which convinced his government that the king was suffering from temporary insanity. Eventually, and with much reluctance, the regular army of royal physicians agreed to stand aside to allow an "expert" in mental illness, the Reverend Dr Francis Willis, to treat the king. Willis was rector of St John's, Wapping, where he also ran a private lunatic asylum as a sideline with his son John. On 5 December 1788 Dr Willis and his son John arrived at Windsor armed with state-of-the-art equipment for the treatment of mental illness: a straitjacket, iron clamps, a chair and a length of rope. The "treatment" they gave King George was so bestial that it probably caused him to have a complete nervous breakdown. George III's misfortune, however, was a gold mine for the dreadful Willises. In spite of them, the king had a couple of remissions, for which Willis and his son claimed full credit. Parliament struck official medals to celebrate and voted them huge annual pensions for life. Willis Snr was later invited to Portugal to "cure" their mad Queen Maria. He failed, but returned £10,000 richer and with an unrivalled reputation as physician to the crowned basket cases of Europe.
7. Dr Theodor Morell was Adolf Hitler's personal doctor from the mid 1930s onwards. Morell's bizarre regimen for curing the Führer's ailments comprised a combination of medications which almost certainly had disastrous effects on his mental state. As Hitler was a strict vegetarian he also suffered terribly from flatulence, a problem which Morrell treated by giving him Dr Köster's anti-gas pills, a medication which contained a mixture of strychnine and belladonna. Morell also prescribed

his "golden" tablets, containing huge amounts of caffeine and a highly addictive amphetamine called pervitin. Large doses of the latter are now known to cause disorientation, hallucinations, convulsions and coma: Hitler was known for his schizophrenic states and irrational outbursts. In September 1940 he threatened England with an air raid in which he specified that a million kilograms of bombs were to be dropped. He later amended the figure to 400,000 kilograms because on reflection the original quantity, arrived at under the influence of Morrell's pills, struck him as excessive. A subsequent personal physician, Dr Geising, discovered in 1944 that the Führer had been cumulatively poisoned over a period of many years with a variety of drugs in a "truly horrifying concentration". Dr Geising was not himself entirely blameless: in 1944 he treated Hitler's cold with a 10 per cent cocaine solution, and in his last days he gave him large quantities of cocaine drops for an eye complaint.

8. Britain's most infamous "doctor" in recent history was Muhammed Saeed. The bogus Bradford G.P. was granted a licence after arriving in the UK from Pakistan, and in spite of his history of obvious and occasionally laughable incompetence was mysteriously allowed to work for the National Health Service for 30 years before he was finally rumbled. "Dr" Saeed was finally jailed for five years in 1992 after variously prescribing to his 3,000 patients shampoo to be taken internally, creosote for a tooth complaint, sleeping pills to be taken three times a day, cough mixture to be rubbed into the skin, and suppositories to be taken orally.
9. The Irishman Sir William Arbuthnot Lane, a surgeon of Guy's Hospital, London, began the most painfully misguided medical fad of the century: surgical removal of the human colon. Lane's life was dominated by two great passions: part-time ballroom

dancing and human bowels. He believed the latter to be the seat of all known medical problems. Lane advised his patients to oil their colons daily with a pint of cream and to sleep flat on their stomachs, and made the remarkable discovery that red-haired women were naturally immune to constipation. His greatest contribution to medical science came in 1903, when he found that the human colon was surplus to requirements – merely a useless tube of tissue and muscle full of nasty smells. Lane set about testing his hypothesis by ridding the world of colons. No anus was safe from Lane: patients who came to see him for minor ailments would have their colons removed and tossed into the incinerator as a matter of routine. Before long his theory became fashionable, and surgeons all over the country agreed that the humble colon was responsible for a whole range of diseases, including cancer and tuberculosis. The fad lasted for about 10 years, until some doctors became suspicious and Lane was discredited.

10. Queen Victoria spent much of her reign in the hands of the mysteriously incompetent court physician Sir James Clarke, a man described by Lord Clarendon as "not fit to attend a sick cat". In 1839 Clarke was involved in a court scandal which became known as "The Flora Hastings Affair". The queen's young, unmarried lady-in-waiting Flora Hastings fell ill with a swollen stomach, convincing several people, including the queen herself, that she was pregnant. To prove her innocence, Miss Hastings agreed to a humiliating internal examination by the queen's doctor. Clarke reported that although he could not find evidence of pregnancy, he could see no other good reason for her swollen stomach. He then produced a bizarre medical statement which concluded that although Flora Hastings was still a virgin it didn't necessarily mean that she was not pregnant. He had come across a few cases in

his time, he explained to the queen, of pregnant virgins. This was all the queen needed to hear, and she set about making life for her lady-in-waiting as miserable as she possibly could. The truth became evident a few months later when the girl died in agony from a tumour on her liver. Clarke's career should have been terminated, but the queen retained his services. When her husband Prince Albert fell ill in November 1861, Dr Clarke was on hand again to assure both the prime minister, Lord Palmerston, and the queen that the Prince Consort was suffering from no more than a nasty cold, and that there was absolutely no need for concern. Within six weeks Prince Albert was dead. Clarke said later that with hindsight he thought he recognized typhoid symptoms. He was wrong in this, too, because the Prince Consort almost certainly died of cancer.

10 vertically challenged heads of state

1. King Pepin the Short – three feet, six inches.
2. Pope Greogory VII – four feet, one inch.
3. Charles III of Naples – four feet, five inches.
4. Attilla the Hun – four feet, six inches.
5. Joseph Stalin – five feet, four inches.
6. Napoleon Bonaparte – five feet, four inches.
7. President James Madison – five feet, four inches.
8. General Franco – five feet, four inches.
9. Queen Anne – four feet, nine inches.
10. Queen Victoria – four feet, ten inches.

History's 10 Biggest Fashion Mistakes

1. See-through clothes: all the rage in Imperial Rome during the reign of Nero. The clothes exposed both the breasts and the genitals. The trouble was, noted Seneca, "our women have nothing left to reveal to their lovers in the bedroom that they have not already shown on the street."
2. The codpiece: essential fashion accessory for Renaissance man, designed to fit around the male member like the finger of a glove, and worn throughout Europe in the fifteenth century. Contemporary fashion critic Michel de Montaigne wondered: "What is the purpose of that monstrosity that we to this day have fixed to our trousers, and often, which is worse, beyond its natural size through falseness and imposture?" Probably it was originally devised to facilitate the armoured knight's call to nature.
3. Flea cravats: for about 200 years, from the fourteenth century onwards, English ladies wore special fur collars. The accessory was designed to attract fleas, thus luring them away from the rest of their clothing.
4. False eyebrows: in the eighteenth century both men and women wore sets of mouseskin eyebrows stuck on with fish glue.
5. Bound feet: the Chinese fashion for foot-binding dates from the thirteenth century and the Empress Taki. She was born with a club foot, and her courtiers took to binding their own feet in cloth to imitate her. Before very long tightly bound, deformed feet became highly desirable in Chinese women. Their husbands encouraged foot-binding because their crippled wives were less likely to run away.

6. Erection restrainers: Queen Victoria's consort Prince Albert gave his name to a form of body-piercing, once fashionable amongst Victorian gentlemen, whereby erections could be restrained by a row of small hoops.
7. Exposed genitals: until Edward VI passed a law in 1548 banning any man below the rank of lord from exposing "his privy member and buttokkes", fashion in medieval England dictated that all should expose their naked genitals below short-fitting tunics. If the genitals weren't big enough a chap could wear padded flesh-coloured falsies, or braquettes.
8. Soliman's Water: the top brand name beauty lotion of the sixteenth century, applied to the skin to eliminate spots, freckles and warts. It was highly efficient, although applying a blowtorch to your face would have had similar consequences. The chief ingredient of this lotion was mercury, which burned away the outer layers of skin and corroded the flesh underneath. One side effect was that it made teeth fall out even more quickly than was usual at this time.
9. Radiation beauty treatments: one of the most popular items to be found in North American beauty parlours in the 1920s were X-ray machines, designed to remove unwanted facial and body hair. Radiation was also touted as a cure-all for every imaginable disease: products available included radioactive toothpaste for whiter teeth and better digestion, radioactive face creams to lighten the skin and radium-laced chocolate bars. A brisk trade in radioactive patent medicines thrived well into the 1930s. One of the most popular preparations was radium water, promoted in the US as a general tonic and known as "liquid sunshine". It was responsible for the deaths of

several thousand people. In 1932 Frederick Godfrey, the "well-known British Hair Specialist", was advertising a radioactive hair tonic, and as late as 1953 a company in Denver was promoting a radium-based contraceptive jelly.

10. Coloured teeth: in sixteenth-century Italy the most fashionable women coloured their teeth. Russian women always dyed them black.

10 Phobias of the Famous

1. Harriet Martineau, Edmund Yates, Wilkie Collins and Giacomo Mayerbeer: taphophobia (fear of premature burial). The dread of being buried alive was so widespread in the nineteenth century that over 200 books were written on the subject, and societies were formed to prevent it. The writer Harriet Martineau left her doctor £10 with instructions that he should make sure she was well and truly deceased before her burial by cutting her head off. The novelist Edmund Yates similarly left a 20 guinea fee for any surgeon kind enough to slit his jugular vein before interment. The novelist Wilkie Collins always carried a letter with him, imploring anyone finding him "dead" to contact the nearest doctor for a second opinion.
2. Nicolae Ceauşescu and Marlene Dietrich: bacillophobia (fear of germs). The former Rumanian dictator and his wife once staged a "walk-about" for publicity purposes, which required them to shake a few hands and kiss small children. The secret police selected a few volunteers beforehand and had them locked up for weeks and regularly disinfected in readiness for the big day. Marlene Dietrich's obsession led her to be known by Hollywood insiders as "the Queen of Ajax".
3. Natalie Wood, US actress: hydrophobia (fear of water). She drowned in 1981.
4. Sigmund Freud: siderodromophobia (fear of trains).
5. Samuel Johnson: lyssophobia (fear of insanity). Johnson often begged his wife to lock him in his room and shackle his legs because he was convinced he was going mad.
6. George Bernard Shaw: coitophobia (fear of sex). Shaw

lost his virginity to an elderly widow at the age of 29. He was so shocked by the experience that he didn't bother to try it again for another 15 years.

7. King Louis XV: cypridophobia (fear of syphilis). He took to sleeping with very young girls, aged between 14 and 19, because it reduced his chances of catching it.
8. Maximilian Robespierre: haematophobia (fear of blood). Thanks to the French Revolutionary the guillotine in the Place de la Révolution in Paris was in almost continuous use. Robespierre himself was extremely squeamish, however, and couldn't bring himself to look at the blood stains on the street cobbles.
9. Robert Schumann, German composer: metallophobia (fear of metal). He especially disliked keys.
10. Queen Christina of Sweden: entomophobia (fear of fleas). The mentally unbalanced seventeenth-century monarch had a four-inch cannon built so that she could spend most of her time firing tiny cannonballs at the fleas in her bedroom.

10 Eponymous Body Parts

1. Alcock's canal (in the pelvis).
2. Scarpa's triangle (in the thigh).
3. Poupart's ligament (in the groin).
4. Santorini's muscle (in the face).
5. Bell's nerve (in the chest).
6. Douglas's pouch (behind the uterus).
7. Willis's circle (at the base of the brain).
8. Vater's ampulla (the end of the bile duct).
9. Schwann's sheath (in the central nervous system).
10. Lieberkühn's crypts (intestinal lining).

10 Alarming Dental Practices

1. Ancient Egyptians cured toothache by splitting open the body of a live mouse, then laying it, still warm, along the patient's gums. Hippocrates recommended a toothpaste made of three mice and the head of a hare.
2. The first-century-AD Greek scholar Pliny claimed that toothache could be prevented by eating two mice a month. He also recommended "pervasive green frogs, burnt heel of ox, toads and worms" as a cure for halitosis. The Romans also relieved toothache by tying toads to their jaws, and made toothpastes and mouthwashes from urine. Apparently the very best piss was Portuguese.
3. A popular seventeenth-century cure for toothache involved the application of sweat from the anus of a cat which had been chased across a ploughed field.
4. An original method of tooth extraction was perfected by Dr Monsey, Resident Physician to the Chelsea Royal Hospital, home of the Chelsea Pensioners. He took a strong piece of catgut, wound one end around the patient's tooth then threaded the other end through a specially prepared bullet with a hole drilled through it. The bullet was loaded into his revolver and fired.
5. Early British dentures were mounted sets of human teeth extracted from corpses. The fashion for wearing dentures made from real human teeth went hand-in-hand with the rise of body-snatching in the first half of the nineteenth century. "Toothing" in the early nineteenth century was big business, and the teeth of the dead became valuable

commodities. Many body-snatchers took to "toothing" as a lucrative way to spend their spare time. Tons of teeth from the dead of the American Civil War were shipped to England to be worn by the rich and the fashionable. Later there was a craze not just for dentures made from human teeth, but for human teeth transplants – teeth removed from one set of gums and surgically implanted into someone else's. Although it was dangerous and encouraged poor people to sell their own perfectly good teeth for pennies, the practice lasted until shortly before World War I. Artificial dentures were invented at the end of the nineteenth century by an English dentist who disliked handling the teeth of dead men. Cheap celluloid teeth were also briefly popular, but they never really caught on because they were highly inflammable and likely to spontaneously combust if you smoked.

6. The eighteenth-century London dentist Martin Van Butchell promised "gums, sockets and palate formed, fitted, finished and fixed without drawing stumps or causing pain" – a bold claim, given that his technique amounted to hitting prospective patients over the head with a large stick, or blowing a trumpet in the patient's unsuspecting ear seconds before a tooth was to be pulled. Van Butchell was chiefly famous for his dead wife. Ever since her demise in 1775, the late Mrs Van Butchell had been embalmed with oil of turpentine and camphorated spirit of wine and left on display in his sitting room in a case with a glass lid.
7. When the Russian Czar Peter the Great saw a bad tooth being pulled he was suddenly consumed with a burning desire to become an amateur dentist. Overnight the czar's retinue of 250 courtiers became unwilling accomplices to his new hobby. He carried out spot-checks on the mouths of anyone who happened to be passing, and if any tooth looked suspect he whipped it out. No one turned him

down: the screams of his patients only made him more determined to get it right next time. He was an incredibly strong man, and it was not unusual for him to get carried away and accidentally remove gums as well. The czar kept the teeth in a little bag and would often show off his collection to visitors.

8. The writer Thomas de Quincey (1785–1879) started taking opium for a toothache he suffered while at Oxford, thus beginning a lifelong addiction. In his mid-20s he was taking 8,000 to 12,000 drops of opium daily. The remedy worked: eventually all his teeth fell out and he had to live on liquids.
9. In 1995 a dentist from Tennessee, Stephen Cobble, was charged with professional incompetence following the death of a patient. Former patients also complained that he had given them check-ups by having his assistant rub their backs, stomachs and arms; sedated patients by administering injections to their groins and navels; transferred C-section scar tissue to treat a jaw disorder; made a patient stand with one foot on a stack of magazines, and prescribed a diet of beef, salt and eggs and a quarter-pound of butter daily.
10. A 26-year-old man from Leeds, Walter Hallas, had a dread of dentists. In November 1979, while suffering in agony from toothache, Hallas persuaded a friend, Mark Waldron, to punch him on the jaw, cowboy-style, thus knocking out the tooth. His friend obliged with a punch which sent Hallas reeling backwards to the floor, fracturing his skull. Mr Hallas died in hospital from his injuries six days later.

10 Radical Cures for Baldness

1. In 1916 the Viennese professor Ludwig Steinach became famous for his revolutionary claim that the male vasectomy was a cure for baldness and loss of virility. The process, known as "Steinaching", attracted thousands of patients to the professor's clinic, including Sigmund Freud. None recovered their hair but many were afflicted by serious psychological problems and poor health, including testicular cancer.
2. Ancient Egyptians tried to cure hair loss with viper's oil and bats' ears.
3. The Chinese believed that they could prevent hair loss by eating rat flesh.
4. In Tudor times it was believed that dog or horse urine, rubbed into the scalp, reduced hair loss.
5. A currently popular Panamanian remedy known as "bladder syrup" claims to cure baldness, impotence and bad teeth. The medicine is made from monkey bladders, green tea and honey, and costs $4 an ounce.
6. Mexicans rub wax extracted from killer bees to cure baldness and haemorrhoids: one simply rubs it into the problem area.
7. Many Norwegian farmers still favour a traditional cure for baldness, available since the nineteenth century. It involves coating the head with cow dung for 20 minutes twice weekly.
8. In seventeenth-century England, before wigs became fash-

ionable for both sexes, bald men would sew clumps of false hair inside the rims of their hats.

9. The founder of the Ford Motor Company, Henry Ford I, always washed his hair in water containing rusty razor blades: he apparently believed that rusty water was a hair restorer.
10. There is no known cure for male pattern baldness which will leave you with your testes intact. Baldness relies upon the male testicular hormone testosterone, therefore castration offers the only plausible answer. The side effects of castration include loss of body hair, a falsetto voice, a tendency to obesity, insomnia, a weak bladder and poor eyesight.

12 DIY Operations

1. Thirty-two-year-old Italian Armando Botalezzi was rushed into hospital in October 1994 after attempting a nose job with a pair of pliers and a kitchen knife. Botalezzi explained later that he couldn't afford plastic surgery and had decided to "whittle it down a bit" himself. He said he would have been successful if only he hadn't kept fainting at the sight of his own blood.
2. In 1994 a 28-year-old cripple who couldn't wait to have his left leg amputated by the NHS decided to do something about it himself by laying his withered limb on a railway line in front of a train. Former landscape gardener Ian Hudson of Winnall, Winchester had damaged his leg in a motorcycle accident six years earlier. In spite of 20 operations he still had to hobble around with a special boot, calliper and crutches. After watching a slow-moving railway maintenance vehicle slice his leg off cleanly above the knee, Mr Hudson said that he had no regrets and was looking forward to having his brand new artificial leg fitted.
3. In 1995 26-year-old Terry Grice from Grand Rige, Florida carefully constructed a wooden clamp with which to hold his penis and testicles in place, then sliced them off with a circular saw. Grice said later that he did it because

he was depressed. He recovered from his state of depression long enough to throw the severed organs into the back of his pick-up truck and drive 50 miles to the nearest hospital to have them sewn back on.

4. Workmates of a 52-year-old Brazilian lumberjack, Luciano Bastos, were hugely impressed when their colleague, having lost his right hand in a logging accident in 1994, refused to make a fuss and simply fitted himself out with a hook. Not another word was spoken about the ordeal, until he tried to take his hat off and accidentally removed his eye.
5. In 1994 43-year-old Miguel Arroya of Barcelona chopped both his ears off with a butcher's knife so that he would no longer have to listen to his nagging mother-in-law. He discovered almost immediately that he could still hear her.
6. In the eighteenth century blood-letting was the most widely used cure-all in medicine, and the single most profitable source of income for surgeons. It became less lucrative in the nineteenth century with the invention of a DIY blood-letting kit which allowed patients to open their arm veins. One day Queen Caroline of Bavaria tried it, opened up a main artery in her arm by mistake and bled to death.
7. Britain's first prime minister, Sir Robert Walpole, ate about 180 pounds of soap over a period of several years in an attempt to get rid of a stone in his bladder.
8. Police were baffled by a flash fire which swept through the Chelsea flat of Norik Hakpisan in October 1982, burning the 24-year-old student alive. It later transpired that Hakpisan had perished during an unsuccessful attempt to cure his severe case of haemorrhoids with a can of petrol – a traditional cure, according to his family.

9. French postman Jean Cellise bled to death in Toulouse in 1994 after cutting himself open to check that his doctors had removed his appendix properly.
10. The wealthy nineteenth-century British MP and country squire Jack Mytton of Halston, Shropshire, died aged 38 after sustaining injuries while setting fire to his own nightshirt in an attempt to cure his hiccough. Before the horribly burned Mytton expired, he remarked: "Well, the hiccough is gone, by God."
11. The Milwaukee cannibal Jeffrey Dahmer admitted at his trail in February 1992 that he had performed DIY lobotomies on some of his victims in the hope of turning them into "zombie sex slaves".
12. West German Heinze Isecke cured his hiccoughs in 1975 by throwing himself from a hospital window. He had become depressed after being afflicted by non-stop hiccoughs over a period of about two years. It was estimated that his 36 millionth hiccough was the last straw.

10 Bowel Problems

1. King Edmund Ironside: reign curtailed when an assassin thrust his longsword up the Saxon king's fundament.
2. King Edward II: assassinated by having a red-hot poker thrust up his rectum.
3. Samuel Pepys: "Wind doth now and then torment me about the fundament extremely."
4. King Louis XIV: flatulence. It was said that he conveyed his admiration for his sister-in-law the Duchess of Orleans by doing her the honour of farting loudly in her presence.
5. Martin Luther: suffered from chronic constipation.
6. King Ferdinand I of Naples: constipation. The daily bowel movements of the eighteenth-century monarch were an utterly serious business: he always insisted on having a crowd of people around to keep him entertained while he strained. His father-in-law, the Austrian Emperor Joseph, was one of many who became privy to these unusual audiences, and noted later, "We made conversation for more than half an hour, and I believe he would still be there if a terrible stench had not convinced us that all was over." Ferdinand evidently also offered to show his father-in-law the fruit of his labours for closer inspection.
7. French Emperor Louis Napoleon III of France: suffered from a variety of ailments, including dysentery, gonorrhoea and a huge bladder stone. He commanded his troops at the Battle of Sedan in 1870 with towels stuffed inside his breeches to act as king-size nappies.
8. Queen Victoria: she ate too quickly, mixed malt whisky with claret, and was a martyr to persistent flatulence.
9. Adolf Hitler: flatulence. His personal doctor Theodore

Morrell gave him "anti-gas" medication to allay the Führer's embarrassment.

10. Elvis Presley: became addicted to Freenamint chewing gum whilst attempting to overcome his severe constipation.

8

Causes of the *Black Death* according to the Church

1. Jews poisoning the wells.
2. Going to the theatre.
3. Olive oil.
4. Lust for older women.
5. The use of dice.
6. Talk of sex.
7. Hanging out with witches.
8. Wearing winklepicker shoes.

10 Contemporary Cures for Bubonic Plague

1. Wash the victim in goat's urine.
2. Apply the entrails of a new-born puppy to the victim's forehead.
3. Drink menstrual blood.
4. Pierce your testicles.
5. Inhale fumes from a latrine.
6. Commit incest on an altar.
7. Smoke tobacco.
8. Apply dried toad to the bubo.
9. Eat the pus-filled boil of plague victims.
10. Eat a little treacle after rainfall.

The Great Unwashed: 10 Historical Stinks

1. Ludwig van Beethoven had such a disregard for personal cleanliness that his friends had to take away his dirty clothes and wash them while he slept.
2. The Chinese communist leader Chairman Mao decided early in his career never to take a bath or to brush his teeth – the latter on the grounds that tigers never brushed their teeth, either. He achieved an epic personal hygiene problem which grew steadily worse as the years went by. As a septuagenarian he had several young concubines rub his body down with hot towels.
3. The Bombay religious mystic Ramasubba Sitharanjan, who eschews personal hygiene as proof of his faith to his followers, claims not to have bathed, shaved or brushed his teeth in 65 years.
4. St Francis of Assisi listed personal filthiness among the insignia of piety, in line with the early teachings of the Christian Church, which held that dirtiness was next to Godliness and that bathing was an evil, ungodly vanity punishable by an eternity in hell. A fourth-century Christian pilgrim boasted that she hadn't washed her face for 18 years. St Anthony never washed his feet and

St Abraham didn't wash his hands or feet for 50 years. St Sylvia never washed any part of her body except her fingertips.

5. Czar Peter the Great, renowned throughout Europe for his occasional personal hygiene, was once described as a "baptized bear". He was incredibly dirty and smelly even by eighteenth-century standards, and blissfully unaware of rudimentary table manners or even basic potty training. When the czar and his courtiers visited London, onlookers noted that they intermittently dripped pearls and lice as they walked.
6. When the Prussian King Frederick the Great grew older and more eccentric he took on a major personal hygiene problem. His clothes remained unchanged for years and he shuffled in rags around his palace, which came to resemble a vagrant's squat, ankle-deep in places in excrement provided by his pack of beloved Italian greyhounds. When he died the shirt on his back was so rotten with sweat that his valet had to dress him in one of his own shirts for the burial.
7. Louis XIV was an enthusiastic lover, but his advances were a trying time for those mistresses with a keen sense of smell. When his doctor ordered him to bathe for medical reasons, the French king tried to get out of it by pretending he had a terrible headache as soon as he became immersed in water, and he vowed never to repeat the experience again. In all he took only three baths in his lifetime, each of them under protest.
8. Genghis Khan's Mongol warriors were a superstitious bunch who believed that washing was a sacrilege. There was also a more practical reason for their lax approach to ablutions: the thick crust of dirt which covered their

bodies helped them withstand temperatures as low as minus 43 degrees F. Khan's men used their lack of hygiene as a weapon of psychological warfare: their enemies could smell the festering Mongol hordes long before they could see them and were often paralysed with fear by the time they arrived.

9. The 11th Duke of Norfolk was renowned as one of the richest and the smelliest men in England. In his entire life the "Dirty Duke" never once voluntarily bathed: when his servants found it impossible to occupy the same room as him they used to get him blind drunk and quickly bathe him before he regained consciousness.
10. Although the French King Henri IV was known, unusually for the time, for being a stickler for changing his shirts regularly, he still went around his court "smelling like carrion". When his fiancée, Marie de Médicis, met him for the first time, the stench almost made her faint.

Xenophobe's Itch:
7 Names for **Syphilis**

1. French Pox (England, Italy and Spain).
2. The Naples Disease (France).
3. The Italian Disease (France).
4. The German Disease (Poland).
5. The Polish Disease (Germany and Russia).
6. Dutch Pox (Portugal).
7. The Portuguese Disease (Persia and Japan).

15 Exotic Phobias

1. Aeronausiphobia: fear of vomiting secondary to airsickness.
2. Apotemnophobia: fear of amputees.
3. Bolshephobia: fear of Bolsheviks.
4. Bromidrosiphobia or bromidrophobia: fear of body odor.
5. Defecaloesiophobia: fear of painful bowel movements.
6. Eurotophobia: fear of female genitalia.
7. Geniophobia: fear of chins.
8. Ichthyophobia: fear of fish.
9. Medomalacuphobia: fear of losing an erection.
10. Papaphobia: fear of the Pope.
11. Peladophobia: fear of bald people.
12. Taeniophobia: fear of tapeworms.
13. Venustraphobia: fear of beautiful women.
14. Walloonphobia: fear of the Walloons.
15. Zemmiphobia: fear of the great mole rat.

12 Inappropriate Cures

1. The seventeenth-century crack German surgeon Wilhelm Hilden advised the use of post-operative balm made from powdered mummy, earthworms, iron oxide, pig brains and moss from the skull of a man who had been hanged under the sign of Venus. The truly innovative part of Hilden's prescription was that this mixture was to be applied not to the wound, but to the weapon that caused it.

2. In the sixteenth century most learned people were convinced of the magical medical properties of bezoar stones, hard secretions often formed in cows' stomachs or goats' gall-bladders. The ground-breaking French barber-surgeon Ambroise Paré offended many traditionalists, especially the French King Charles IX (who was also a big bezoar fan), when he announced that the stones were completely useless. Paré decided to set up an experiment to prove his point. A cook who had been convicted of theft and sentenced to public strangulation was offered a choice between receiving his sentence and swallowing a lethal poison along with a bezoar stone, which was thought to be a perfect antidote. He chose the latter and died after lingering in agony for seven hours. King Charles concluded from this experiment that the bezoar stone was a fake.
3. Jean Nicot, a French ambassador in Portugal, became famous in 1560 for giving his name to the remarkable new wonder drug nicotine, an antiseptic and universal cure-all which would put an end to ulcers, bites, headaches, colds and rheumatism. A distinguished English doctor hailed Monsieur Nicot's discovery as "one of the best and surest remedies in the world" for apoplexy and giddiness. Tobacco has also been used at various times since to

cure asthma, gout, labour pains and even cancer.

4. Early suggested cures for syphilis included intercourse with a virgin, rubbing dung into the male organ and bathing in horse urine. The only regular precaution taken to avoid venereal disease in Elizabethan times was the washing of genitals in vinegar. Eighteenth-century cures for venereal disease included a sound thrashing, or having the penis wrapped in the warm parts of a freshly dismembered fowl.
5. Although morphine is one of the most highly additive drugs known (only 20 to 25 days' usage will produce a morphine junkie), it was used until the early twentieth century as a general painkiller for the most benign of ailments, including colds and minor headaches. At the beginning of the century the US had over 3,000 High Street stores selling over 50,000 different opium-based drugs over the counter. Morphine and opium were so widely used on the battlefield during the American Civil War – the former as a painkiller and the latter as a recreational drug – that opium addiction became known as the "army disease". When the US Congress introduced total prohibition in 1919, the American medical profession recommended morphine as an ideal substitute for alcohol. During Prohibition about 35,000 Americans were killed by drinking moonshine and other forms of illegal liquor. For the wives of alcoholics Sears Catalogue offered their morphine-based White Star Liquor Cure, which the loving spouse would use to drug her husband's coffee so that he would pass out instead of going to the local bar. Although the liquor cure was highly addictive, help was at hand with the Sears Narcotic Cure, featured on the same page of the catalogue.
6. The eighteenth-century English cure for mumps was to lead the patient, in the halter of an ass, around a pig-sty three times.
7. Until the sixteenth-century French surgeon Ambroise Paré proved it unnecessary, the standard cure for male hernias was castration.

8. The most popular cure for leprosy in the Middle Ages was to bathe in the blood of a dog. If a dog wasn't available, a two-year-old infant would do.
9. When radiation was first discovered in the nineteenth century it was immediately pronounced to be as harmless and beneficial as sunshine, and so began a medical craze for radiation treatment of the most trivial ailments. For a period of around 40 years, into the early part of the twentieth century, large numbers of people were needlessly exposed to lethal doses of radiation for such minor problems as ringworm and acne. Women were treated for post-natal depression by having their ovaries irradiated.
10. The nineteenth-century New York physician Dr Thomas Spencer pioneered a cure for cholera that involved plugging the patient's anus with sealing wax.
11. Until laws passed in the early 1900s prohibited false claims on medicine labels, US and British manufacturers were creative with their ingredients. Lead and arsenic were often combined with baking powder or gelatin. Although the families of people who were killed by these "curative" concoctions could sue, the courts usually sided with the manufacturers, handing down the verdict of "buyer beware." Soothing Syrup for infants and young children was laced with highly dangerous narcotics and killed about 15,000 English children every year. Dr Rupert Welk's Radiated Fluid for Cancer contained radioactive materials which resulted in many terrible deaths. Other medicines included Microbe Killer, Kick-apoo Indian Sagwa, Dr Kilmer's Swamp Root and Pinkham's Vegetable Compound.
12. Although the solvent Oil of Turpentine is more suited to cleaning paint brushes than treating illness, it was regularly prescribed by doctors in the eighteenth century after they discovered that bladder stones dissolved when placed in turpentine. "Turps" is highly poisonous and if ingested causes kidney damage and eventual death.

10 Famously Ugly People

1. The Greek philosopher Socrates was known for his uncannily pig-like features, a fact which he was happy to acknowledge. A Greek contemporary who practised physiognomy – the ancient science of judging a person's character by their appearance – once deduced from Socrates' face that the great man was a drunkard and a brute. When Socrates' followers violently objected to this, he intervened and announced that the reading was, in fact, quite correct.
2. Attila the Hun, the warrior leader who attacked the crumbling Roman Empire in the fifth century, was known to have been short, squat and exceptionally ugly. He nevertheless took 12 wives, and died of a heart attack while bedding a beautiful virgin.
3. The notorious "Habsburg Jaw" was a congenital malformation which blighted many Catholic royal families of Europe, but especially the royal family of Austria, for centuries. The disorder began in the fifteenth century with Maximilian of Habsburg, son of the Austro-Hungarian Emperor Frederick III. Maximilian was a remarkably ugly prince, with a large hooked nose, thick lips and a very pronounced underbite which made his jaw stick out. Disastrously, he married a close relative, Princess Mary, who also had thick lips and a pronounced underbite. These features subsequently became the predominant physical characteristics in both the Spanish and Austrian branches of the Habsburgs, a problem made much worse by the royal habit of inbreeding.

4. The butt of the very first sexist "paper bag" joke was probably the unfortunate Miss Tannakin Skinker, who lived in northern Germany in the early seventeenth century. She was born to wealthy parents, and had a perfectly normal body. However, her features earned her the unflattering nickname "the pig-faced lady". The girl's deformity was kept a secret by her parents for years, but news of her condition leaked out and a flood of voyeurs flocked to the family home. Against all odds, her family tried to increase her eligibility rating by dressing their daughter in the finest and most expensive clothing and throwing in a dowry of about £40,000. One young man, undaunted by the stories circulated by people who had seen the girl, commented: "Put her head in a blacke bagge and what difference between her and another woman?" As soon her veil was lifted, however, he went the same way as all the other enterprising suitors and ran away in horror. Miss Tannakin lived out her days a single woman.
5. The ruthless French revolutionary Jean-Paul Marat suffered from a variety of unsightly and disfiguring skin diseases, picked up during the years he spent hiding in cellars and sewers. Marat had to spend most of his time in the bath to obtain relief from his problem. He was in his bath-tub when he met his death: Charlotte Corday severed the aorta near his heart with a sharpened table knife.
6. All Britain's Hanover kings were noted not only for their ugliness but also for the plainness of their wives and mistresses. George III's wife, Queen Charlotte of Mecklenburg-Stretz, was so physically repulsive that it was suggested at the time that the king's bouts of madness were brought on by the trauma of having sex with her. When she arrived in England to take her throne, Londoners greeted

her with cries of "pug-face". When Charlotte requested a translation, she was told that it meant "God Bless Her Majesty". A few years later, when the king and queen were out riding in a horse-drawn trap, the cart overturned, breaking the queen's nose. This accidental remodelling of her features was noted to have been a considerable improvement.

7. Frederick North, the 2nd Earl of Guildford and Britain's prime minister from 1770 to 1782, was considered "the ugliest man in London". North was a huge man, swollen by dropsy and with thick lips and two protuberant eyes, through which he could barely see. He generally neglected his appearance to the point where his clothing and personal hygiene "always gave offence". On a trip to Africa, North asked the Dey, the ruler of Algiers, if he could see some of the women of his harem. It was an unusual request, which the Dey considered long and hard before replying: "He is so ugly – let him see them all."
8. Julia Pastrana, a Mexican who lived in the mid-nineteenth century, is said to have been the ugliest woman in history. For most of her adult life she was exploited as an international freak-show exhibit by her ruthless husband and manager, who married her to ensure that he had sole rights of ownership. When she became pregnant he even made money by selling tickets to the birth. The deformed child died stillborn and the mother died soon afterwards. For the husband, grief at losing his family came a poor second to the shock of losing his livelihood. He had Julia Pastrana and her child embalmed and placed in a glass case, and set off on a lucrative world tour.
9. Joseph Biggar, the nineteenth-century parliamentarian who invented "obstruction" and the Commons guillotine, is said

to have been the ugliest Tory MP of all time. Biggar had a hunchback, "a face like a gargoyle", bony hands and abnormally large feet, and suffered from a major speech impediment. He also took to wearing in the Commons a bizarre foul-smelling waistcoat fashioned from an unknown species of animal skin. When Biggar rose to make his maiden speech, a startled Benjamin Disraeli turned to a colleague and said: "What's that?"

10. Joseph "John" Merrick, the uniquely malformed "Elephant Man" discovered and cared for by the famous London surgeon Dr Frederick Treves, may have suffered from a combination of genetic skin and bone disorders, but probably not the one bearing his nickname. For many years it was assumed that Merrick suffered from multiple neurofibromatosis, now commonly called Elephant Man disease, a particularly horrific genetic disorder which causes eruptions of bone growth, causing bubbles of bone to grow from the sufferer's skull and skeleton. Recent three-dimensional scans of the skeletal remains of the unfortunate Victorian celebrity now suggest that he suffered from an extremely rare disorder called Proteus Syndrome, of which only 100 cases have ever been reported worldwide. The non-inherited disease, first identified in the 1970s, is triggered by proliferating cells that cause abnormal bone growth in the skull and in some body tissues. Merrick's bones continue to be the subject of research at their home in the London College of Medicine Museum.

12 EPONYMOUS ILLNESSES

1. James Parkinson (Parkinson's Disease, 1817).
2. William Stokes and Robert Adams (Stokes-Adams attack, 1826).
3. Sir Charles Bell (Bell's Palsy, 1828).
4. Thomas Hodgkin (Hodgkin's Disease, 1832).
5. Sir Dominic Corrigan (Corrigan's pulse, 1832).
6. Prosper Ménière (Ménière's Disease, 1850).
7. Guillaume Dupuytren (Dupuytren's contraction, 1851).
8. Thomas Addison (Addison's Disease, 1855).
9. John Hughlings Jackson (Jacksonian epilepsy, 1875).
10. Sergei Korsakoff (Korsakoff's Syndrome, 1887).
11. Max Wilms (Wilms' tumour, 1899).
12. Aloius Alzheimer (Alzheimer's Disease).

The Wonder of You: 10 Revealing Facts about the Human Condition

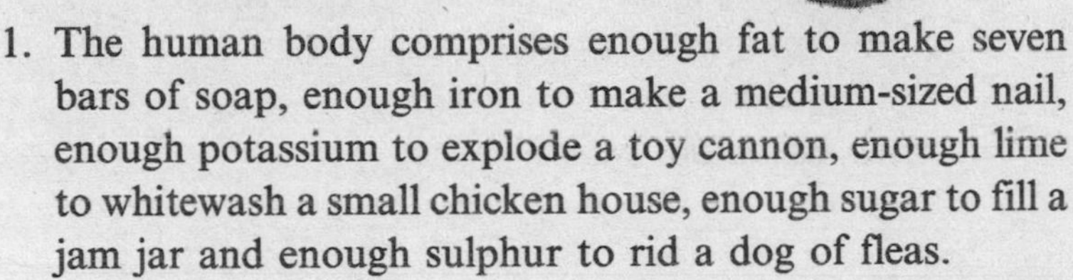

1. The human body comprises enough fat to make seven bars of soap, enough iron to make a medium-sized nail, enough potassium to explode a toy cannon, enough lime to whitewash a small chicken house, enough sugar to fill a jam jar and enough sulphur to rid a dog of fleas.
2. Your complete skeleton is worth between £2,500 and £4,000 to a medical student; your skull alone would fetch about £250.
3. Your mouth produces about one litre of saliva per day.
4. Demodox folliculorum has eight stumpy legs and a tail, is about a third of millimetre long and loves nothing more than to recline in the warm, oily pits of your hair follicles. Most adults have this mite, usually on the head and especially in eyelashes, and often in nipples.
5. You have about 4,000 wax glands in each ear.
6. The average British adult stool weighs about 4 ounces. About half of the bulk of your faeces comprises the dead bodies of bacteria which live inside your gut.
7. The average male foot exudes half a pint of sweat each day.
8. If it wasn't for the slimy mucous which clings to and lines

the walls of your gut, your stomach would readily digest itself.

9. The average person will pass about 1,100 gallons of urine in a lifetime.
10. A man weighing 150 pounds would provide enough meat to make a meal for 75 cannibals in one sitting.

10 Historical DEFORMITIES

1. Moses was a reluctant public speaker, who described himself as "heavy of mouth". He had a major speech impediment, and probably suffered from a cleft lip and palate. In Exodus 6:12:30 Moses describes his mouth as having "uncircumcised lips".
2. Anne Boleyn had six fingers on her left hand, and three nipples. If King Henry VIII's charges against her of adultery and incest had failed he planned to use this as evidence to have her burned as a witch.
3. Marshall Talleyrand had a deformed leg, the result of being dropped by his nurse.
4. John Keats had an unusually small head.
5. Lord Byron had a club foot shaped like a cloven hoof.
6. Napoleon had only one testicle.
7. Kaiser "Bill" Wilhelm II had a stunted and withered left arm, the result of a complicated breech birth.
8. Josef Stalin's left foot had webbed toes and his left arm was noticeably shorter than his right.
9. Josef Goebbels had a club foot. His left leg was eight centimetres longer than his right. He was born with the disability, but the official version was that it was the result of a childhood illness. The possibility that one of the architects of the Nazi movement had a genetic defect didn't sit too well with the prevailing ideology.
10. According to Soviet medical reports, Adolf Hitler did indeed have only one ball.

10 Famous *Drug* Addicts

1. Admiral Horatio Nelson: opium addiction.
2. William Wilberforce, slave trade abolitionist: opium addiction.
3. Lord Liverpool, British prime minister: ether addiction.
4. Clive of India: opium addiction.
5. Sigmund Feud: cocaine addiction.
6. Czar Nicholas II, the last Russian czar, spent the final two years of his reign high on a cocktail of addictive drugs. He took cocaine for colds, opium and morphine for stomach complaints and hallucinogens, obtained from a herbalist. Visitors were shocked by his appearance and remarked on his dull eyes, dilated pupils, hollow cheeks, vacant smile and his apparent lack of concern about the impending crisis.
7. Sir Winston Churchill: barbiturates. His personal physician, Lord Moran, supplied him with a bewildering variety of chemical stimulants and depressants with little or no warning about the probable effects. As prime minister in the 1950s Churchill became totally dependent on barbiturates, especially after his stroke in 1953, always mixing them with copious quantities of alcohol. Churchill had nicknames for his drugs – majors, minors, reds, greens and Lord Morans.
8. Anthony Eden: amphetamine addiction. The British prime minister probably became dependent during a long and painful blockage of his biliary tract in the early 1950s. He carried with him at all times a box containing a variety of chemicals, including morphine. Throughout the Suez crisis Eden acknowledged that he was "practically living on Benzedrine". Close advisers noted that Eden seemed to be permanently "in a state of acute intoxication". In September 1956 the Israeli Ambassador reported that Eden talked excitedly and ceaselessly over lunch. His medical consultant confided to a member of his

cabinet that the prime minister "could not live on stimulants any more". Regular doses of amphetamine are highly dangerous, and even small doses can lead to paranoid psychosis. By 1956 Eden had become obsessed with the Egyptian President Nasser and was given to hysterical outbursts at the mention of his name. According to some of his friends, Eden was under the delusion that Nasser was a reincarnation of Hitler.

9. Hermann Goering, Commander-in-Chief of the Luftwaffe, was a lifelong drug abuser who spent much of World War II "in a near comatose state of narcotic stupor". Long before the war, in 1925, the Swedish authorities had certified Goering a dangerous drug addict and locked him an asylum, where he attacked a nurse who refused to give him morphine. By 1937 he was hooked on Codeine, a morphine derivative commonly found in pain-killing tablets and cough mixtures. When he was captured in 1945 his daily intake averaged 100 tablets. In pre-war Nazi Germany cocaine was hugely popular with the rich and powerful. Some historians have made a connection between the delusions of strength and paranoia suffered by cocaine-abusers and similar traits displayed by Nazi leaders: it has even been speculated that Hitler may have been on a cocaine trip when he decided to conquer Russia.
10. Leonid Brezhnev, the comatose Soviet leader, spent the last 10 years of his life as a tranquillizer and sleeping-pill junkie. His prolific drug abuse accelerated the ageing process and caused massive damage to his central nervous system. Brezhnev's public appearances were so famous for their lack of animation that they inspired widespread rumours that he was already dead. His assistants later admitted that during a state visit to East Germany in 1979 they had to set the drugged president on his feet and propel him forwards as though they were "kick-starting a car".

12 PRESIDENTIAL ILLNESSES

1. George Washington was in his early 60s during his second term of office and succumbed to progressive senile dementia. He was noted to be emotionally unstable, confused and out of touch with reality before his presidency ended in 1797. Washington had a morbid fear of premature burial and left instructions that after he died he was to be laid out for three days just to be on the safe side.
2. Andrew Jackson suffered throughout his life from an irritating skin disease called the "bit itch".
3. Before the advent of anaesthetics and antiseptic practices, James K. Polk survived a urinary stone operation at the age of 17, but it left him sterile.
4. Zachary Taylor fell ill at the Washington Monument on 4 July and died suddenly a few days later. The official cause of death was gastroenteritis – inflammation of the stomach and intestines. Some historians continued to believe, however, that Taylor had been murdered and probably suffered arsenic poisoning; so 141 years after his death his remains were exhumed and samples of hair and fingernail tissue were removed for study. The findings disproved the murder theory.
5. Chester A. Arthur, remembered only for his nickname "Elegant Arthur", as he owned 80 pairs of trousers and changed clothes several times a day, discovered he was dying of Bright's Disease, a fatal kidney condition, after serving about one year in office. He died

a year after leaving the presidency in 1886.

6. Grover Cleveland had a large cancerous growth on his upper palate which was secretly operated on without even his vice-president knowing what was going on. The evident problem with his mouth was explained as "severe toothache".
7. William Howard Taft suffered from chronic obesity, weighing 24 stones and four pounds when he came to office. He owned a special bathtub big enough for four average-sized men: he got stuck in it on his Inauguration Day and had to be prized out. Taft's wife Helen found his obesity repulsive and refused to have sexual relations with him.
8. Woodrow Wilson was in the middle of a lecture tour in 1919 when he had a major stroke, resulting in brain damage and paralysis and turning his trademark radiant smile into a frightening leer. As Wilson lay seriously ill and incapacitated in the White House for seven months, the US government effected a major cover-up. Twenty-eight bills during this period were passed without the president's signature. Whenever he was required to receive visitors, he was propped up in a chair, his useless left arm hidden from view. An aide would whisper the names of his guests in his ear so that he could greet them. Wilson's illness was kept a secret from the American public for years after his death.
9. As a young man, Warren G. Harding had several nervous breakdowns. He died in office from a myocardial infarction.
10. Franklin D. Roosevelt's polio was the biggest public deception in the history of presidential illnesses, pulled off with the full co-operation of the press. Newsreels never

showed him being wheeled or carried, and of the 35,000 photographs of Roosevelt in the Presidential Library, only two show him in a wheelchair.

11. Dwight D. Eisenhower suffered from arteriosclerosis and acute intestinal obstruction. He had a major heart attack which required emergency treatment just 18 months into his presidency in 1955, but apparently made a full recovery. In November 1957 he also suffered a stroke, which affected his speech.
12. John F. Kennedy carefully nurtured his image of robust good health to disguise the fact that he suffered from Addison's Disease, a deficiency of the adrenal glands which was physically debilitating and led to emotional instability and depression. He was treated for many years with a type of steroid associated with psychiatric side-effects including depression, mania, confusion and disorientation. Two other side effects of steroid abuse are massively increased appetites for food and sex – both signs noted in Kennedy. He also suffered from a bad back and was given repeated local anaesthetics containing a derivative of cocaine. It is likely that he was also hooked on amphetamines. Nine years after his death, Kennedy's personal doctor, Max Jacobson, known to his show-biz patients as "Dr Feelgood", was struck off after being found guilty on 48 counts of professional misconduct, mostly involving the illegal prescription of amphetamines or "speed" to his patients. The Kennedy family have taken unusual steps to ensure that the former president's medical records are not disclosed for many more years to come.

The Top 10 Causes of Madness in the Eighteenth Century*

1. *Moving into a new home.*

2. *Squeezing a pimple.*

3. *Old age.*

4. *Childbirth.*

5. *The menstrual cycle.*

6. *Shrinkage of haemorrhoids.*

7. *Misuse of mercury.*

8. *Disappointment in love.*

9. *Masturbation.*

10. *Bloodletting.***

*As listed in the standard text on the subject of madness, written by the leading French physician Jean Esquirol.
**Particularly confusing to a medical profession which still believed bloodletting to be a cure for madness.

’Roid Rage: 20 Famous Haemorrhoid Sufferers

1. Alexander the Great.
2. Charles Dickens.
3. King Edward VII.
4. T.S. Eliot.
5. Gerard Manley Hopkins.
6. Francis Kilvert.
7. Martin Luther.
8. Marilyn Monroe.
9. Emperor Nero.
10. Napoleon.
11. Edgar Allan Poe.
12. Alexander Pope.
13. Thomas de Quincey.
14. Viv Richards, West Indian cricketer.
15. Percy Bysshe Shelley.
16. Socrates.
17. Lytton Strachey.
18. Queen Victoria.
19. Evelyn Waugh.
20. The Duke of Wellington.

They said they were ill:

Ex-hypochondriacs

1. Florence Nightingale.
2. Queen Victoria summoned her court physician up to six times a day. He was surprised to receive a telegram from the queen while he was away on his honeymoon informing him that "the bowels are acting fully".
3. Otto von Bismarck.
4. King George IV frequently complained to his court doctors that he was dying.
5. Charles Darwin took to his bed for months at a time, complaining of headaches and giddiness.
6. Howard Hughes kept all his urine in jars, which were labelled and catalogued.

8 Health Problems that helped Napoleon meet his Waterloo

1. *Pituitary dysplasia.*
2. *Prolapsed piles.*
3. *Constipation.*
4. *Syphilis.*
5. *Extreme fatigue.*
6. *Colic.*
7. *Peptic ulcer.*
8. *Cystitis.*

10 Historic Operations

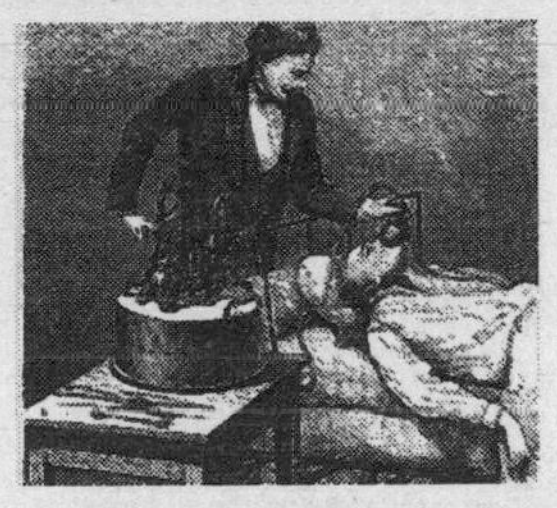

1. In 1881 US President Garfield was shot twice by the assassin Charles Guiteau. One bullet grazed Garfield's arm but the other lodged itself somewhere inside his body. He was rushed to the White House, still conscious, and over the next 80 days 16 doctors were consulted on the president's condition. The first doctor, Willard Bliss, jabbed a finger into the wound, then inserted a non-sterile probe to find the bullet. Bliss didn't find the slug, but did so much damage with his probe that it misled physicians who arrived later into believing that this was the path made by the bullet. They concluded that the missile had penetrated the liver and that surgery would therefore be of no use. An army surgeon-general then stuck his unwashed finger into the wound as deep as he could, and was followed by the navy surgeon-general, who probed with his finger so deeply that he actually punctured the liver – an organ which the bullet had not hit. They concluded that the president would be dead within 24 hours. Garfield's fever rose and he was put on a diet of milk and brandy. Meanwhile, the surgeons continued to poke and prod inside the president's body with their fingers. At this point Alexander Graham Bell was called in to help find the offending missile with a crude metal detector. After several passes, Bell announced that he had located the bullet, and doctors decided to cut Garfield open to remove it. What Bell's equipment had actually located was the metal spring under the mattress.

The bullet continued to elude them. The deep and by now badly infected wound, coupled with possible blood poisoning, caused Garfield to have a massive and fatal heart attack several days later. The bungling surgeons incorrectly attributed death to the rupturing of a blood vessel in his stomach. At the president's autopsy, examiners determined that the bullet had lodged itself some way from the spine and that Garfield would have survived if the doctors had only left him alone. Charles Guiteau argued at his trial that he did not kill the president and that the doctors were responsible for the president's death, but he was sentenced to death and hanged on 30 June, 1882.

2. Gruesome pioneer attempts at blood transfusion were made in the seventeenth century long before it dawned on anyone that blood-type compatibility was quite important. On 23 November 1667 members of the Royal Society gathered to witness the transfusion of 12 ounces of sheep's blood into the unfortunate Reverend Arthur Coga. Samuel Pepys recorded in his diary: "The patient speaks well, saying that he finds himself much better, as a new man . . . but he is cracked a little in his head." The Rev. Coga died soon afterwards.
3. Pepys himself experienced the only internal surgical operation available before the nineteenth century – lithotomy, or removal of a bladder stone. The diarist was trussed on his back with wrists tied to ankles, while the surgeon probed his urethra with a catheter, following it with a bigger probe to locate the stone. A large cut was made near the patient's groin, then the surgeon cut through the perineum and, reaching into the bladder, extracted the stone. The operation took at least one hour and nearly half the patients didn't survive it. Pepys was

only 22 years old when he was operated on for a stone "as big as a tennis ball" by the leading lithotomist, Thomas Holister. The diarist was quite happy with the outcome of the operation, although it left him sterile, and afterwards he often passed "gravel" in his urine, which he tried to cure by drinking neat turpentine.

4. When Charles II had a fit while shaving in 1685, he was lucky to be treated with the finest medical advice of the day. He was attended by 14 physicians who drew blood, forced him to vomit violently and gave him a strong laxative. Then they shaved his head, applied blistering agents to his scalp, put special plasters made from pigeon droppings onto the soles of his feet, fed him bezoar stones (much-prized gallstones from the bladder of a goat) and made him drink 40 drops of extract from a dead man's skull. He died two days later.
5. In 1686 King Louis XIV of France had a terrible operation for anal fistulas. Twice he was sliced open without any form of anaesthetic, but the word from the palace of Versailles was that he endured the operation heroically. A group of French nuns at the cloister of Saint-Cyr heard of his recovery and celebrated by writing a song, *Dieu Sauvez le Roi*. A travelling Englishman heard the tune, copied it down, and when he got it home translated it into *God Save the King*. Thus the British National Anthem evolved from a hymn written to celebrate a successful operation on the French king's piles.
6. Admiral Horatio Nelson had a terrible fear of sea-sickness, which stayed with him throughout his naval career. He was also an opium addict. His problem dated back to the amputation of his right arm, without anaesthetics, on board the *Theseus* on 25 July 1797. Nelson was so upset by

the feel of the cold scalpel against his flesh that he ordered all amputations performed on ships under his command to be performed with warm knives. After his arm had been removed he was left alone to recover with an opium pill and a shot of rum.

7. In 1846 the famous engineer Isambard Kingdom Brunel accidentally swallowed a gold half-sovereign, which lodged in his windpipe and stayed there for six weeks. After vomit-inducing drugs failed to dislodge it, his surgeon attempted a tracheotomy to keep the airway open while he tried to remove the coin, but this also failed. The coin was finally expelled by a more basic method: the engineer was strapped to a hinged table, tilted to a 45-degree angle, then thumped hard in the back. Much to Brunel's relief the coin shot forward and hit his teeth.
8. Before the discovery of anaesthetics, when the only two important qualifications for a good surgeon were fast hands and an iron stomach, it was often a close call as to who suffered the most, surgeon or patient. By and large surgeons were humane men who worked in the certain knowledge that despite their best intentions they were inflicting the most appalling pain on their patients. The most accomplished English surgeon of his day, Sir Astley Cooper, once burst into tears when a sick child smiled confidently at him just as he was about to operate. Queen Caroline's personal surgeon, William Chiselden, threw up before every operation, and always armed his assistant with a watch to try to keep the duration of his operations down to under three minutes. Although many operations took about an hour, Napoleon's famous chief surgeon, Dominique Lorrey, could amputate a leg in under 15

seconds. The nineteenth-century Scottish surgeon and part-time body-snatcher Robert Lister was described as "the finest surgeon in Europe". Lister's personal best for a leg amputation was 28 seconds, although while achieving this record he accidentally cut off two of his assistant's fingers and the patient's left testicle.

9. If the official records of such events are to be believed, royal patients are not only a lot braver than the rest of us when they have to go under the surgeon's scalpel, but their breeding also makes them rather more courteous. After George IV had a sebaceous cyst removed from his head in 1821, entirely without the aid of anaesthetics, he casually enquired of the surgeon, Astley Cooper: "So, what do you call these tumours?" As a mark of the king's gratitude, plain Astley became Sir Astley. When Queen Victoria had a particularly nasty axillary abscess drained, she came round from the chloroform and remarked: "A most unpleasant task, Professor Lister, most pleasantly performed."

10. The first amputation ever carried out under anaesthetic was performed on 7 November 1846 in Massachusetts General Hospital, when a 21-year-old servant girl, Alice Mohan, parted with her right leg. The operation was carried out by Dr George Haywood, assisted by Andrew Morton and his new invention, the ether inhaler. When the amputation was successfully completed, Haywood was understandably pleased with himself and couldn't resist showing off. He leaned over the girl and said: "I guess you've been asleep, Alice." The patient replied: "I think I have, Sir." "Well, you know why we brought you here," said Haywood. "Are you ready?" The girl replied that she was, at which point Haywood plucked the leg

from the sawdust where it lay and waved it triumphantly under her nose, saying: "It's all done, Alice!" There is no record of her reply.

12 Popular Parasitic Infestations

1. The parasite *cryptosporidium*, which can cause severe diarrhoea, occurs naturally in British tap water. About 10,000 cases are reported each year, one-fifth of which require hospital treatment.
2. Several types of worm found in nearly all raw fish, especially fish used in Japanese sushi, live in the human brain.
3. The human body can happily accommodate a tapeworm up to 10 metres long. The tapeworm cannot breed without exiting then re-entering the host.
4. The three types of body lice which most enjoy human company are *pediculus humanus* (the head louse), *pediculus humanus corporis* (the body louse) and *phthirus pubis* (the pubic louse, or "crab").
5. Up to 155 different types of yeast colonies exist on your skin at any one time. You have roughly the same number of bacteria and other organisms on your skin and hair as there are people on earth. One of the most populous strains, *pityrosporum ovale*, lives in and around your nose, with a population density of up to half a million per square centimetre. There are now 25 known types of venereal, or sexually transmitted diseases which are harmful to mankind, variously caused by viruses, bacteria, parasites, mites, yeasts, chlamydiae and fungi. Close cousins of the gonorrhea bacteria live in your mouth and throat.
6. Athlete's foot is caused by a parasitic fungus. The most severe cases of athlete's foot are treated with amputation of the toes.
7. More than 90 per cent of the population are carriers of the herpes virus.

8. You can catch pubic lice during sexual intercourse, from lavatory seats, bed linen or moulting pubic hairs.
9. Parasites can flourish in virtually every organ or tissue in your body, but some species target specific parts. Guinea worms live beneath your skin, roundworms go for your lungs or muscle tissue, and flukes head for your bloodstream, your liver, your intestine or your lungs.
10. Hydatid cysts are formed in the larval stage of the tapeworm. They commonly exist in dogs, although a dog can pass them on to humans with a simple lick of the hand. Once this cyst is inside the human host it can swell to the size of a football.
11. The bacterium *streptococcus A* is found in 10 per cent of the population. In some people – doctors don't know why – it develops into necrotizing fasciitis, the so-called flesh-eating bug which eats away at the fat under the skin at the rate of several inches an hour. It usually results in the need for drastic surgery.
12. Guinea worm disease develops within a year of a person's ingesting water fleas infected with the larvae, at which point worms up to three feet long emerge from painful blisters.

60 Work-related Health Problems

1. Baker's Eczema.
2. Billingsgate Hump (a problem for fish porters).
3. Boilermakers' Deafness.
4. Bricklayers' Itch.
5. Bricklayers' Anaemia.
6. Biscuit-Makers' Dermatitis.
7. Budgerigar Fanciers' Lung.
8. Bullmans' Hand.
9. Cable-Makers' Rash.
10. Chain-Makers' Cataracts.
11. Cigar-Makers' Cramps.
12. Cigarette-Cutters' Asthma.
13. Cobblers' Mouth.
14. Combers' Fever.
15. Confectioners' Dermatitis.
16. Coolie Itch.
17. Cornpickers' Pupil.
18. Cotton Mill Fever.
19. Cotton-Twisters' Cramp.
20. Cotton-Weavers' Deafness.
21. Covent Garden Hummy (curvature of the spine).
22. Dairyman's Itch (caused by a form of VD found in cows, horses and sometimes dogs).
23. Deal-Runners' Shoulder.
24. Diamond-Cutters' Cramps.
25. Dockers' Itch.
26. Dustmen's Shoulder.
27. Feather-Pluckers' Disease.
28. Fireman's Eye (afflicts potters who fire kilns, not firemen).
29. Fish-Handlers' Disease.

30. French Polishers' Dermatitis.
31. Gold-Smelters' Cataracts.
32. Fish-Handlers' Disease.
33. Glassworkers' Cataract.
34. Grocers' Itch.
35. Harpists' Cramps.
36. Hatters' Tremor.
37. Hodman's Shoulder.
38. Miners' Bunches (hookworm, also known as Tile-Makers' or Tunnellers' Disease).
39. Miners' Elbow.
40. Mushroom-Workers' Lung.
41. Nailmakers' Cramps.
42. Nuns' Bursitis.
43. Paddyfield Foot.
44. Paprika-Splitters' Lung.
45. Printers' Asthma.
46. Pork Finger (afflicts abbatoir workers).
47. Potters' Rot (lead-poisoning).
48. Poultry-Pluckers' Finger.
49. Seal Finger (unique to sealers and whalers).
50. Shipyard Conjunctivitis.
51. Shoemakers' Cramps.
52. Sugar-Cane-Cutters' Cramps.
53. Swineherds' Disease.
54. Tailors' Ankle.
55. Tea-Tasters' Cough.
56. Tripe-Scrapers' Disease.
57. Tulip Finger (afflicts market gardeners).
58. Upholsterers' Mouth.
59. Wool-Sorters' Disease (anthrax, also known in France as "Bradford Disease").
60. Weavers' Bottom.

5
SAINTS & SINNERS

10 Holy Relics

1. The personal evacuations of the Grand Llama of Tibet were considered so holy that his followers wore samples of his excrement around their necks as holy relics. His urine was also considered a powerful prophylactic, and his courtiers would mix it in their food.
2. At least 13 churches worldwide claim to own Christ's foreskin. Pope Innocent III declined to rule on which was the genuine artefact on the grounds that God alone knew the truth.
3. King Henry VII was given St George's left leg as a present.
4. Sri Lanka has a temple dedicated to one of the Buddha's teeth.
5. In the nineteenth century there were three holy navels of Christ on display in churches at Rome, at Lucques and at Chalones-sur-Marne.
6. The brain of St Peter was for several decades housed above an altar in Geneva, until it turned out to be a pumice stone.
7. St Peter's nail-clippings have surfaced in a dozen churches in Europe.
8. The body of the Welsh saint, Teilo, was at one time miraculously housed in three different locations.
9. At least 60 churches claim to be the respository of the Virgin Mary's breast milk.
10. The chamber-pot used by the late-fourteenth century saint Giovanni Columbini was renowned for its miraculous healing properties. After his death, the pot emitted a fragrant odour. A young lady suffering from a severe facial disfigurement smeared the contents of the chamber pot over her face, and was cured.

10 Politically Incorrect Politicians

1. The Holy Roman Emperor Henry VI liked to cheer up his troops by having nuns stripped and smeared with honey, then decorated with feathers and sent on horseback through the ranks of cheering men.
2. The president of Uganda, Idi Amin (or, to accord him his full title, "Lord of All the Beasts of the Earth and Fishes of the Sea and Conqueror of the British Empire in Africa in General and Uganda in Particular") had over 250,000 people murdered or executed between the time he seized power in 1971 and the day he was deposed in 1979. One of Idi Amin's two favourite hobbies was erecting statues all over Uganda to his two greatest idols, Queen Victoria and Adolf Hitler; the other was crushing the genitals of his victims with his bare hands. To save time, Amin handed out a mass murder contract to his private police force, the implausibly named State Research Bureau, who rounded up candidates and murdered them, then informed the families that for £150 they would lead them to the bodies. The scheme became such a huge success that neighbours complained about the ceaseless din of machine-gun fire at SRB headquarters. To keep the noise

down, Amin bribed his prisoners to execute themselves by clubbing each other to death with 16-pound sledgehammers. The scale of Amin's campaign of terror against his enemies was so immense that it ran into logistical problems. A former government employee, Francis Kalimazo, was at a wedding when he learned of his own "death" on the radio, and quickly fled when he realized that he was part of the backlog. Dinner guests at Idi Amin's State House in Entebbe were treated to some unscheduled entertainment by their host one evening in August 1972, when between courses Amin vanished into the kitchen and returned with the frozen head of his former commander-in-chief, Brigadier Hussein. Amin screamed abuse at the head and threw cutlery at it, before asking his guests to leave. His foreign policy was also marked by eccentricity. In 1978 Amin planned a full-scale invasion of neighbouring Tanzania, but first decided to lull Tanzania's President Julius Nyerere into a false sense of security. He sent Nyerere a telegram which read, "I love you so much that if you were a woman I would consider marrying you." Amin was a former heavyweight boxing champion of Uganda. When his country was being overrun by Tanzanian troops, he suggested that he and Julius Nyerere settle the war between them in the ring, with Mohammed Ali as referee. To mark the anniversary of his military coup in 1977, Idi Amin invited the former prime minister Edward Heath to fly to Uganda "with his band" to play before him during the celebrations. He once refused to attend the Commonwealth Games unless the queen sent him a new pair of size 13 boots.

3. Joaquin Balaguer became president of the Dominican Republic in 1966 with the help of US marines who feared

another "Cuba". He remained in power for the next 30 years, thanks to ballot box fraud. He travelled the countryside in a vehicle with a glass tower, from which he handed out gifts ranging from sweets and bicycles to money and plots of land. Known to foreign diplomats as the Wizard of Id, he marked the 500th anniversary of Columbus's visit by spending a ruinous amount of money on a gigantic white lighthouse in the shape of a crucifix. When the lighthouse was first switched on it caused a massive and disastrous drain on the national grid (unnoticed by the 60 per cent of his people who still do not have electricity). Although blind, deaf and 89 years old, in 1996 he challenged a civil servant suspected of fraud to a duel, but changed his mind at the last minute and settled for a speech in parliament instead.

4. The ideas of the Chinese leader Mao Tse-Tung, called Mao Thought, became the official ideology of the Chinese Communist Party at their seventh Congress at Yanan in the spring of 1945, the same year he received the title of Chairman. On Mao's instructions, elderly people accused of being class enemies were beaten to death on trains, on buses and on the street. At the height of Mao's reign of terror the Babaoshan crematorium in Beijing had a three-day backlog of corpses. The entire senior faculty at Zhongshan University was hauled to the front entrance of the campus in the middle of the night and hanged from the trees in a mass execution. Many of Mao's homicides were dressed up to look as if the victims had taken their own lives. The favourite method of suicide was by jumping from a high window, but other methods were common, including drowning in lakes or rivers, hanging, leaping in front of trains and drinking concentrated insecticide. Mao

was also responsible for the world's worst-ever famine, a disaster which killed an estimated 43 million of his countrymen. His so-called Great Leap Forward in the late 1950s was a suicidal socialist farming programme based on a similar plan which had already failed Josef Stalin. Throughout the famine Mao refused to believe that his policies were not working. At one point he even doubled his country's grain export. Mao compounded the problem by mobilizing the entire Chinese nation to wipe out China's sparrow population, with the explanation that sparrows were eating the country's cereal crops. Over a period of 48 hours about 80 million Chinese took to the streets and fields and banged woks and gongs until the birds dropped dead of exhaustion. It was a popular move, because the Chinese loved fried sparrow. Without the sparrows to control worms and other pests, however, agricultural disaster followed. With the natural food cycle altered, even more people starved to death over the next three years. According to Chairman Mao's personal physician, Dr Li, the communist leader was almost certainly mad throughout his entire leadership. In contrast to his early days, when he maintained a purposely spartan lifestyle, Mao grew fat, chain-smoked, and seldom got out of bed before noon. He would frequently summon his ministers to meetings in the middle of the night, rarely bothered to get dressed and spent most of his time in bathrobes: he only ever wore his official Mao uniform when there were cameras around. In the late 1960s Mao confessed to his aides that he hoped the US would drop a nuclear bomb on a province of China and kill between 10 and 20 million Chinese people. This would show the rest of the world, he explained, just how crazy the Americans were.

5. Haiti's president, "Papa Doc" Duvalier, was an expert in violence and intimidation, but his speciality was fraudulent elections. When his countrymen went to the polls in 1961 they found printed at the top of each ballot sheet the words "Docteur François Duvalier, President." When the votes were counted it was announced that Papa Doc had been unanimously re-elected on the basis that his name appeared on every ballot paper. A few years later he used a familiar tactic to prolong his stay in office *ad infinitum*: when Haitian voters were asked: "Do you want your president elected for life?" the answer was a convenient and resounding "Yes": there wasn't room on the ballot sheet to print a "No" box. Duvalier had the Lord's Prayer rewritten for use in Haitian schools:

   "Our Doc, who art in the National Palace for life, hallowed be Thy name by present and future generations. Thy will be done in Port-au-Prince as it is in the provinces. Give us this day our new Haiti, and forgive not the trespasses of those anti-patriots who daily spit upon our country . . ."

   "Papa Doc" claimed that he could predict the future from his late-night conversations with a severed human head, which he kept in a cupboard in the presidential palace. It belonged to one of his former army officers, Blucher Philogenes, who had led a doomed CIA-backed invasion of Haiti in 1963. When he needed advice on matters of state, however, he got it by sitting in his bathtub wearing a black top hat and consulting the entrails of a dead goat. Duvalier died in 1971 and was replaced by his son "Baby Doc".
6. Francisco Lopez, president of Paraguay from 1862 to 1870, was probably the most memorable of all South

America's transient dictators. An extremely ugly and obese man – one of the more flattering descriptions of him was "a tidal wave of human flesh" – Lopez had a Napoleonic fixation, and kept one hand tucked inside his jacket at all times. His fiercesome Irish wife, Eliza Lynch, influenced most of his political decisions. He was utterly ruthless in all matters, to the point of having his 70-year-old mother publicly flogged and executed because she confessed to him that he was a bastard. He spent most of his reign waging a hopeless war against Paraguay's neighbouring enemies Argentina, Brazil and Uruguay, and trained his men so hard that many didn't live long enough to see battle. His misguided war effort, combined with his refusal to allow any of his men to surrender, reduced the male population of Paraguay by nine-tenths. Due to Lopez's incompetence the military situation grew worse, so he organized a spying system which encouraged every third man in his army to spy on his comrades, and to shoot anyone, including officers, who showed any sign of cowardice. The resulting widespread paranoia among the ranks led to many of his men marching into battle backwards because they feared their own side more than the enemy. When his senior commander found himself surrounded and facing certain defeat, he opted to blow his own brains out rather than face his president, but missed and only shot one eye out. When things started to go badly Francisco Lopez organized a mass suicide pact and ordered the entire population of his nation's capital Asunción to march off into the jungle with him. He changed his mind at the last minute and ordered the national treasure to be thrown off a cliff into a deep jungle, instead. To ensure secrecy, the treasure was swiftly followed by all the witnesses. In 1870 Lopez declared himself a saint of the Christian Church. When the matter was put to the bishops of Paraguay, the 23 who admitted they were not keen on the idea were shot. "Saint" Francisco was duly anointed, and the date officially entered the Christian calendar.

7. North Korea's leader Kim Il Sung was the last great dictator of south-east Asia to organize his entire country around cult worship of his personal leadership. He once compelled the entire population of North Korea to wear lapel badges with his face on them, and had every road in North Korea built with an extra lane for his sole private use.
8. The former novice monk Pol Pot, leader of Cambodia's notorious guerilla movement Khmer Rouge, adopted the most extreme line on communist ideology ever known when he tried to purge Cambodia of all western influences and to revert the state to a mythical peasant past. He abolished money, cities and anything else he considered to be tainted by capitalism. In three genocidal years, beginning from his Year One in 1975, he had between two and three million people killed, some of them clubbed to death with shovels for the decadent imperialist crime of wearing spectacles.
9. Colonel Mengistu Haile Mariam was among the leaders of an Ethiopian military coup in 1974, and became president three years later. He unleashed his "red terror" against so-called counter-revolutionaries in 1977, picking mostly on children and young students; many hundreds were massacred. He allowed parents to buy the bodies back for burial, a scheme known as "paying for the bullet", and had the tortured bodies of his political

opponents displayed on television. He resigned and fled in 1991. A year later police found the remains of the former Emperor Haile Selassie buried under Haile Mariam's office floor.

10. Jean-Bedel Bokassa, self-styled emperor of the former French colony of the Central African Republic, was another dictator with a Napoleonic fixation. He seized power in 1965, and although his country was officially one of the poorest in the world, quickly established a reputation for recklessly squandering money on personal indulgences. He blew £10 million – about one-third of the annual national budget – on a bizarre 48-hour coronation binge to celebrate his "promotion" from president to emperor in 1977. Although all the world's top political leaders were asked to attend, most, including Britain and the US, returned Bokassa's invitations. However, many foreign dignitaries, including ambassadors from Italy and West Germany, did turn up to the imperial banquet held in the capital, Bangui. What they didn't know was that Bokassa had arranged to have 12 selected inmates from Bangui prison butchered and served to his dinner guests.

Appalling Pontiffs: History's 20 most unconventional Popes

1. Pope Damasus I (366–84) left nothing to chance in his campaign to became pope. He hired a gang of hit-men to storm the Julian Basilica and murder the nearest rival for the job and all his supporters. Damasus had a reputation as a ladies' man, and was nicknamed "the matron's ear-tickler", but he surrounded himself with an entourage of sexually ambiguous young men. Damasus was tried, convicted and sentenced to death for adultery by a synod of 44 bishops in 378 AD, but was subsequently acquitted by the emperor.
2. Pope John XII (955–63), known as John the Bad, was bisexual and allegedly an avowed atheist. He had dozens of lovers of both sexes, including one of his father's former concubines. He turned his papal home, the Lateran Palace, into a brothel and was accused of summoning the devil during one of his more rampant orgies. He and a gang of his friends also liked to molest female pilgrims in the basilica of St Peter: when a cardinal pointed out that this wasn't theologically sound practice, the pope had him castrated. A tribunal found Pope John guilty *in absentia* of various crimes, including incest, adultery and murder, and he was

excommunicated. Eventually His Holiness was bludgeoned to death with a hammer by an irate husband, after being caught in the act of copulation with the man's wife. When news of the ex-pope's death reached Rome it was noted that he was lucky to have died in bed, even if it wasn't his own.

3. Pope Stephen VI (896–7) made it apparent on his election that he had not been on the best of terms with his predecessor, Pope Formosus. After Formosus had been buried for about nine months, Pope Stephen gathered together some of the Roman clergy into a synod and had his rotting corpse exhumed and carried into the hall. Clothed in full pontifical vestments, the body was seated in a chair while a terrified deacon stood by the corpse as defence attorney and a series of charges against the late pope was read. The "Cadaver Synod" then condemned Formosus, his ordinations were declared invalid, and the three fingers used by a Pope in blessing were cut off. The body was then buried in a pilgrims' cemetery; a gang later dug it up and threw it into the Tiber. Stephen did not survive for very much longer. A few months later an insurrection removed him from office, whereupon he was dressed in a monk's habit, thrown into a dungeon and strangled.
4. Pope Sergius III (904–11) enjoyed sex with underaged girls and, according to the historian Baronius, was "the slave of every vice". When Sergius was 45 he took a 15-year-old mistress, Marozia: the affair produced a son who went on to became Pope John XI.
5. Pope John XIII (965–72) used the equestrian statue of the former Emperor Marcus Aurelius, the biggest bronze Roman statue in existence, as a gibbet, when

in 965 he hanged a city prefect from it by his hair. John was condemned as an adulterer who "defiled his father's concubine and his own niece". Just like his dad, Pope John XII, John XIII was said to have have been murdered by an enraged husband after being caught in a sex act with his wife.

6. Pope Joan. The legend of the female pope has been doing the rounds since the thirteenth century. According to various versions of the story, in the eleventh, twelfth or thirteenth century the Church accidentally elected a woman, often thought to have been English, masquerading as a monk, who ruled for two years as Pope John. Her secret was discovered only after she gave birth prematurely during a procession from St Peter's Church in Rome. Shocked Church elders declared the street out of bounds, and subsequent popes have avoided it ever since. The details of the story of St Joan have become greatly embellished over the centuries but the basic premise that there was a female pope was acknowledged by the Catholic Church until the nineteenth century, when the legend was used by Protestants to attack the papacy. Intriguingly, the Vatican's Chair of St Peter, the ancient red marble throne on which popes were ceremoniously inaugurated, had a hole in the seat which made it resemble an elaborate commode. It is said that the seat was designed that way to allow new popes to be sex-tested: according to custom, upon the election of a new pope a junior cleric would be positioned below the "groping chair" to feel the pontiff's testicles. Some accounts assert that this procedure was adopted as a consequence of Pope Joan, but it could also have been to check that the new pope had not been castrated, as

Church law decreed that a pontiff had to be "sexually intact".

7. The only Portuguese pope, John XXI (1276–7) was also the only doctor ever to become pontiff. In the mid thirteenth century, largely on the strength of a medical treatise in which he prescribed lettuce leaves for toothache, lettuce seed to reduce sex drive and pig dung to stop nosebleeds, he was appointed physician to the Vatican. While receiving his medical advice three popes, Gregory X (1271–6) Innocent V (1276) and Adrian V (1276) died in quick succession. The doctor was duly elected pontiff, possibly in the hope that his medical skills would enable him to live longer than the previous three. Within 12 months of his election, however, the roof of his new palace fell in, crushing him horribly. He died six days later. The accident came as a huge relief in some quarters of the Vatican where it was believed that he was the anti-Christ.
8. Pope Benedict IX served three terms as pontiff (1032–44, 1045, 1047–8), the first of which he began when he was only 12 years old. Dante estimated that under Pope Benedict the papacy reached an all-time low in immorality and debauchery. Benedict grew up to be a murderer who allegedly dabbled in bestiality, witchcraft and Satanism, and threw wild bisexual orgies. When the pope was 23 he survived an attempt to strangle him at the altar during Mass. Benedict eventually married his cousin and sold the papacy to his godfather, Gregory VI.
9. The midget Pope Gregory VII (1073–85) tried to stamp out sin within the Church, including clerical marriages and the keeping of mistresses by priests. His campaign against moral abuse and heresy was stepped up a notch

when he announced that he thought it a bad thing for people to read the Bible – it might provoke thought, said Gregory, and free thought led to heresy. His private life was another matter. He took great pleasure in scourging himself and enjoyed watching others being scourged. He also had a girlfriend, Countess Mathilda, whose German husband, Godfrey the Hunchback, retaliated by spreading stories that the pope was an atheist. In fact the Roman Catholic Church didn't adopted celibacy as a code for the priesthood until 1095, at the Council of Pacernza, and even then it was only a device to raise money. The reigning pope, Urban II, introduced the *callagium*, a sex tax which allowed clergymen to keep mistresses provided they paid an annual fee to the papacy. The immediate effect of the ban on concubines was a huge rise in clerical homosexuality. Three hundred and fifty years later Pope Innocent VIII became known as "The Honest" because he admitted that he had fathered several bastards. He owned up to disprove a rumour going around Rome at the time that he was a woman. Pope Alexander III (1159–81) attempted to reinforce the ban on clerical mistresses but found it particularly difficult to enforce in England. The pope was determined to appoint a celibate Archbishop of Canterbury, but was disappointed to discover that the man he chose for the job, a monk called Clernbald, had 17 illegitimate children in one village alone. The Bishop of Lincoln, meanwhile, was worried about the moral health of England's nunneries, and developed his own method of testing nuns to find out if they were living up to their chastity vows. He went around the convents, fondling nuns' breasts to observe their reactions.

10. Pope Anacletus (1130–8) had a prostitute for a mistress, committed incest with his sister and a few other female relatives, and had a disturbing habit of raping nuns.
11. Pope Boniface VIII (1294–1305) got rid of his predecessor, Pope Celestine V, by locking him up in Fumone castle leaving him to die of starvation. Boniface was an atheist who had numerous gay lovers and was eventually tried for heresy, rape, sodomy and eating meat during Lent. He didn't attend his trial and escaped punishment, but went mad soon afterwards and committed suicide. Later, Pope Clement V had Boniface's body exhumed and burned as a heretic.
12. Clement VI (1342–52) was a famously dissolute and extravagant pope, described by Petrarch as "an ecclesiastical Dionysus with his obscene and infamous artifices". When the pope's confessor warned him that he must give up his dozens of mistresses, Benedict explained that he had got into the habit of sleeping with whores as a young man and continued to do so now on the advice of his doctors. When Clement died 50 priests said Mass for the repose of his soul for nine consecutive days, but it was generally agreed that this was not going to be nearly enough to prevent the dead pope from going directly to hell.
13. Pope John XXIII (1410–15) was a former pirate who became a priest the day before he was crowned pope. After obtaining the papacy through force of arms he went on to reign as a brutal libertine. In 1415, at the Council of Constance, Pope John was charged with 54 offences, including piracy, murder, rape, sodomy and incest. Of the 70 original charges, 16, said to have been "of the most indescribable depravity", were dropped –

not out of respect for the pope, but in the interests of public decency.

14. Pope Pius II (1458–64) had been a well-known author of erotic literature, and had fathered about 12 illegitimate children.
15. Pope Sixtus IV (1471–84) is best known for building the Sistine Chapel. His less artistic achievements included six illegitimate sons – one of them the result of an incestuous relationship with his sister – and sanctioning the papal bull which unleashed the Spanish Inquisition and the subsequent burning of thousands of heretics.
16. Pope Alexander VI (1492–1503), Rodrigo Borgia, was reputed to have committed his first murder at the age of 12, and earned fame for his reign of astonishing profligacy and especially his sexual voracity, and the unashamed advancement of four of his illegitimate children. He died of accidental poisoning, probably prepared by his son Cesare and intended for a couple of cardinals they were dining with; Alexander inadvertently drank to their health from the wrong cup. After his death the Borgia apartments in the Vatican were sealed off and remained closed until the nineteenth century.
17. Pope Julius II (1503–13), who commissioned Michelangelo to paint the ceiling of the Sistine Chapel, was a paedophile and spent much of his time with rent boys and male prostitutes.
18. Pope Leo X (1313–21), also a great patron of both Michelangelo and Raphael, was promiscuously homosexual. When he was elected he was suffering so much from terrible ulcerations of his anus that he had to be carried into the conclave on a stretcher. It was Pope Leo

who provoked Martin Luther to nail his 96 theses to the door of the church in Wittenburg denouncing Church corruption.

19. Pope Paul III (1534–49) is famous for excommunicating Henry VIII and for placing England under interdict. He also poisoned several relatives, including his mother and his niece, to gain control of his family inheritance, and enjoyed an incestuous relationship with his daughter. He killed a couple of cardinals and a Polish bishop to settle an argument over a theological point, and was probably Rome's biggest ever pimp: Pope Paul kept a roll of about 45,000 prostitutes, who paid him a monthly tribute.
20. Pope Julius III (1550–55) specialized in sodomizing young boys, and appointed several handsome teenage boys as cardinals. He hit a new low in bad taste when he took as his bed companion his own illegitimate son, Bertuccino. Cardinal della Casa's famous poem *In Praise of Sodomy* was dedicated to Pope Julius.

10 Doomsday Cults

1. The Panacea Society was founded to promote the writings and beliefs of the early-nineteenth-century London seer Joanna Southcott. In 1814 Miss Southcott, a 64-year-old virgin and part-time fortune-teller, announced that she was pregnant and about to give birth to a new messiah, known as the Shiloh. The world would end soon after the birth and only her followers would be saved. Twenty-one doctors examined Miss Southcott at her home in Manchester Street, Marylebone, of whom 17 concurred that the seer was either pregnant or "probably" pregnant. Dozens of people camped outside her front door to wait for the impending miracle. Sadly, the new messiah failed to arrive on the expected date and Miss Southcott died 10 days later. Her followers were largely undismayed by the failure of the prophecy, deciding that the child had gone to heaven and would return later. Helen Exeter, founder of The Panacea Society, announced that the messiah would return in 1914, but didn't live to see her forecast fail, as she was drowned early that year. The Society now pins its hopes on a locked and sealed box, once belonging to Southcott, which it believes will reveal the date of Christ's return. Unfortunately, the box may only be opened in the presence of all the bishops of the Church of England. In 1997 The Panacea Society took out a series of newspaper advertisements de-

manding that the bishops assemble to open the box.

2. Edgar Cayce (1877–1945) was an American Nostradamus known as "the sleeping prophet" because of his habit of going into a trance to predict the future or heal the sick. Although Cayce's track record was so erratic that he was obliged to keep up his day job selling photographic supplies, he had one notable success just before the 1929 Wall Street Crash, when he advised a client against investing in the stock market because he saw "a downward movement of long duration". Cayce is also said to have foreseen World Wars I and II, the independence of India, the state of Israel and the assassination of President Kennedy. He also predicted the fall of communism in China, that California would fall into the sea in 1969, and that Christ would return after World War III, in 1999. In the year 2000, Cayce predicted, the earth's axis will shift and mankind will be destroyed by flooding and earthquakes. Cayce's followers, the Association for Research and Enlightenment, keep the great man's memory alive from their base at his former home in Virginia.
3. In 1957 the Rev. Mark Prophet from Washington D.C. was visited by a holy spirit which instructed him to found an organization called the Summit Whitehouse, an heroic theological mixture, mostly of fundamental Christianity and eastern mysticism. When the Rev. Prophet died in 1967 the torch was taken up by his wife Elizabeth Wulf, or Guru Ma, as she is now known to her disciples, who renamed the cult the Church Universal and Triumphant and moved it to a remote Montana ranch, patrolled by armed guards. Members of the movement are expected sign away all their money and property to the organization and to conform to a strict regime, which controls sex

even between married couples. Ex-members claim that the cult held people at the ranch against their will or brainwashed them. In the 1980s the cult built a massive bunker and began to stockpile arms to withstand a nuclear war, which Guru Ma predicted would occur in 1990. When the year passed without the promised apocalypse she denied setting any date for the catastrophe, claiming that she had merely pointed out that the world was in great danger from imminent disaster. The cult continues to maintain both bunker and arsenal just in case.

4. The Jehovah's Witnesses know more than most about forecasts of millennial doom: they have been forecasting the imminent apocalypse since about 1872, the year they were founded in Pittsburgh by businessman Charles Russell. His followers – about four to five million worldwide, including about 250,000 in the UK – are taught that the Battle of Armageddon will happen quite soon, and will be followed by God's Kingdom on Earth. All will die except Jehovah's Witnesses, who will live with Christ for another 1,000 years. After this period the dead will be raised, of whom the most righteous 144,000 will live in heaven while the remainder exist in earthly paradise. Russell originally employed a complex mathematical system to determine that Armageddon would occur in 1874. Two uneventful years later, he revised his date to 1914. After Russell's death in 1916 he was succeeded by "Judge" Rutherford, who advised the Witnesses that the new date for Armageddon was 1925, later updating it to 1975. Following a mass walk-out of members in early 1976 the church has been reluctant to speculate as to a new date.
5. The US-based Morris Cerullo World Evangelism Orga-

nization employs satellite and cable TV to spread the message that the return of Christ, the end of civilization as we know it and the destruction of all sinners will occur in the year 2000. The sect has set itself a target of saving one billion souls before the millennium, via Morris Cerullo's hard-sell *Victory* TV show, which encourages regular donations from viewers (apparently, $10 is the cost of converting a Jewish soul). The movement has an estimated 800,000 followers worldwide.

6. The apocalyptic Japanese sect Supreme Truth, one of about 183,000 cults currently operating in Japan, was formed in 1987 and predicted the end of the world in 1997. Its blind leader, Shoko Asahara, a self-confessed fan of Adolf Hitler, justifies indiscriminate mass murder through belief in *poa*, a Tibetan Buddhist term for reincarnation to a higher existence. Asahara taught his followers that a *poa* killing relieved victims from everyday life and the accumulation of more bad *karma*. Child members were only allowed to wash once a week, ate frugally and were subject to solitary confinement for bad behaviour. Some had their eyebrows dyed green and were forced to wear special battery-powered headgear, designed to produce the same electronic frequency as their leader's own brainwaves. Under Asahara's command his followers built a chemical plant to produce 70 tons of the lethal Nazi-invented gas Sarin. He also manufactured various other drugs, including barbiturates and truth serum, and ordered the production of 1,000 automatic rifles and one million bullets in preparation for his apocalyptic war against the Japanese government. The deadly toxin was released in five Tokyo subway stations on the morning of 20 March 1995,

killing 11 people and injuring more than 5,500 others. The cult is also suspected of a similar gas attack in June 1994 in Matsumoto, a town north of Tokyo, that killed seven people and wounded 144. It is believed that both gas attacks were test runs for a much bigger assault, planned as part of an attempt to wipe out the entire population of Japan's major cities.

7. Claude Vorilhon was an ordinary 27-year-old French sports journalist until 1972 when aliens, or "Elohim", revealed to him that he was the product of an extraterrestrial gang-rape on his mother Marie, and that he was now the last of a long line of alien prophets, which included Buddha, Mohammed and Jesus. Vorilhon, renamed Raël, was given a mission to save his followers from "the age of Apocalypse", which had begun in 1945 (the year of Raël's birth) and would probably end in nuclear war very soon. The Raëlians hope to achieve "higher planetary consciousness" by building an embassy in Israel, at which the Elohim will reveal themselves to the world's governments. No precise date has been given for the apocalypse, but the Raëlians warn that if the embassy isn't built by 2030 the consequences will be cataclysmic. The movement banks 10 per cent of the income of its 30,000 members worldwide.
8. In the 1970s "Reverend" Jim Jones believed himself to be the reincarnation of both Jesus and Lenin, and preached his vision of an impending nuclear holocaust, which would wipe out the most of the world (except parts of central and South America) by the year 2000. Jones set up a People's Temple in San Francisco and sat back to await Armageddon, meanwhile preparing his growing band of followers for an act of "revolutionary suicide".

By 1977 he had moved his "church" to Guana, South America, where, in the isolation of the jungle, he created his dream community, Jonestown. In November 1978, a US Congressman, Leo Ryan, visited Jonestown to investigate alleged human rights abuses. Jones had Ryan and his party killed, then ordered his 900 followers to perform ritual suicide by drinking from a tub of Kool Aid laced with a deadly cocktail of cyanide and tranquillizers. The Reverend Jim put a bullet through his brain.

9. The Reorganized Church of Jesus Christ of the Latter-Day Saints comprised six American families led by Jeffrey Lundgren, or Jeb7, as he preferred to be known. In 1987 Lundgren settled with his cult in a 15-acre farm in rural Ohio, and trained his disciples for holy war while having excrement rubbed all over his body as he preached about the impending apocalypse. One of the families, the Averies, were singled out as a sacrifice to appease God. The entire Avery family was thrown in a pit under the barn of the cult's ranch and shot with a Colt 45. After the killing Lundgren and his immediate family fled and eventually relocated in Jackson County, Missouri. Two years later, one of the cult members reported the Avery murders to Kansas City police. On 7 January 1990 Lundgren, his son Damon and his wife Alice were arrested in a motel room in National City, California, where police uncovered an arsenal of weapons. Lundgren was sentenced to death and his wife and 19-year-old son received five consecutive life terms for the killings.
10. In 1990 a Ukrainian journalist, Marina Tsvygun, realized that she was the incarnation of Christ on earth, changed her name to Maria Devi Christos and began a holy

crusade against the evil influence of bar codes in Russia. Ms Tsygun pointed out that all bar codes contain three sets of thin bars, each set representing the number six and together representing the biblical Number of the Beast. She predicted an apocalyptic end to mankind in the year 2000. She and many of her followers were rounded up and imprisoned, convicted of criminal damage and inciting mass disorder.

10 Greats

1. Xerxes the Great (519–465 BC), king of Persia: famously harsh ruler much hated by his subjects until his assassination in a palace intrigue.
2. Pompey the Great (106–48 BC): Roman general who sparked a civil war by opposing Julius Caesar. Subsequently fled to Egypt, where he was murdered.
3. Herod the Great (73–4 BC): ruler of Palestine at the time of Christ's birth. Mostly known for his hard line on first-born babies and so unpopular with Christians that he was "smitten by God and eaten of worms".
4. Mithridates the Great (died 63 BC), king of Pontus: an utterly ruthless leader, who resisted Rome's advances into Asia Minor.
5. Alexander the Great (356–23 BC), king of Macedonia, conquered most of the known world. Renowned for his unthinking cruelty: on one occasion, when he needed a bridge, he demolished an entire nearby village and threw it into the river, thus providing a means of passage. He died of alcoholism, aged 32.
6. Clovis the Great (466–511), king of the Franks: massacred the Romans, mutilated the Visigoths and beat up the Germans to build a united French kingdom.
7. Otto the Great (983–1002): became Holy Roman Emperor when he was three and was dead before his 22nd birthday.
8. Catherine II the Great (1684–1727), German-born empress of Russia: enjoyed a legendary sex life and made advances to young soldiers when she was well into her 60s.
9. Peter the Great (1672–1725), czar of Russia: brilliant but cruel despot, who had his own son tortured to death. After a lifetime of alcoholism, he died of syphilitic dementia.

10. Frederick the Great (1712–86), king of Prussia: the third son born to his parents, but the first named Frederick to survive infancy. Two earlier Fredericks were dead: the first from having his fragile head crammed into a crown during the christening, the second from shock when the guns saluting his birth were fired too near his cradle. Frederick went on to enjoy a lifetime of ceaseless war-making and a reputation for ruthless military organization. He was also known for his dubious sex life and body odour.

No nearer my God than Thee: 25 Dead Atheists

1. Diagoras "the Atheist" of Melos, fifth-century BC Greek poet, threw a wooden image of a god into a fire, remarking that the deity should perform another miracle and save itself. Athens outlawed him and offered a reward for his capture, dead or alive. He lived out his life in Spartan territory.
2. Socrates, Greek philosopher.
3. Christopher Marlowe, English dramatist and poet (1564–93): "I count religion but a childish toy, and hold there is no sin but ignorance."
4. David Hume, Scottish philosopher and historian (1711–76): "When I hear a man is religious, I conclude that he is a rascal."
5. Thomas Jefferson, American president, author, scientist and architect (1743–1826): "I do not find in orthodox Christianity one redeeming feature"; "Religions are all alike – founded upon fables and mythologies"; "The day will come when the mystical generation of Jesus, by the Supreme Being as His father, in the womb of a virgin, will be classed with the fable of the generation of Minerva in the brain of Jupiter."
6. James Madison, American president (1751–1836): "Religious bondage shackles and debilitates the mind and unfits it for every noble enterprise."
7. Napoleon Bonaparte, French emperor (1769–1821): "Re-

ligion is excellent stuff for keeping common people quiet."

8. Lord George Gordon Byron, English poet (1788–1824).
9. Percy Bysshe Shelley, English poet (1792–1822): thrown out of Oxford University for writing *The Necessity of Atheism* in 1810. "If God has spoken, why is the world not convinced?"
10. Karl Marx, German political philosopher and economist (1818–83): Religion is "the opium of the people, which made this suffering bearable".
11. Marion Evans (George Eliot), English novelist (1819–80).
12. Samuel Clemens (Mark Twain), American author and humorist (1835–1910): "Faith is believing something you know ain't true"; "It ain't the parts of the Bible that I can't understand that bother me, it is the parts that I do understand"; "If there is a God, he is a malign thug."
13. Thomas Hardy, English author (1840–1928): "After two thousand years of mass, We've got as far as poison gas."
14. Friedrich Nietzsche, German philosopher (1844–1900): "God is dead."
15. Thomas Edison, American inventor (1847–1931): "Religion is all bunk"; "I have never seen the slightest scientific proof of the religious ideas of heaven and hell, of future life for individuals, or of a personal God."
16. Sigmund Freud, Austrian physician and pioneer psychoanalyst (1856–1939): "It would be very nice if there were a God who created the world and was a benevolent providence, and if there were a moral order in the universe and an after-life; but it is a very striking fact that all this is exactly as we are bound to wish it to be"; "In the long run, nothing can withstand reason and experience, and the contradiction religion offers to both is palpable."
17. George Bernard Shaw, Irish playwright (1856–1950):

"The fact that a believer is happier than a sceptic is no more to the point than the fact that a drunken man is happier than a sober one."

18. Clarence Seward Darrow, American lawyer (1857–1938): "I don't believe in God as I don't believe in Mother Goose."
19. Herbert George Wells, English author (1866–1946).
20. Vladimir Ilich Lenin, Russian revolutionary leader (1870–1924).
21. Bertrand Russell, British philosopher, mathematician, and social critic (1872–1970): "I am myself a dissenter from all known religions, and I hope that every kind of religious belief will die out"; "Religion is based . . . mainly on fear . . . fear of the mysterious, fear of defeat, fear of death. Fear is the parent of cruelty, and therefore it is no wonder if cruelty and religion have gone hand in hand . . . My own view on religion is that of Lucretius. I regard it as a disease born of fear and as a source of untold misery to the human race."
22. Albert Einstein, German-born theoretical physicist (1879–1955): "I do not believe in a personal God and I have never denied this but have expressed it clearly. If something is in me which can be called religious then it is the unbounded admiration for the structure of the world so far as our science can reveal it."
23. Sir Charles Chaplin, British-born actor, director, and producer (1889–1977): "By simple common sense I don't believe in God, in none."
24. Jean-Paul Sartre, French philosopher and author (1905–80).
25. Gene Roddenberry, creator of *Star Trek* (1921–91): "For most people, religion is nothing more than a substitute for a malfunctioning brain."

10 Facts about the Church you are least likely to hear in Sunday School

1. The Book of Esther is the only book in the Bible which neglects to mention God.
2. Although the Church frowned on adultery from the beginning, it didn't get around to banning sex with animals until the Council of Ankara in AD 314.
3. The modern confessional box was invented in the Middle Ages to help prevent women from being sexually assaulted by priests.
4. The early Christian Church held that the Virgin Mary was impregnated through her ear. Paranoia about aural sex was so widespread that the naked ear was considered sexually explicit, hence the fashion for tight-fitting wimples.
5. The Catholic Church accepts cannibalism as a justifiable means of saving one's life.
6. Onan, the son of Judah, "spilled his seed" in the Old Testament (Genesis 38:8–10), thus becoming the Bible's sole masturbator. The passage is the basis for the Church's unreserved condemnation of masturbation for centuries, and gave rise to the expression Onanism, a term for self-abuse which was still popular in Victorian times.
7. The Old Testament book Ecclesiasticus recommends clearing the stomach by throwing up before or during a big meal to make room for more food.
8. The Bible was full of lepers. It was written at a time when

any skin defect, even a bad case of acne, was likely to get people branded as a leper and shunned by society. Most "lepers" were probably sufferers of syphilis. As they would also, to all intents and purposes, be written off as dead, they would have a requiem mass sung for then, as was the custom for all living lepers.

9. In the twelfth and thirteenth centuries the Church declared a holy war on cats, because they were ambassadors of the devil. After two centuries of persecution, the cat population of Europe was decimated, and there followed an explosion in the rat population, bringing with it the Plague. The Catholic Church duly reversed its position on cats, and issued a new proclamation that anyone caught abusing a cat would be excommunicated.
10. At one time you could be excommunicated for wearing a wig.

10 Spectacular Sadists

1. The conquests of Genghis Khan, which covered most of the known world, were marked by acts of breathtaking cruelty. He once stormed the town of Termez and slaughtered all the inhabitants. As one old woman was about to be killed, she begged Khan's soldier for mercy in return for a pearl, which she said she had swallowed for safe-keeping. The old woman was promptly disembowelled and several pearls were found. When Khan heard about this he ordered that all the dead should be opened up and their stomachs inspected. He was not entirely without compassion, however: he once decided that a defeated foe, who turned out to be an old childhood friend, should be spared a bloody execution. He had him rolled in a carpet and kicked to death, instead. When Khan died in battle, his followers followed his strict order that his eventual death should be kept a secret until his son Ogatai was safely installed. Khan's final victims were the bystanders who innocently spotted his funeral procession as it passed by. They were all put to the sword.
2. The insane Raja of Akalkot reigned over the Indian state of Porbandor in the mid nineteenth century. His mental condition was brought to the attention of the British rulers one day when, on a whim, he lopped off the ears and nose of a courtier.
3. Tamburlaine, a descendant of Genghis Khan, was considered the most violent of all the Mongol leaders. He celebrated his conquest of Sabzawar in 1383 by having 2,000 prisoners buried alive; later that year he had 5,000 people beheaded at Zirih and used their heads to build a pyramid. In India he massacred about 100,000 prisoners, and in 1400 he had 4,000 Christians buried alive. It was said that Tamburlaine was a somewhat humourless man: in fact, he had anyone who cracked a joke put to death immediately. He conquered an empire stretching from Turkey to India and to

Moscow in the north, but it broke up soon after his death.

4. When the king of Siam wanted to have some of his relatives murdered he was reminded of an inconvenient Siamese tradition which forbade the spilling of royal blood on the ground. He had them pounded to death with a mortar in a large pestle instead.
5. The Indian Maharajah of Jaipur declared a 15-mile exclusion zone around his capital where he alone was allowed to hunt. He had poachers tortured by pushing ground hot chillies into their rectums.
6. The king of Fiji once punished a servant girl by making her watch him dine on her roasted amputated arm.
7. In the Indian state of Baroda in the nineteenth century, the maharajah had criminals executed by standing elephants on their heads.
8. Although the Gospels' description of Christ's death is the most famous account of crucifixion, it was a commonplace method of execution, widely used throughout the Middle East. As if a lingering death by suffocation on the cross wasn't enough, it was usually augmented by whatever torture took the executioner's or the mob's fancy, including breaking the legs, stoning or flaying. The Emperor Nero particularly liked to amuse himself by nailing his victims up in different positions: upside-down was a big favourite.
9. Czar Ivan IV (the Terrible) came to power in 1547, and after a serious illness when he was 23 years old became given to bouts of random and spectacular brutality. He would often foam at the mouth like a rabid dog and tear clumps of his hair out until his scalp bled. He specialized in inventing ingenious deaths for his enemies. When the archbishop of Novgorod was suspected of organizing an uprising against him, Ivan had the entire population, about 50,000 people, tossed into a freezing river, then had the archbishop sewn into a bearskin and hunted to death by a pack of

hounds. He had his treasurer boiled to death in a caldron, and his imperial chancellor was strung up while Ivan's friends took turns to hack pieces off him. When he conquered Withenstein he had the defeated Finnish leader roasted alive on a spit. On his deathbed he repented and became a monk.

10. The Indian Maharajah Jay Singh of Alwar, a notorious paedophile and a personal friend of King George V, used live babies or elderly widows as tiger bait. In 1933 the polo-playing maharajah had a bad game and blamed his horse, which had stumbled and thrown him. As an audience of British VIPs watched, the maharajah poured a can of petrol over the polo pony and set fire to it.

12 Ways to Achieve Sainthood

1. St Denis is the patron saint of syphilis and of Paris. Legend has it that after he was beheaded, St Denis walked for quite some distance carrying his head. He is not to be confused with St Fiacre, the patron saint of non-specific venereal disease, a job he combines with looking after haemorrhoid sufferers. After an altercation with a non-believer, St Fiacre sat down heavily on a rock, miraculously leaving the impression of his buttocks upon it. Christian haemorrhoid sufferers subsequently discovered that they could get relief by sitting where St Fiacre had rested.
2. St Agatha is patron saint of Malta, bell-makers, diseases of the breast, earthquakes, fire and sterility. In the third century she defended her virginity against a high-ranking Roman, was sent to prison and had her breasts cut off. These were later restored by divine intervention. She was then put in a brothel, where her virginity miraculously remained intact; burned at the stake, but failed to ignite, then finally beheaded. Sicilians honour her feast day every year by carrying an image of her breasts through the streets.
3. The feast day of St Lawrence is 10 August. He was roasted alive on a spit, but faced his death heroically, telling his torturers: "Turn me over – I'm cooked on that

side." St Lawrence is now the patron saint of rotisseurs.

4. St Apollonia is the patron saint of dentists. She achieved martyrdom after running into a mob of Egyptians, who pulled her teeth out one by one because she refused to renounce her faith.
5. St Dympna is the patron saint of mental illness. She was raped by her father, who then murdered her when she tried to escape. Her remains were placed in a crypt in Gheel, Belgium. A number of mad and mentally handicapped people who visited her shrine were cured.
6. Blessed William of Fenoli, whose feast day is 19 December, was a monk in the thirteenth century. One day, when he was returning from the fields with a mule, he was attacked by robbers. William defended himself by ripping off the leg of his mule, clubbing his attackers with it, then restoring the leg and continuing his journey.
7. The feast day of saints Eulampius and Eulampia, the brother and sister martyrs, is celebrated on 10 November. The couple survived being boiled in oil, moving 200 astonished onlookers to convert to Christianity on the spot. Immediately, all 200 converts were beheaded.
8. St Nicholas is the patron saint of Russia, children, pawnbrokers, unmarried girls, perfumiers and sailors. He was a bishop in south-western Turkey at some point in the fourth century, and is purported to have restored to full health three decapitated children. St Nicholas is also said to have been such a pious baby that he abstained from his mother's milk on Wednesdays and Fridays.
9. St Catherine is the patron saint of wheelwrights and philosophers and the namesake of a small firework. She lived in Alexandria, Egypt in the fourth century, and

protested against the ill-treatment of Christians by the Emperor Maxentius. He had her sentenced to death on a spiked wheel. Divine providence intervened and the wheel broke, causing spikes to fly off and kill her persecutors. The emperor had her taken off the wheel and beheaded, whereupon milk flowed from her severed arteries.

10. The feast day of St Swithun is 2 July. To demonstrate his awesome self-control, he liked to sleep chastely between two beautiful virgins.
11. The feast day of St Simeon the Stylite is 5 January. The first and most famous of the "pillar hermits", he was known for his thrift, and for living on top of a column for 30 years. He demonstrated his divinity by standing on one leg for a year, and tying a rope around his waist so tightly that his lower body became putrefied and infested with maggots. He then ate the maggots, saying: "Eat what God has given you." He passed out, but was revived with a few lettuce leaves. St Simeon bowed in prayer one day and fell off his pole to his death.
12. The feast day of St Catherine of Siena is 29 April. She overcame her fear of bubonic plague victims by drinking a whole bowl of pus.

Terrible Turks: 10 All-Time most Deranged Ottoman Sultans

1. Mahomet III (1595–1603) murdered his 19 brothers (all aged under 11), and almost clogged up the River Bosphorus with the bodies of his father's pregnant mistresses. In his spare time he enjoyed watching women's breasts being scorched off with hot irons.
2. Osman II (1618–22) enjoyed archery practice on live pageboys.
3. In the first five years of his reign, Murad IV (1623–40) had about 25,000 men put to death, many of them by his own hand. Murad set himself a target of taking 10 lives a day, beheading anyone who annoyed him, no matter how trivial the offence, and enjoying daily target practice with his long-barrelled gun on innocent passers-by who strayed too close to his bedroom window. He once chanced across a party of women who were enjoying a picnic, and had them all drowned because they were making too much noise. He killed one of his own doctors by forcing to him to swallow an overdose of opium, and murdered a musician for humming a Persian tune. He broke up illegal assemblies by banning the smoking of tobacco or the drinking of wine or coffee after the hours of darkness (punishable by immediate hanging or impalement). His dead victims were left in the street as a warning to anyone else who fancied a smoke or a late drink. Wherever he travelled, his stopping-off points were usually marked by the spot execution of smokers. Even on the

battlefield, nicotine addicts weren't safe. Murad had his own soldiers beheaded or hanged and quartered, and would sometimes crush their hands and feet and leave them helpless in no-man's land.

4. One night, in a fit of madness, Ibrahim (1640–8) had his entire harem put into sacks and drowned.
5. Mahomet IV (1648–87) appointed an historian called Abdi to write a running biography of his reign. One evening, the sultan asked Abdi what he had written about his reign that day. Abdi replied that he hadn't written anything, as nothing particularly noteworthy had happened. Mahomet calmly picked up a hunting spear and impaled him with it. "Now," he told Abdi, "thou hast something to write about."
6. Ahmed III (1703–30) was known for his tulip fetish. The sultan's obsession with the bulb became so exaggerated that this entire period in Turkish history became known as the Tulip Age. It began as a harmless hobby, when Ahmed imported 1,200 different rare bulbs from Mongolia for his gardens. Eventually he came to value his tulips more than he valued human life. Guests were forbidden from wearing clothes that didn't match the sultan's tulips on pain of death. Turkey's ruling class, eager as always to imitate the sultan, competed in the cultivation of tulips, and the wealthiest men in Turkey ruined themselves financially in an effort to throw the best tulip parties. Horticultural secrets were guarded as jealously as state secrets. Rare blooms became the most coveted possessions of the rich and were used to bribe public officials. Ahmed's obsession with tulips became a such a massive drain on Turkey's treasury that he was deposed in 1730.
7. Mahmud I (1730–54) was completely insane when he

came to the throne, and went straight into the harem, where he remained for much of his 24-year reign. Perversely, for a man who could have had any woman in the empire, he preferred to play peeping Tom, hiding behind a grille to watch the girls bathe.

8. Abdul Aziz (1861–76) a deranged megalomaniac, was physically huge and had a sex drive to match. His first action as sultan was to order a bigger bed and increase the number of women in his harem to 900. Earlier in his reign he was noted for his insane extravagance: his personal civil list accounted for 15 per cent of Turkey's entire annual expenditure. He was the first sultan to travel to Britain and to be entertained by the royal family. While he was there, he ordered dozens of pianos, which he planned to strap to the backs of his servants, so that he could hear music wherever he went. He bought locomotives, even though he had no tracks to run them on, and several iron-clad ships, which never sailed. He had the history of Turkey re-written, expunging every military defeat that had ever taken place and deleting all references to Christianity or the French Revolution. When he discovered that one of his employees was also named Aziz, he passed a law which made it illegal for anyone else to share his second name (an act comparable to banning the name Brown in England). He finally developed a thing about black ink, and had every government document re-written in red. He took to spending his time playing soldiers with real troops, making them stage nocturnal mock battles in the palace grounds, while he watched through a window. Britain's gallant Crimean War ally was finally struck off Queen Victoria's Christmas card list when he began indiscriminately butchering Christians. Up until this

point the random massacres of his own subjects had been passed off as wild exaggeration; this time, however, the sultan was careless, and committed the murder under the noses of the world's press.

9. Murad V (1876) enjoyed the briefest reign of any Ottoman sultan. Murad was a mentally unstable alcoholic, incapable of appearing in public, let alone performing any sort of official function. After three months, an Austrian doctor and a Turkish court physician jointly signed a document declaring that the sultan was incurably mad, and he was quietly locked away.
10. Abdul Hamid II (1876–1909) was variously known as The Red Sultan (for the amount of blood he shed), The Ogre of Yilditz Kiosk (after his fortress bolt-hole overlooking the city), or Abdul the Damned. The sultan's downfall was genocide: he supervized the methodical and systematic slaughter of at least one million Bulgarian and Armenian men, women and children. News of the massacre leaked out of Turkey, but when the bloodshed finally reached the streets of Constantinople his own subjects decided to remove him. The Young Turks who overthrew him decided that they must lead by example, and that he should be treated with the constitutional decorum befitting an ex-leader of the Turkish Empire. The vile Abdul was allowed to shuffle off into a comfortable retirement with a few young concubines to keep him company.

10 PROPHETS

1. The Duke of Edinburgh. A group of villagers in the New Hebrides islands, in the Pacific Ocean, is dedicated to the worship of Prince Philip. The villagers believe that Queen Elizabeth II's husband will one day cure all known diseases and grant them eternal youth. The Duke's 200 followers expect that on his return he will resume his rightful place among them, wearing the traditional penis gourd, and restore paradise on earth. They also believe that Philip secretly runs the Commonwealth and has been able thus far to conceal his true identity from his wife.
2. André Ivanov formed a sect called Skoptzy in Russia in 1757. One of the fundamental beliefs of the cult was the virtue of castration, taking as its tenet Matthew 19.12: ". . . and there be eunuchs which have made themselves eunuchs for the kingdom of heaven's sake". Ivanov had himself and his 13 disciples castrated, and although the cult leader was subsequently arrested and banished to Siberia, the authorities failed to halt the spread of the Skoptzy cult. As late as 1875 there were still at least 5,000 known male members of the sect.
3. Baghwan Rajneesh. The Indian mystic was famous for his fleet of Rolls-Royces, interesting theories on sex, personal greed and tax evasion. Baghwan (the name means "master of the vagina") studied and taught philosophy at the University of Jabalpur, India, where he developed a form of meditation. In 1974 he opened an ashram in Poona, but he moved in 1981 to a 126-square-mile site in Oregon, where he acquired a reputation for extravagance and dubious sexual practices. His spiritual needs included the use of a private swimming pool with computer-controlled heating, a private plane and anything up 96 Rolls-Royces. He died in 1990, possibly of AIDS, by

which time his movement had been renamed "Osho". The cult has now been taken over by financial opportunists, who have turned it, more or less, into a holiday resort for stressed Western executives.

4. David Koresh (né Vernon Howell). The Branch Davidian cult was an offshoot of the much larger Seventh Day Adventist movement. Like the Adventists, Branch Davidians believed in the imminent apocalypse, but they were disappointed when this failed to happen according to the script, in 1959. In 1986 Koresh became leader of the cult, after a pilgrimage to Jerusalem, from which he returned declaring himself the "sinful Messiah". In February 1993 members of the local militia laid siege to the Branch Davidian headquarters in Waco, Texas and were fired on by cult members; four militiamen died. On the 51st day of the siege, as FBI agents mounted a final assault, the compound broke out in flames, killing 86 people inside. The US government claimed that Koresh had ignited the flames and had the compound booby-trapped so that it would go up in a fireball.
5. Joseph Smith. The New York State farmworker was visited in the 1920s by a vision of God and by an angel called Moroni, who revealed to him the whereabouts of secret buried golden plates. On these plates it was written that Christ had appeared in America and appointed the disciples. Smith translated the plates and wrote the Book of Mormon. He was then visited by John the Baptist, who ordained Smith into the priesthood of Melchzdek. Smith began his own cult, The Church of the Latter Day Saints, but was murdered in 1844. His successor, Brigham Young, was widely persecuted and derided for his beliefs, especially polygamy, and decided to lead an exodus of Mormons west. They settled in Salt Lake City, and the Mormon Church now owns most of Utah, a large part of Hawaii and

land in Canada, as well as the Marriott hotel chain, the Beneficial Life Assurance Company, quite a few TV and radio stations and several million bicycles.

6. Joseph di Mambro. A middle-aged Frenchman claimed that in a previous life he had been a member of the Knights Templar, a medieval organization created by French crusaders in Jerusalem. Di Mambro founded a New Age cult in Canada, called the Order of the Solar Temple. During ceremonies his followers wore Crusade robes and held in awe a sword said to have been given to di Mambro 1,000 years before. Later investigation revealed that 69-year-old di Mambro had moved to Canada because of tax problems in France and that he had convictions for fraud. He claimed that his daughter Emanuelle was a "cosmic child" and had been conceived without sex. When a couple in the cult called their own son Emmanuel, di Mambro declared it the Antichrist and ordered the family's murder. This was carried out shortly before the whole cult decamped from Canada to Switzerland. Di Mambro's cult has, to date, claimed 69 victims in two mass suicide rituals. It first became newsworthy in October 1994, when 53 people committed suicide simultaneously in Switzerland and Canada. The victims, including children, were variously shot in the head, asphyxiated with black plastic bags and poisoned. It was believed that di Mambro had died in a fire so that he could lead his followers, through death, to the planet of Sirius, although it has been rumoured that he faked his own death. The second mass suicide ritual took place shortly before Christmas 1995. Swiss and French authorities had been alerted to the possibility of ritual suicide when 16 known cult members disappeared from their homes, some of them leaving behind handwritten notes expressing their intentions of killing themselves. On 23 December, in a remote

part of the French Alps, police discovered 16 charred bodies arranged in a star formation, with their feet pointed to the ashes of a fire. The victims had been stabbed, asphyxiated, shot or poisoned. Two of the dead were the wife and son of French ski champion and millionaire businessman Jean Vuarnet. Computer records seized by Canadian police in Montreal showed that some cult members had personally donated over $1 million to di Mambro.

7. Adolfo de Jesus Constanzo. This Cuban cult leader and part-time male model managed a drug-smuggling enterprise in Matamoros, Mexico, where he and his partner Sara Aldrete became extremely successful, largely because of their practice of ritually sacrificing their drug trade rivals. Few cared about the missing drug dealers because it was generally assumed that they were simply victims of a drug war. It was quite a different matter, however, when they decided to sacrifice a white American. The cult members abducted Mark Kilroy, a college student on his spring break, and killed him in their border ranch, Santa Elena. Kilroy's body was dismembered and his heart, genitals and spine were used to make a "magic stew". His disappearance triggered an all-out police search around the border, and the authorities soon became alerted to rumours of weird rituals practised in Rancho Santa Elena. Excavation of the ranch premises quickly revealed a large number of dismembered bodies, and several members of the cult were arrested. By this time Constanzo and Aldrete were hiding in an apartment in Mexico City. Police discovered their hideaway and surrounded the apartment, and after an exchange of gunfire Constanzo and a male lover were shot dead by another cult member, just before the police moved in.
8. Ervil LeBaron, a disaffected senior Mormon, founded an

offshoot cult: the Church of the Lamb of God. LeBaron murdered at least 20 people over a 20-year period in the 1970s and 1980s. Most of the victims were rival polygamists and Mormons. Although LeBaron himself died in prison in 1981, the killings were continued in his name by his followers for years afterwards.

9. Yahweh Ben Yahweh (God, son of God, né Hulon Mitchell). An outwardly respectable multi-million-dollar businessman and a prominent member of the Miami Chamber of Commerce, Mitchell founded the extreme racist cult "Church of Love", a murderous sect which preached that the American blacks were the true Jews, living in the land of the "white devil". Members dressed in white robes, took the last name Israel and followed a kosher diet. To become part of the "Brotherhood", a secret inner group within the sect, a member was required to murder a "white devil". The cult is accused of a reign of terror and the slayings of at least 14 people, including the beheading of an ex-member and the fire-bombing of a Delray Beach neighbourhood. Many of the details of the sect's activities come from Robert Rozier, a former US football player, who was arrested in 1986 in connection with four of the killings.
10. George King. In 1954 the Shropshire taxi driver was visited by aliens who informed him that Jesus was alive and well and living on the planet Venus, and that furthermore he had been selected by the Hidden Masters to become "the Voice of the Interplanetary Parliament". King's mission on earth was to represent spirituality in its battle with materialism. In his quest he would be assisted by the Hidden Masters, who would occasionally lend support by visiting humanity in their flying saucers. King changed his name to Sir George King, OSP, PhD, ThD, DD, Metropolitan Archbishop of the Aetherius Churches, Prince Grand Mas-

ter of the Mystical Order of St Peter, HRH Prince De George King De Santori, and Founder President of the Aetherius Society. He now lives in Los Angeles with his wife, Lady Monique King, Bishop of the American Division.

Rome's 9 most Ideologically Unsound Emperors

1. Tiberius (14–37 AD) was such a well-respected torturer that many of his prisoners committed suicide as soon as they were accused of anything, rather than bother waiting for the trial. He became bored with the array of tortures in fashion at the time, and decided to invent a few of his own. One of his favourites was to force the victim to drink vast quantities of wine until the bladder was at maximum pressure, then tie up his genitalia with a lute string. His favourite pastime was sodomizing young boys. If they protested he had their legs broken.
2. Gaius (Caligula) (37–41 AD) grew up in an army camp as a favourite of his father's soldiers. The troops nicknamed him "Caligula" (Little Boots) after the child-size military boots he wore in the camp. As a boy, Caligula became sexually fixated with his sister Drusilla and was once caught in bed with her. He became profoundly insane after a severe illness in AD 37, probably encephalitis, and from that point on his reign was marked by his cruel and maniacal whims. Caligula was prematurely bald, and so sensitive about his lack of hair that he made it a capital crime for anyone to look down from a high place as he passed by. When he ran out of money he found novel ways of raising cash, including opening his palace as a brothel and forcing high-ranking members of the senate to pay 1000 gold pieces each to have sex with his sisters. They were

then ordered to send their wives and daughters to work in the palace brothel. Caligula demanded that he be worshipped as a god and set up a special temple with a life-sized gold statue of himself. His reign was terminated when one of his guards ran a sword through his genitals, while another murdered his wife and dashed out the brains of his baby daughter against a wall.

3. Nero (54–68 AD) had crucified Christians covered in tar and set alight to form avenues of glowing human torches for spectators heading to the Christians versus Lions contests. Unlike Tiberius, Caligula and Claudius before him, however, Nero didn't enjoy watching men die: he couldn't stand the sight of spilled blood. He preferred to order his enemies to commit suicide (they usually did). After having his first wife murdered, he became besotted with his beautiful second wife Poppaea, and wrote a song about her long auburn hair. Three years after the wedding day, however, while Poppaea was pregnant, they had a tiff, during which Nero accidentally kicked her to death. The emperor was grief-stricken, but found consolation soon afterwards in a young male slave named Sporus who, he believed, closely resembled the late Mrs Nero. The emperor had him castrated and they lived together as man and wife. To rid Rome of Christians, Nero blamed them for the fire which burned down much of the city, and which he probably started himself. The citizens of Rome were not fooled: the senate condemned Nero to the death of a common criminal. Rather than face being stripped naked, tied to a post and flogged to death, Nero stuck a dagger through his throat.
4. Vitellius (69 AD) perfected the Roman art of disgorging food by sticking a feather down his throat between courses so he could binge all over again (see 10 Historical Figures you

would Least Want to Share a Dinner Table with). He was also known for bizarre culinary creations. The most famous of these was known as "Minerva's shield", an enormous dish assembled on a vast silver platter. Vitellius deployed the Roman navy to scour the four corners of the known world for ingredients, which included peacock brains, pike livers and flamingo tongues. The emperor eventually handed over the government of Rome to a freed slave so that he could concentrate on eating.

5. Domitian (81–96 AD) extracted confessions from people he suspected were plotting against him by holding a blazing torch under the prisoner's genitals. Courtiers guilty of even the mildest criticism were crucified upside down. His inevitable assassination in AD 96 was almost a carbon-copy of Caligula's death – he was stabbed in the genitals.
6. Commodus (180–92 AD) was arguably the most psychotic and murderous of all the Roman leaders. He was a transsexual who occasionally suffered delusions that he was Hercules. He collected all the dwarfs, cripples and freaks he could find in the city of Rome and had them brought to the Colosseum, where they were ordered to fight each other to the death with meat-cleavers. Commodus carried a club with him which he used to bludgeon pinioned prisoners. He also liked to try his hand in the gladiator pit, where, unsurprisingly, he always emerged unscathed. He often took the heads of his slain victims with him into the senate as a warning to anyone who might consider opposing him.
7. Heliogabalus (218–22 AD) was a mad teenage transsexual, who indulged in human sacrifice – killing thousands of young boys and girls – and ritual castration. He was part of a cult which worshipped the Syrian sun-god El-Gabal and encouraged deviant sexual practices shocking even to Ro-

man senators. He erected a huge stone phallus and demanded that Romans worship it, and was famous for making important staff appointments based solely on the size of the individual's sexual organs. Although Heliogabalus married five times in four years, he also indulged a private fantasy that he was a female prostitute, and set aside a room in his palace where he would hide behind a curtain and solicit passers-by. His unfortunate "clients" were expected not only to humour him, but also to pay well for the privilege. As a precaution against assassination he had various poisons and devices hidden around his palace so that he could take his own life. Heliogabalus finally pushed his luck too far when he broke Rome's most sacred law, by sexually violating the Vestal virgins, priestesses of the goddess Vesta, who celebrated celibacy. After a four-year rule, he was murdered by the Praetorian Guard as he sat on the toilet. His body was weighed down and dumped in the River Tiber.

8. Constantine (306–37 AD). The first Christian Emperor of Rome spent most of his life, like Heliogabalus, as a follower of the sun-god El-Gabal, and was baptized only at the very end of his life, when he was too elderly to sin any more. Constantine married twice, killed his son Crispus by his first wife and had his second wife murdered in her bath. He also had his brother-in-law and his 11-year-old nephew murdered. The Christian Church was keen to accommodate their new patron and took a lenient line on the emperor's adulterous personal life, ruling that it was perfectly acceptable for a man to take a mistress or two, provided his wife was barren. Neither of Constantine's wives was barren and the emperor didn't confine himself to just the one mistress, but it was a compromise that satisfied both Constantine and

the pope. However, Constantine never relinquished the title Pontifex Maximus as head of the Roman state's pagan cult.

9. Valentinian I (364–78 AD) was proclaimed emperor after the death of Jovian. He named his brother Valens co-emperor, and took the western portion of the empire for himself. Althogh he had great success against the invading Germans, he was manically cruel, and survived by feeding his enemies to two caged she-bears. He was often subject to inexplicable fits of rage, one of which resulted in a burst blood vessel and the emperor's death.

6
ODDS & SODS

10 Zealous Officials

1. In 1994 the regulatory authority for funeral parlours in Massachusetts suspended the licence of undertaker Robert Miller for two years. They were acting upon complaints that he had dug up the remains of two cremated bodies because relatives of the deceased failed to pay their funeral bills promptly.
2. In January 1994 in Riga, Latvia, five local bus inspectors beat a 33-year-old man named Smits to death for failing to produce a valid bus ticket.
3. In 1994 Los Angeles city officials ordered a strip club owner to remove the stage upon which nude dancers performed. The authorities ruled that the stage was not wheelchair-accessible for disabled nude dancers, although they admitted that no such dancers had yet come forward.
4. In 1996, in preparation for the first death-row hanging in 50 years – that of William Bailey – officials at the Delaware Correctional Centre fixed non-skid safety strips to each of the 23 steps leading to the outdoor gallows.
5. In February 1994 the Philadelphian state weights and measures officials served notice of a violation on topless dancer Crystal Storm. The officials had ascertained that Miss Storm's bust measurement was only 50 inches, and not her advertised measurement of "127", which Miss Storm later claimed was in centimetres.
6. In 1992 the South Carolina social services department sent a letter addressed to a recently deceased person: "Your food stamps will be stopped effective March 1992 because we received notice that you passed away. May God bless you. You may re-apply if there is a change in your circumstances."

7. When the city of Kirtipor in Ceylon fell to the King of Ghorka in 1770, the victorious king ordered an accurate census of the population. His officials followed his order by amputating the noses of the entire population, then counting them.
8. In February 1996 a US coroner complained that ambulance drivers were deliberately delivering obviously deceased people to hospital so that they could bill the county for the fare. Supporting his claim, he cited the case of a recent shotgun suicide victim who was rushed to hospital even though the blast was so effective that it blew both eyeballs out of their sockets.
9. In the nineteenth century, Indian tax collectors persuaded defaulters to pay up by forcing them to drink buffalo milk laced with salt until the victim was half-dead with diarrhoea.
10. In 1988 a US tax court considered the case of Cynthia Hess, who worked under her stage name "Chesty Love" in the US state of Indiana, and her claim of a $2,088 tax deduction on her breasts against depreciation on the surgical implants that boosted her bust to size 56FF. Officials subsequently ruled that the implants were so freakishly large – they weighed about 10 pounds apiece – that Ms Hess's breasts were clearly wholly for business use, because she couldn't possibly derive any personal benefit from them.

Adorable Ewe: 12 Animal Passions

1. One of the least publicized examples of Ice Age cave art depicts a man on skis having sex with an elk. Middle Eastern cave paintings also reveal that men once believed that sex with female crocodiles would bring them success in life.
2. The Incas had laws to prevent llama drivers from having sex with their animals: they enforced them by requiring that llama drivers were escorted by chaperones.
3. Frederick the Great, who never slept with his wife, was rumoured in later years to have been romantically attached to his pack of Italian whippet bitches.
4. The poet Algernon Charles Swinburne claimed he had once copulated with a monkey.
5. In 1857 Warren Drake, a soldier serving in the Utah militia in Echo Canyon, was found guilty of having sexual relations with a mare. A court martial sentenced both Drake and the mare to death. The soldier's sentence was subsequently commuted to exile from the territory; the less fortunate mare was executed.
6. In 1952 a man from Nigeria was accused of committing an act of sexual indecency with a pigeon in Hyde Park. His resourceful defence counsel reminded the judge of a precedent in the 1930s, when a man was accused of buggering a duck: on that occasion the accused had escaped scot-free after pointing out that a duck was a fowl, not a beast, and that he was therefore innocent of the charge of bestiality. The case against the Nigerian was dismissed, although he was fined £10 for taking the pigeon home and eating it.

7. In December 1993 James Humfleet, 33, was charged with the murder of his uncle, Samuel Humfleet. According to the accused he became angry after stumbling across his uncle having sex with one of the two pit bulls belonging to the owner of the trailer in which they had been partying.
8. A father of four, Mohammed Pervez from East Ham, London, was placed on probation for two years in May 1996 for buggering a horse. The Old Bailey was told that when police arrived they found the accused trying to flee from the field with his trousers around his ankles, and that the horse was in a state of "physical trauma".
9. In Key West, Florida, Patricia Wyatt called local police to report a stray pot-bellied pig having sex with her husband's new Harley Davidson. While trying to mate with the motorcycle's front wheel, the 50-pound pig scratched the paintwork, causing at least $100 damage. Animal control officers were uncertain as to what action to take against the pig. The bike's owner, Walter Wyatt, complained: "His crime is an alleged sex act against a Harley. We don't even know if that's a felony."
10. A man from Silver Spring, Maryland became infected with rabies in 1996 after he admitted having sex with a deceased racoon. He was charged with animal cruelty.
11. In Lebanon a man may legally have sex with an animal so long as it is female.
12. In August 1996 a court in Eagleville, Tennessee, charged a man with indecent exposure when it was discovered that the state had no law to apply to the act of having sexual intercourse with a miniature horse.

10 Paranoid Rulers

1. Emperor Qin Shi Huangdi unified China under the Chin dynasty in the third century BC. China's first emperor maintained his rule with a combination of enthusiastic wall-building to keep out his external enemies, and removing the tongues, hands, feet and genitalia of his enemies within. To ensure that no unfavourable comparisons were made between his and earlier regimes, he ordered the burning of all China's history books and decapitated 160 academics. The extraordinarily ruthless emperor had a favourite punishment: sawing his victims in half at the waist. Qin took his paranoia with him to his grave. His giant mausoleum was guarded by 8,000 life-size terracotta soldiers, to ward off the ghosts of the thousands of people he had wronged in his lifetime.
2. Emperor Nero was famous for his vanity and his cruelty, and for living in permanent fear of plots against him. He had hundreds of suspected enemies murdered, including his mother Agrippina. His fears were eventually justified when he was overthrown by a military revolt: he slit his own throat to avoid a lynch mob.
3. Paranoia was a state of mind which occurred naturally for Russia's ruling czars, but Ivan the Terrible's condition was more extreme than most. Violent punishments, meted out to real or imaginary enemies, became the hallmark of the latter years of his reign. A Russian nobleman, accused of casting spells against the czar, was personally burned alive by Ivan. Archbishop Leonidas of Novgorod, also suspected of plotting against the czar, was sewn inside a bearskin and thrown to a pack of hounds. The 50,000 or so townspeople of Novgorod were drowned beneath the ice of the Volkhov. His state treasurer was alternately immersed in freezing and boiling water until his skin peeled completely away. Ivan once tipped red-hot soup over the head of his court jester, then ran a sword through him because he screamed in pain.

4. Czar Paul I saw subversion everywhere, even in the way his people dressed. In 1797 he created a law forbidding his subjects to wear round hats, top boots, straight pants or shoes with laces – modern dress which had become associated in the czar's mind with the French Revolution and progressive political ideology. To enforce this regulation a couple of hundred armed troops were sent on to the streets of St Petersburg with orders to attack anyone who didn't conform to the dress code. People were stripped of clothing where they stood in the streets: shoes, hats, breeches and waistcoats were ripped to shreds or confiscated. The czar censored his own family's mail, closed down all private printing presses and deleted from the Russian dictionary the words "citizen", "club", "society" and "revolution". His police spies attended parties and concerts, even in private houses. Paul had every cab-driver in St Petersburg banished because one of them had been found carrying a gun. He passed another law which required everyone to get out of the carriage they were in whenever he passed by. Most people hid when they saw him coming. Under his mother, Catherine the Great, St Petersburg had become the third most fashionable city in Europe; under Paul it became a ghost town. He imposed a nine o'clock curfew and blockaded all exits from the capital. It became almost impossible to move without being harassed by the czar's police. Under Paul's instructions, one of Russia's finest buildings, the New Summer Palace in St Petersburg, was pulled down; on the site a new residence was built: Michael Castle, an ugly, thick-walled fortress with battlements, a moat and drawbridge. Shortly after moving into his new home Paul was strangled in a palace coup.
5. King Eric XIV of Sweden suffered from schizophrenia and extreme paranoia. He was convinced that all Sweden's noblemen were plotting against him, and took to stalking the palace with his sword drawn, ready to use it against anyone he could pick an argument

with. He saw subversion everywhere: even a sudden movement or a cough could result in bloody death. He suspected smartly turned-out servants of intending to seduce the court ladies, and had them put to death. Hundreds of Swedish noblemen were sentenced to death on trumped-up charges of treason, and Eric even stabbed to death his former tutor, believing him to be talking about him behind his back. With Sweden's prisons packed with noblemen awaiting death sentences and the country degenerating into chaos, Eric was finally proved right when his two younger brothers, John and Karl, joined forces to have him arrested and subsequently assassinated by poisoning.

6. King Henry Christophe of Haiti insisted on drawing attention to his country's chief export by having himself anointed with chocolate syrup. He was obsessed with his security, and ordered his entire personal bodyguard to prove their loyalty to him by marching over the edge of a 200-foot cliff to certain death. Those who disobeyed were tortured and executed. The king then decided to tighten security by having himself a new castle built at the top of a high mountain, fortified by 20 cannon. One by one the men required to drag the huge guns up the mountain dropped with exhaustion, and were executed on the spot. In all, the exercise cost the lives of about 20,000 men. When the mad king's subjects finally rebelled against him in 1820 he cheated a lynch mob by shooting his own brains out.
7. Sultan Abdul Hamid II was the last of the great rulers of the Ottoman house of Osman. As his two predecessors had both been deposed, he came to the throne a very nervous man. Although he surrounded himself with a bodyguard of several thousand tall Albanians, he considered security at his palaces to be far too relaxed, and set about building a new, impregnable palace from scratch. To create this new hiding place he had two Christian cemeteries cleared on a hillside at Yilditz and secured the services

of a dozen architects. Each architect was detailed to build just one 12th of the palace, working in complete ignorance of the work in progress of the other 11. In effect, the sultan built himself the world's most elaborate prison. Every wall was mirrored so that he could see the people around him from any angle; every door was lined with steel; every room was connected by a secret underground passage, which only Abdul Hamid knew about. He had a thousand loaded revolvers hidden around the palace, including one at each side of his bath. Many rooms were booby-trapped: at the flick of a switch, cupboards facing the entrance of the room would fly open and trip mechanically controlled revolvers. The palace was surrounded by a fake town – a labyrinth of buildings including fake shops, each of which was manned by the sultan's spies. The fortress town of Yilditz was filled with about 20,000 secret agents, with orders to spy on the sultan's bodyguards and on each other. The only spies that the sultan truly trusted were the hundreds of caged parrots which were hung on street corners, trained to squawk if they saw a stranger. The sultan's greatest phobia was of poisoning. He refused water unless it had been drawn from his secret spring and brought to him in a sealed container. The business of drinking milk was similarly tricky: his was the only dairy herd in the world with a 24-hour bodyguard. All his food was prepared behind iron bars and bolted doors. Each dish was then divided into three portions: the first was tasted by the Chief Chamberlain, "Guardian of the Sultan's Health and Life", the second was given to a cat or a dog. If both parties lived, the third portion was delivered on a sealed tray. The food was usually left uneaten, because the sultan really trusted only vitamin pills. He was a chain smoker, and even his cigarettes had to be pre-tested. Tobacco was bought cheaply and randomly, in case the sultan's supply of finest Turkish leaves had been got at. His cigarettes were then hand-rolled by his most trusted eunuch, who would be required to take the first drag. Every garment that Abdul Hamid wore had first to be "warmed" by a eunuch in case someone had attempted to poison his clothing. The sultan always carried with him a pearl-handled revolver. He was a nervy, jumpy little man, and a crack shot to boot – a lethal combination. No one dared put their hands in their pockets in his presence: to do so would be an invitation to the sultan to take a pot shot. When one of his gardeners made too sudden a bowing movement, Abdul Aziz quickly blew his brains out. When one of his own daughters gave him a playful shove from behind, he spun around and shot the girl dead before realizing who she was. On his very rare excursions outside Yilditz, he always travelled wearing a steel-lined fez and a shirt of chainmail, crouched inside his specially built armoured carriage, with one of his young sons on his knee as a "human shield". Eventually he retreated almost permanently into the company of his concubines, but even in the harem he found opportunities for paranoia. He had a life-sized wax effigy of himself placed behind a gauze curtain to make it look as though he was always watching them. Whenever news reached him of assassination attempts elsewhere in Europe he took it very personally, banning all mention of them in the press – with absurd consequences. When the king and queen of Serbia were butchered and tossed out of a bedroom window in 1903, the Turkish press solemnly reported that they had both died of indigestion.

8. After succeeding Lenin as ruler of the Soviet Union in 1924, Joseph Stalin ensured his survival for the next 30 years by ruthlessly removing all political rivals, and with the help of his secret police established his personal dictatorship over the party and country. Between 1934 and 1939 he had virtually the entire Communist Party élite executed, and placed millions in forced labour camps. In one day in December 1938 "Uncle Joe" signed 3,182 death

warrants. After the death of his second wife, he became deeply paranoid, refusing to trust his oldest personal and political friends, or even close family relatives. He withdrew to his Kremlin apartment, pathologically shy of public appearances. Stalin was about to launch his biggest leadership purge yet when he died suddenly of a brain haemorrhage on 5 March 1953.

9. King Carol II of Rumania, Queen Elizabeth II's German cousin, proclaimed himself Royal Dictator of Rumania in 1938, promptly abolishing party politics and cancelling the Rumanian Constitution. He suspected his own mother of plotting against him, and had her placed under 24-hour surveillance. King Carol had whole buildings demolished, including a large section of the Rumanian royal palace, so that the sights of his machine-guns could get a clear line of fire at the approaches to his residence. It didn't matter to him that the buildings happened to be most of the Rumanian royal palace.
10. President Macis Nguema was ruler of Equatorial Guinea from 1968 to 1979, during which time he was responsible for an escalating reign of terror, which wiped out more than 10 per cent of his country's 350,000 population. He methodically exterminated his real or imagined enemies, including 10 of his original 12 cabinet members, averaging about one political killing per week. He ordered the assassination of the ambassador to the United Nations, had a priest frozen to death in a refrigeration truck, left a prominent intellectual tied and gagged in the Sahara desert, and amputated the fingers of his government statistician because "he couldn't count". He surrounded his palace with an electric fence, banned Catholicism and had his own portrait placed above the altars of all Guinea's churches. In 1976 he announced that his fellow countrymen had just six months to give up their Christian names for African ones. Nguema was overthrown in 1979 and executed.

10 Royal Soubriquets

1. Constantine the Copronymous, Byzantine Emperor. So-named because at his christening in 718 the baby Constantine defecated in the baptismal font.
2. Pepin the Hunchback, ninth-century Frankish prince.
3. Alfonso the Fat, thirteenth-century king of Portugal.
4. Pedro the Cruel, fourteenth-century king of Castile.
5. Ethelred the Unready, king of England. At his christening, baby Ethelred urinated in the font and defiled the holy water. This was taken as an unlucky omen that he would be unfit to rule.
6. Stephen the Fop, fourteenth-century Bavarian duke.
7. Louis the Fat, Grand Dauphin, son of King Louis XIV of France.
8. Otto the Idle, king of Prussia. Never set foot in his homeland, and once attempted to sell it.
9. Henry the Impotent, prince of Castile. So-named for his inability to consummate his marriage with his wife, due to a deformity of his foreskin.
10. Selim the Grim, sultan of Turkey.

Europe's 10 All-Time Most Insane Monarchs

1. King Christian VII of Denmark displayed symptoms of mental illness consistent with schizophrenia, although he may also have been brain damaged by tertiary syphilis inherited from his father, King Frederick V. Physically puny, Christian was a sado-masochist who indulged in self-mutilation and violent wrecking sprees around his palace, often beating his head against walls until he drew blood. He had a fascination with public executions and secretly attended dozens of them in disguise. Christian played mock executions, and had a rack made for himself, on which he lay while his friend Conrad Holcke beat him until he was unconscious. With a gang of courtiers, he stalked the streets of Copenhagen by night, brandishing a spiked watchman's club. For the last 20 years of his life he lived in seclusion and in complete mental derangement. He was dragged out to make the odd ceremonial appearance when affairs of state demanded it, but was otherwise immured in his palace. For most of his long reign the people of Denmark were completely unaware that they had a lunatic on the throne. Little was known of the king's mental condition outside royal circles, and most Danes blamed their king's aversion to public appearances on the fact that he was being kept a prisoner and was being maltreated or drugged. Even when the full story broke years later, Danish history books taught that King Christian VII had simply become a little odd because he had been sexually abused by pageboys when he was a child. He was, however, awarded honorary degrees by both Oxford and Cambridge universities.

2. King Ludwig II of Bavaria was the most famous son of the House of Wittelsbach, a distinguished German royal family with a long tradition of mental instability. Ludwig's reign was dominated by two obsessions: his expensive patronage of the composer Richard Wagner, and his even more expensive hobby of erecting fantastic mock medieval castles, which came to be known as Ludwig's "sick children". After failing to fund his escalating building programme by sending begging letters to the crowned heads of Europe, he planned a series of major bank robberies. In despair in 1873 he planned to sell Bavaria and instructed a minor government official to go away and find a few thousand square miles of foreign land on which Ludwig could start up a new kingdom from scratch and live undisturbed, "completely independent of seasons, men and needs of all kinds". With the Bavarian treasury in a state of near bankruptcy, and with Ludwig's behaviour growing increasingly eccentric, the government pronounced that the king was suffering from advanced paranoia, was incurably insane and was incapable of exercising his duties. It was decided that he should be deposed and placed under restraint. Ludwig eluded permanent incarceration, however, by drowning himself in Lake Stern shortly after his arrest.
3. King Otto I of Bavaria became king when his elder brother, Ludwig II, was pronounced insane and removed from the throne. Otto was even more unstable than Ludwig II, but while his elder brother earned notoriety by organizing pan-European bank robberies and building fantastic castles, Otto's mental illness manifested itself in the less notable activities of barking like a dog, shouting abuse and occasionally taking pot shots at people with a

rifle through his bedroom window. After Ludwig's demise Otto reigned in name only from his cell in Castle Fürstenried guarded by a few medical attendants for 27 years, while his uncle Luitpold took charge of Bavaria as prince-regent. It was said that the king's screams could often be heard outside the castle. King Otto was removed from the throne a few months before the start of World War I and replaced with his cousin, who reigned as Ludwig III.

4. King Charles VI of France was insane for most of his 30-year rule, which (fortunately for England) also coincided with the 100 Years' War. Early in his reign he was struck down by a mystery illness which made his hair and nails fall out. He made a complete physical recovery, but lived in mental derangement thereafter, often given to bouts of extreme violence. He became convinced that his legs and his anus were made of glass, and refused to travel by coach in case they shattered. He eventually became so unstable that his wife, Queen Isabeau, decided that it was too risky to share a bed with him, and ordered one of her servants, Odette de Champdivers, to wear her clothing and take her place. The king slept with her regularly, never once noticing the difference. When he discovered that his wife had taken a lover, however, the king had the man drowned in the River Seine. Despite many creative attempts by his court physicians to find a cure for the king's condition, including trepanation and crude shock treatment, Charles VI died insane.
5. King George III, the best known "mad" British monarch, was mentally ill for just three or four relatively brief periods during his 60-year reign. George became apparently mentally unbalanced in 1788–9, again in 1801, in 1804, and then from 1810 until his death 10 years later. At

first it was thought that the king was suffering from "flying gout", a mysterious Georgian affliction which was thought to be relatively harmless unless you were unfortunate enough to get it in your head. Many of the best-known stories about the king's behaviour stem from a pamphlet published in 1789 by Philip Withers and containing many myths and politically motivated lies about the king's eccentricities. Some are repeated to this day, including the one about George shaking hands with an oak tree, having mistaken it for Frederick the Great. The final attack came in October 1810, shortly after celebrations to mark the 72-year-old king's golden jubilee. Although the first three breakdowns were followed by apparently complete remissions, in 1811 the king's physicians were compelled to testify to parliament that George III was irretrievably insane. The precise nature of his illness remains unproven, although "madness" theories have gone in and out of fashion. His final illness was almost certainly senile dementia, a natural condition unconnected with his earlier attacks.

6. Queen Maria I of Portugal displayed signs of incipient insanity from a very early age, probably the result of centuries of inbreeding within Portugal's royal family, the House of Braganza. In 1788 a smallpox epidemic carried away several people who were close to Queen Maria, including her confessor and a few of her immediate family, most notably her son José. It was believed that the combined shock of these deaths tipped her mind completely over the edge. She took to wearing children's clothes and became violently unstable. The English traveller and diarist William Beckford arrived at the Portuguese court in 1794 just as the queen was having one of her

turns. Beckford reported "the most horrible, the most agonising shrieks . . . inflicting upon me a sensation of horror such as I never felt before." The Braganza family sent to London for a specialist in the treatment of insanity, and hired the Rev. Francis Willis, fresh from his inept but apparently successful treatment of George III. Although none of his advice worked, Willis returned home with a consultancy fee of £10,000. The Portuguese people were kept in ignorance about the queen's condition, and in 1807 she was quietly smuggled off to Brazil so that her subjects wouldn't discover that insanity had again struck their royal family.

7. King Frederick William I of Prussia, the "sergeant-major" king, is known to posterity for his freakish army of giants and the way he terrorized everyone, including his own family. He was related to King George III and suffered from a variety of similar illnesses, including gout, piles, migraine and terrible stomach cramps. Unlike George III, whose illness was sporadic, Frederick William was a pathological tyrant almost all his life. The king's favourite weapon was his ever-present rattan stick, which he used to thrash anyone in sight. Everyone got the same treatment, including members of his own household. At meal-times he threw plates and cutlery and attacked his servants, starved his children or spat in their food. He regularly beat and degraded his son, Prince Frederick, later Frederick the Great. When the prince rebelled, the king taught him a lesson by forcing him to watch the execution of his best friend, then ordered that the severed head and body be left to lie for hours beneath his son's window to let the message sink in. The king had intended to kill his son as well, but backed off in the face of

international opposition As his reign continued he became progressively more violent. He kept two pistols by his side, loaded with salt, which he would fire at his servants if they didn't move quickly enough. One valet had his eye shot out, another was crippled. His courtiers were so afraid of him that when one of them was summoned to the king's private quarters he dropped dead with fright. The king's behaviour on the parade ground was even more intimidating. One of his army majors, humiliated by a thrashing from the king, drew his gun and shot himself through the head.

8. Czar Paul I of Russia, whose four-year reign saw Russia into the nineteenth century, was most spectacularly insane Russian monarch. He was small and very ugly, with a disproportionately large head and a saddle nose typical of sufferers of congenital syphilis. It wasn't until a few months after he became czar, at the age of 43, that his dangerous insanity became evident. His first act as czar was to have the body of the man he wrongly believed to be his father, Peter III, exhumed from a crypt at the Alexander Nevsky Monastery: by this time Peter III had been dead for 34 years. The rotting corpse was dressed in one of Peter's elaborate military uniforms, robed in ermine and taken to the throne room at the Winter Palace. It was seated on the throne and the imperial crown was placed on the skull. Paul's courtiers and officials were instructed to pay obeisance to the "true czar", the rightful occupant of the throne, usurped by his evil wife Catherine. There followed a double funeral, as the body of Peter III and Catherine were laid side by side so that their remains could mingle. Czar Paul did not have Peter III's genes, but he did inherit his obsession with Prussian militaria. His

officers grew to fear his unpredictability so much that they got into the habit of saying a final farewell to their wives and families before going on parade. For no apparent reason the czar once ordered an entire regiment on a 2,500-mile march, which took two years to complete and killed hundreds of horses. As Paul's relatively brief reign progressed he became more crazed, suffering increasingly from what he called his "black butterflies". In 1801 he was strangled in a palace coup.

9. King Frederick William IV of Prussia, Kaiser Wilhelm II's great-uncle, was the only Hohenzollern "soldier king" incapable of riding a horse. He succeeded to the throne in 1840, and from early in his reign suffered mental disturbance, a condition which was aggravated in the 1850s when the king suffered a series of strokes. When the king's behaviour became markedly more erratic, his younger brother Wilhelm was asked to step in as temporary regent. In 1858 it became apparent that the king's "softening of the brain" was irreversible and he was certified insane. For the next two years the by now extremely short-sighted king spent much of his time wandering around the Sans Souci Palace gardens, colliding with trees. The last official act of King Frederick William IV, just before he was officially declared insane, was to consider and ratify 13 death sentences.

10. Thanks to centuries of inbreeding, Queen Juana the Mad of Spain came to the throne mentally unhinged, and spent days on end wandering around the palace mumbling incoherently, vacant and childlike. She was driven completely insane by her faithless and mostly absent husband Philip the Handsome. When her beloved Philip died, aged 28, she resolved to see more of him in future, and to this

end had his body embalmed and kept by her side for several weeks, even at mealtimes and in bed at night. For the next 46 years her husband's corpse was always at hand, buried just outside her palace window, where she would gaze at his grave for hours on end. For the last three decades of her reign she remained a virtual prisoner in her castle, considered a danger to herself and her servants, who were frequently attacked by the queen. She died aged 76, under the regency of her son, Charles.

10 Homosexual Monarchs

1. King Edward II (1308–27). His favouritism towards his lover Piers Gaveston infuriated his wife Queen Isabella, especially when Edward gave his boyfriend most of her best jewellery. When Gaveston was assassinated by English nobles, Edward began an affair with Hugh Despenser, the son of an earl. The king was eventually taken prisoner by the queen's followers and was killed by having a red-hot poker thrust up his rectum.
2. King Richard II (1377–99) was known for his effeminate court and his fantastic gemstone-covered ball gown. He had an open homosexual affair with Robert de Vere, Earl of Oxford. When de Vere died the king had a breakdown and became completely inactive. He was deposed and murdered.
3. King Henry III of France (1574–89) wore ball gowns while chasing pretty French boys around his court. His followers, a gang of young male courtiers known as Les Mignons, copied him slavishly in every detail, painting their faces and wearing their hair long and piled high on their heads.
4. King James I (1603–25) was forever molesting the young men chosen as his bedroom attendants: a court diarist noted the king strolling with a boyfriend, his fingers "fiddling about his codpiece". The king was also very small, frequently drunk, never washed, had a terrible speech impediment and died of dysentery.

5. Czar Peter the Great of Russia (1682–1725) was an energetic and random seducer of either sex. There was always at least one available young man in court who was only there "for the pleasure of the czar", and he commissioned the Saxon artist Danhauer to paint a picture of his favourite male pages in the nude. A black slave lover, Abraham Hannibal, was known at court as "the Negro of Peter the Great".
6. King Gustav III of Sweden (1771–92) was shot dead at the opera in 1792 by his former page boy and lover Johan Ankartstrom.
7. King William III of Orange (1689–1702) was England's last known gay king, renowned for his terrible temper and his open relationships with male courtiers. Back in Holland he had surrounded himself with a côterie of young male aides, including a captain of the cavalry. Queen Mary's indifference towards him has been interpreted as proof that she was also a lesbian, although it is more likely that she simply found her small, ugly and cold husband repulsive. They died heirless.
8. King Louis XVIII of France (1814–24) was an obese Bourbon whose affections were centred on his captain of his bodyguard, a 34-year-old soldier named Antoine. Louis became totally infatuated with him and showered him with gifts and titles. Later, he formed another close relationship with a Gascon lawyer in his early 30s, Elie Decazes, whom Talleyrand noted resembled "a moderately good-looking hairdresser's assistant". The two were inseparable, the king always referring to him as his "darling child".
9. King Ludwig II of Bavaria (1863–86), the Swan King, liked to dress in silver armour and frolic with his boy-

friend, Prince Paul von Thurn und Taxis. He also had a long-lasting affair with a male servant, Alfonso Wecker, who eventually betrayed Ludwig by telling a commission investigating the king's insanity that Ludwig liked to watch young soldiers being whipped.

10. Czar Ferdinand I of Bulgaria (1908–18), first monarch of the newly independent state, was related on his father's side to Britain's ruling royals, the house of Saxe-Coburg-Gotha, and was also second cousin to Queen Victoria. Six feet tall and heavily bearded, Ferdinand wore women's jewellery, powdered his face and slept in a pink nightgown trimmed with Valenciennes lace. Although he married twice to keep up appearances (and produced an heir, Prince Boris), he spent his days chasing butterflies or seducing his male chauffeurs. The fact that the czar was gay was made apparent to his second wife, Princess Eleonore von Reuss-Köstritz, on their wedding night. When her new husband discovered that they had been assigned a double room, he flew into a furious rage and had it immediately swapped for two singles.

10 Experts

1. The respected ancient Roman physician Pliny taught that the souls of the dead resided in beans.
2. "I tell you, Wellington is a bad general, the English are bad soldiers: we will settle the matter by lunch time" – Napoleon on the eve of the Battle of Waterloo, 1815.
3. Mrs Beeton's *Book of Cookery and Household Management*, regarded as the housewife's bible since it was first published in 1861, contains several potentially lethal recipes, including one for mayonnaise which contains raw eggs. Mrs Beeton went to her grave aged 28 knowing nothing of salmonella.
4. Florence Nightingale steadfastly refused to believe in the existence of bacteria, even as they were wiping out half of her patients.
5. "Everything that can be invented, has been invented" – Charles H. Duell, Commissioner, US Office of Patents, 1899.
6. Ernest Rutherford was the first man to prove that the atom could be split. Although his work is the basis of all modern understanding of nuclear energy, Rutherford never considered it to be of any useful significance.
7. In 1928 MGM boss Louis B. Mayer refused to give a contract to the young cartoon-maker Walt Disney and his creation Mickey Mouse, because a 10-foot-tall rodent on the screen was an appalling idea and bound to frighten pregnant women.
8. In 1943 Thomas Watson, Chairman of IBM, predicted: "I think there is a world market for maybe five computers."

9. In 1962 an executive for Decca Recording Co. rejected the Beatles, informing their manager Brian Epstein: "We don't like their sound, and anyway, guitar music is on the way out."
10. In 1963 a BBC radio producer took aside Andrew Loog Oldham, manager of failed auditionists the Rolling Stones, and advised him: "The band's OK, but if I were you I'd get rid of the singer with the tiretread lips."

Get your Teeth out for the Lads: **10 Libidinous Geriatrics**

1. In September 1996 a male inmate died of a cardiac arrest and five more were treated for palpitations after a 79-year-old woman stripped off in a home for the elderly in Brisbane, Australia.
2. In 1993 a police raid on the A-1 Massage Studio in Oregon, US uncovered a masturbation service offered by two sisters, aged 70 and 73.
3. In 1994 Los Angeles police were alerted to find a peeping Tom. Apparently the man specialized in dressing up as the grim reaper, with a scythe in his hand, and staring through the windows of nursing homes at old inmates.
4. In 1981 French magistrates gave an 80-year-old prostitute a 10-month suspended prison sentence. The Paris court heard that Madame Marie Louise Soccodato had been plying her trade since 1941, although lately business had been dropping off.
5. A 72-year-old doctor caused a sensation in 1889 when he gave a lecture to the French Society of Biology about his discovery of the elixir of youth. Dr Charles Brown-Séquard described how he chopped and ground up the testicles of puppies and guinea pigs, then injected himself with the resulting compound. He announced that he was now physically 30 years younger and boasted that he was able to "visit" his young wife every day without fail. The lecture caused a stir in the medical establishment, albeit briefly: soon afterwards his wife left him for a younger man, and shortly after that the doctor dropped dead from a cerebral haemorrhage.
6. Catherine the Great of Russia was both an insomniac and a nymphomaniac, which was very bad news for the dozens of handsome young soldiers she continued to bed well into her

70s. She advocated sexual intercourse six times a day, had 21 "official" lovers and employed a doctor to examine all new applicants.

7. The Russian surgeon Serge Voronoff started to study Egyptian court eunuchs when it occurred to him that most of them looked remarkably good for their age, and concluded that male sex glands rejuvenated the body. In 1920 he put his theories to the test: he took the testicles of a chimpanzee and grafted them onto a 73-year-old man. Voronoff recorded that his experiment only had "a temporary effect".
8. In accordance with the fashion of the day, unmarried Elizabethan women wore their breasts exposed – a habit Queen Elizabeth herself favoured well into her 70s.
9. Chairman Mao regularly suffered from venereal disease, but refused to be treated or to abstain from sex until the infection cleared. The young girls whom he continued to bed well into his 70s considered catching VD from their chairman a badge of honour and testimony to their close personal relationships with Mao.
10. In Iran in 1994 Mohammad Esmail al-Bahrami, age 105, filed for divorce from his wife, Fatemeh Razavi, age 100.

Building a Better Moose Trap: **10** Inventions that nearly took the World by Storm

1. The distinguished scientist Sir Francis Galbon, a first cousin of Charles Darwin, invented identikit photos, fingerprinting and the science of eugenics. He also invented a pocket counting device which he used to clock the number of attractive women he passed in the street. After many years of dedicated research Galbon's instrument enabled him to compile a "beauty map" of Great Britain, which determined that Britain's ugliest women lived in Aberdeen. Galbon went on to invent a device for measuring the size of African female bottoms, and a ventilating hat which cooled the head by automatically lifting. He also began to experiment on himself with drugs, in alphabetical order, but stopped at C when he discovered what a large dose of castor oil did best.
2. In 1786 a German, S.G. Vogel, invented a cage-like contraption to prevent masturbation. Between 1856 and 1932, 33 devices were registered with the US patents office designed to prevent male masturbation. They included handcuffs, chains and armoured cod-pieces.
3. In 1959 Bertha Dlugi of Milwaukee became the first person to realize the commercial possibilities of a bird nappy (diaper), which would allow pet birds to fly freely around the house without depositing droppings.

4. The Museum of Questionable Medical Devices in Minneapolis, Minnesota is the world's largest display of quackery. Gadgets on view include a machine devised to increase virility and cure prostate problems by electric shock treatment, a foot-powered breast-enlarger, weight-reducing soap and weight-reduction spectacles.
5. Indiana doctor Alpheus Myers patented his Trap for Removing Tapeworms from the Stomach and Intestines on 14 November 1854. Myers' invention comprised "a trap which is baited, attached to a string, and swallowed by the patient after a fast of suitable duration to make the worm hungry. The worm seizes the bait, and its head is caught in the trap, which is then withdrawn from the patient's stomach by the string which has been left hanging from the mouth, dragging after it the whole length of the worm."
6. In 1994 an Italian patented a condom that played Beethoven whenever it tore during use. Lini Missio's prophylactic was coated with a substance that changes electrical conductivity upon rupture, setting off a microchip that produces a sound.
7. In the 1860s the British Patent Office issued a patent for a toilet shooting stick "to assist persons of short stature in personal evacuation".
8. One of the first ever inventions lodged at the British Patents Office was a device for flushing out the Loch Ness monster with a series of electric shocks.
9. In 1914 Natalie Stolp from Philadelphia patented a device to discourage men from rubbing their thighs against ladies in crowded trains. Her spring-loaded undergarment responded to unwanted male pressure

by releasing a metal spike into the offender's thigh.

10. In 1994 the US based Kimberly-Clark Corporation patented chemically realistic synthetic faeces for testing nappies and incontinence garments. The company had concluded that previously used substitute concoctions made from a mixture of mashed potatoes, peanut butter and canned pumpkin pie were inadequate because they separated into liquids and solids more quickly than the real thing.

10 Least Insightful People

1. A 39-year-old American, Bruce Jensen of Bountiful, Utah, sought an annulment to his three-and-half-year marriage in 1986 citing "irreconcilable differences", when he discovered that his wife was a man. The couple first met at the University of Utah Health Sciences Centre, where the soon-to-be Mrs Jensen, real name Felix Urioste, was masquerading as a female doctor. Jensen wed Urioste after the latter claimed to be pregnant with twins after their solitary sexual encounter. Urioste later said the twins were stillborn. He never let Jensen see him naked during their marriage. The deception was uncovered when Jensen filed a missing person report. Police subsequently learned that the absent Mrs Jensen had a record for credit card fraud in Las Vegas, Nevada, and had been arrested while travelling as "a bearded man". Jensen confessed later: "I feel pretty stupid."
2. On 4 July 1776, American Independence Day, King George III wrote in his diary: "Nothing of importance happened today."
3. In 1955 Sam Phillips, owner of a small recording company in Memphis, sold to RCA Records for the sum of $35,000 the exclusive contract he had with a young performer named Elvis Presley. Phillips thereby forfeited royalties on over a billion records.
4. In 1898 the young Albert Einstein applied for admission to the Munich Technical Institute, but was rejected on the grounds that he "shows no promise" as a student.
5. In 1880 a house master at Harrow wrote of the young Winston Churchill: "He is forgetful, careless, unpunctual, irregular in every way. If he is unable to conquer this

slovenliness he will never make a success of public school."

6. In 1889 the editor of the *San Francisco Examiner* published a single article by Rudyard Kipling, but explained that he was unable to accept any more. "I'm sorry, Mr Kipling, but you just don't know how to use the English language."
7. In 1886 prospector Sors Hariezon decided to cut his losses and sell his South African gold claim for $20. Since that day, mines sunk on or near his claim have produced over a thousand tons of gold a year, about 70 per cent of the Western world's gold supply.
8. In 1938 Joe Shuster and Jerry Siegel sold all rights to the comic-strip character Superman to their publishers for $65 each.
9. In 1994 a Chinese TV crew in Hong Kong filmed a documentary on the first open-heart surgery ever performed at the Weifang Medical Institute in Shangdong. The crew were later informed that they would have to reshoot. Hospital officials had belatedly discovered that the open-heart patient was, in fact, a boy who had been admitted for a tonsillectomy.
10. During the First Crusade, a band of desperate religious hysterics marched behind a goose which they believed was filled with the Holy Spirit.

10 Military Eccentrics

1. The US Confederate General "Stonewall" Jackson was a strict Presbyterian known as Deacon Jackson before winning his new nickname at the first battle of Bull Run. He was also highly eccentric. The general believed that one side of his body weighed more than the other, so whenever he walked one arm was raised to restore his balance. He also always stood while eating. When he was a junior officer, he wore his thick army greatcoat throughout a long and very hot summer because he had not received an order to do otherwise. His deep religious convictions also meant that he refused to fight on Sunday. During the thick of the battle of Mechanicsville in 1862 Jackson spent the day praying alone on a nearby hill, refusing to speak to anyone, while his troops took heavy casualties. In 1863 he was mistakenly shot by his own men, and died a week later.
2. One of Wellington's senior commanders during the Peninsular War, Sir William Erskine, had twice been confined to lunatic asylums. Wellington heard of his appointment with stunned disbelief, and immediately wrote to the military secretary in London for an explanation. The secretary replied: "No doubt he is a little mad at intervals, but in his lucid intervals he is an uncommonly clever fellow, and I trust he will have no fit during the campaign, although I must say he looked a little mad as he embarked." During one of Erskine's less lucid intervals he was found at dinner when he should have been defending a strategically important bridge. He eventually sent five

men to defend it: when a fellow officer queried his decision Erskine thought better of it and sent a whole regiment, but pocketed the instruction and forgot all about it. Sir William's mental health wasn't his only problem. His eyesight was so poor that before a battle he had to ask someone to point him in the general direction of the battlefield. He eventually committed suicide by jumping out of a window in Lisbon. Found dying on the pavement, he asked bystanders: "Why on earth did I do that?"

3. The Greek commander General Hajianestis, who led his country's army in the war with Turkey in 1921, was believed at the time to have been completely insane. In fact, he showed a keen sense of self-preservation. Rather than rouse himself to command his troops, he stayed in bed pretending to be dead. Another ploy he sometimes used was to claim that he couldn't get up because his legs were made of glass and they might break if he moved.
4. The Prussian king, Frederick the Great, was renowned for his military genius but had a complete disregard for casualties or human life, including his own. Wounded men were expected to find their own way off the battlefield and back to hospitals as best they could, and were denied rations. As only one in five who entered a Prussian military hospital came out alive, men deserted by the thousand, and hundreds more committed suicide. When his campaign funds ran short Frederick saved money by skimping on his soldiers' uniforms: there was so little material in them that they couldn't be fastened, and many of his men froze to death. Frederick would always open a vein before a battle to calm his nerves, and when the tide turned against him he fought on with a phial of poison ready for suicide. He drank up to 40 cups of coffee a day for several weeks in an experiment to see if it was possible to

exist without sleep. It took his stomach three years to recover. One day, he was surprised to find one of his best soldiers shackled in irons. When he asked why this was so, he was told that the man had been caught buggering his horse. Frederick ordered: "Fool – don't put him in irons, put him in the infantry", then apologized to the soldier for taking his horse away from him.

5. The Civil War General S. Ewell, or Old Bald Head, as he was known by his Confederate troops, was a brave but flawed military leader who harboured the delusion that he was a bird. This problem became apparent whenever he cocked his head to one side, pecked at his food and made chirping noises. To complete the picture, Ewell was also known for his beaky nose.
6. The Mexican general Antonio Lopez de Santa Anna stubbornly observed the tradition of siesta, even in life-threatening situations. In 1836 Santa Anna and his troops found themselves near a wood known to be full of Texan soldiers, but nevertheless insisted on taking their usual afternoon nap. While Santa Anna and his men quietly snoozed the Texans attacked and routed the entire Mexican army in under 20 minutes. Santa Anna escaped, but two years later had a leg torn off in a skirmish with the French. He recovered the leg, and when he eventually became the most powerful man in Mexico he gave it a full state funeral.
7. As commander-in-chief of the Russian army, Czar Paul was able to indulge his childlike obsession with his hero Frederick the Great. He made his troops wear a uniform slavishly copied from the Prussian military handbook, right down to the last detail of old-fashioned gaiters and powdered pigtails, entirely at the expense of military efficiency. The soldiers wore costumes so tight-fitting that breathing

was difficult and fighting practically impossible. Underneath, they wore straitjackets to make them stand erect, and on their heads they wore thick, heavy wigs with iron rods inserted in them to make the hairpiece sit straight. To make his soldiers goose-step perfectly without bending their legs, the czar had steel plates strapped to their knees. The night before a parade his men would labour until dawn to cover their wigs with grease and chalk. They all knew that even a hair out of place could mean arrest, a thrashing or deportation.

8. Queen Victoria's psychopathic father Edward, Duke of Kent, was the most sadistic and the most hated man in the British army. The duke believed that the only way to treat a soldier was to flog him into submission: the added bonus was that he was sexually aroused by the sight of men being whipped (in fact, it made him wet his trousers). Consequently he quickly made his mark as a brutal and tyrannical disciplinarian, who would thrash his soldiers at the slightest provocation. The duke was sent to Gibraltar as colonel of the Royal Fusiliers, and it was there that he first earned his nickname "the beast". From 5AM every day he thrashed, marched and drilled his men into the ground, and the floggings multiplied. When news filtered back to England that the Gibraltar garrison was at the point of mutiny, the duke was quietly removed and sent to Canada. He saw his new posting as a fresh opportunity to inflict even more unnecessary cruelty, and once again he drove his troops to the brink of mutiny with a regime of outrageous punishments. In 1802 the duke was unwisely returned to Gibraltar, this time as governor-general. On the barren rock there was there little else for his dispirited Royal Fusiliers to do except drink, so the flogging duke banned alcohol,

oblivious to the real danger of mutiny. One day one of the frequent deserters from his garrison was caught, and the duke sentenced him to the maximum number of lashings the army rulebook would allow: 999. This time the troops mutinied. Many men lost their lives, many more were seriously wounded. Three ringleaders were executed, others were flogged. The duke was quickly recalled to England, lucky to have escaped with his life.

9. The Duke of Wellington had more on his mind at Waterloo than the small matter of defeating Napoleon. Wellington's ally, the famous Prussian field marshall Leberecht von Blücher, was in the early stages of senile dementia, which frequently caused him to experience bizarre delusions. Blücher once confided to Wellington that he was pregnant and about to give birth to an elephant, and that moreover the cad who had raped him was a French soldier. Von Blücher also took to walking around the room on tip-toe because he believed the French had developed a dastardly plan to burn his feet by heating the floor.
10. Vlad "the Impaler" Tepes, the historical Count Dracula, was renowned for his extraordinary appetite for cruelty, but was considered a military hero in his own country, being a talented general who had defeated their sworn enemies, the Turks. Tepes ruled over Walachia, now part of Rumania, between 1456 and 1476. He had about 20,000 of his enemies impaled on wooden stakes and often drank the blood of his victims. He forced wives to eat the cooked flesh of their husbands and parents to eat their own children. When a large troop of Tartars strayed into his territory he selected three of them and had them fried and force-fed to the others. When Turkish envoys arrived at his palace to sue for peace, he had their hats and coats nailed to their bodies.

10 Milestones in the History of New Laddism

1. 323 BC: Alexander the Great conquers most of the known world, then drops dead, during a drinking contest aged 32.
2. AD 211: The young Roman emperor Heliogabalus has a couple of palace dinner guests suffocated in rose petals for a laugh.
3. 1544: the young Ivan the Terrible amuses himself by throwing live dogs off the Kremilin roof "to observe their pain".
4. 1561: King Philip II of Spain's son and heir Don Carlos, a mentally retarded psychopath who is eventually disinherited, locked up and quietly done away with, has young girls whipped for his enjoyment, has animals roasted alive while he watches, and murders at least six men for some real or imagined slight against him. When he is dissatisfied with a pair of boots made for him, he has them cut into pieces and forces the cobbler to eat them. On another occasion, when some water is inadvertently emptied from a house balcony and splashed near him, he has the occupants executed.
5. 1712: Peter the Great's son Alexis travels to Dresden to marry a German princess. The Elector of Hanover Ernst August notes that the tsarevitch shits in his bedroom and wipes his backside with the curtains.
6. 1741: the Comte de Charolais, cousin of French king Louis XV, orders his coachman to run over any monks he encounters on the road, and shoots a man he sees working on a roof, for the hell of it. The king pardons his psychopathic cousin with the warning: "Let it be understood, I will similarly pardon anyone who shoots you."

7. 1793: the Russian Grand Duke Constantine, a grandson of Catherine the Great, amuses himself by kicking Hussars to death and firing live rats from cannon.
8. 1813: 25-year-old Lord Byron impregnates his half-sister Augusta.
9. 1828: King Miguel of Portugal tosses live piglets into the air and catches them on the point of his sword.
10. 1909: Prince George of Serbia, eldest son and heir of King Peter I, is removed from the line of succession after kicking his valet to death.

10 Creative Applications for Formaldehyde

1. Dr Honoré Fragonard, eighteenth-century anatomist and cousin of the French master Jean-Honoré Fragonard who was famous for his paintings of landscapes and rosy-cheeked cherubs, made sculptures from human and animal cadavers. His pieces, carefully skinned, preserved in formaldehyde and posed, are now on public view in the Fragonard Museum, which comprises three rooms of the National Veterinary School in Maisons-Alfort, on the eastern outskirts of Paris. Fragonard set up the museum himself in 1766, at the school where he worked as a teacher. The school authorities, upset by their employee's nauseating hobby, fired Fragonard in 1771, but decided to keep the museum. Fragonard went on to enjoy a strange celebrity status among members of the French aristocracy, who liked to keep curious objects in their homes. By the time the anatomist died in 1799, aged 66, hundreds of his sculptures were being used to break the ice at the very best dinner parties.
2. By the time Eva Peron died of cancer in 1952 an eminent pathologist had been on stand-by for a fortnight to embalm her. With Eva barely dead he quickly filled her veins with alcohol, then glycerine, which kept her organs intact and made her skin appear almost translucent. Her funeral turned into a riot: as two million Argentinians filed past her coffin, seven people were crushed to death. Eva's husband Juan planned to have her housed in a giant new mausoleum, but he was forced to flee the country, and the body went missing for several years. In 1971 Juan and Eva were touchingly re-united. According to an eye-witness, Eva's corpse was ever-present at the Peron family dinner table along with Juan and his new wife Isabel.

3. Damien Hirst's Turner Prize-winning 1994 show at the Serpentine Gallery in London featured his famous animal exhibits, including *Away from the Flock*, a lamb embalmed in a glass case. Previous works include *Mother and Child Divided* comprising a dead cow and calf bisected in formaldehyde in a glass case, and a cow's head being devoured by maggots, a piece which had to be replaced every 36 hours with a new head.
4. The famous duellist Brian Maguire was a descendant of the ancient Fermanagh family and an officer in the East India Company. When his son George died aged 12 in 1830, Maguire decided to craft a permanent and cherished keepsake: he embalmed the boy himself and kept him in a glass case which he carried with him everywhere, until his own death five years later, of a heart attack.
5. When Enrico Caruso died in 1921 the great Italian opera singer was laid to rest on show in a glass coffin, allowing hordes of fans to ogle at his corpse for the next five years. Five years and several new suits later, his widow decided to give him a more dignified resting place: in a private tomb.
6. Because of a fault in the embalming process, the body of Chairman Mao is shrinking at a steady rate of about 5 per cent a year. The official line given by the mausoleum director is that this is merely an optical illusion caused by the curious lighting effects in the hall which contains his corpse.
7. Ancient Egyptians didn't always bury their dead relatives after their bodies had been mummified. Families often observed the grisly ritual of keeping the body at home with them so that it could be present at meal times; some were kept above ground for several years. There was another reason for this practice: at the risk of ruining appetites and frightening the children, the mummified bodies of dead relatives were valuable assets,

which could be used to guarantee loans: i.e. you could borrow money on the surety of your stiff mother, father, brother or child. Anyone who failed to discharge a debt would be refused a burial of their own.

8. When Bonnie Parker and Clyde Barrow were ambushed in their car and shot to death, their bodies were placed in a Louisiana undertaker's parlour, which was the rear room of a furniture store. The crowds who turned out to see the outlaws were so uncontrollable that the undertaker had to squirt embalming fluid on them to keep them back.
9. Most Russians are prepared to stand in line for hours only for something edible, but Vladimir Ilyich Lenin continues to be a crowd-puller in his new mausoleum at St Petersburg, although neither his reputation nor the queues are quite what they were. Lenin may have been a poor conversationalist since 1924, but the world's most famous embalmee has managed to get through several dozen new suits. Under his blue acrylic tailored three-piece, the father of communism also wears a rubber wetsuit, into which is poured the solution which keeps him from falling apart. Twice a week the parts that show – his hands and face – are painted with fresh embalming fluid, and every 18 months the whole body is lifted out and given a thoroughly good soaking. Every four years a bit of Lenin is scraped off, placed under a microscope and examined for signs of deterioration. About 60 per cent of his body is now made of wax, including his ears: the original pickling wasn't done properly and bits of him have "gone off" since. He also sports a growth of fungus around his neck and the back of his head, which definitely wasn't there when he led the Bolsheviks to power in 1917. When communism was still popular Lenin had to be refrigerated with equipment from a German fish-freezing plant to stop him melting in the body-heat of visiting tourists.

10. When united Italy's first monarch, Victor Emmanuel II, died, Rome's daily paper *Opinione* carried a "live" eye-witness report of the deceased king as he lay in state: "He lies with his face turned slightly to the left. His eyes are closed and his appearance, maintaining a certain look of pride, has taken on an aspect of calm which is enhanced by his natural pallidness. At 7PM this evening the embalming of the royal corpse will begin." The newspaper went on to assure its readers that the embalming process would guarantee that: "the mortal remains of the appearance of our beloved sovereign will be conserved for the benefit of posterity." This confidence was misplaced: owing to a fault in the embalming process the old king very quickly decomposed in his new general's uniform, forcing onlookers to flee with handkerchiefs covering their noses.

10 Women Behaving Badly

1. In 1603, as 30,000 Londoners were dying of the plague, Queen Elizabeth I responded to the national crisis by fleeing with her court to Windsor Castle, where she had a gallows set up, with the promise that she would hang anyone who tried to follow her.
2. Queen Henrietta, wife of the Belgian king Leopold II, kept a pet llama which she taught to spit in the face of anyone who stroked it.
3. The Russian empress Anne was fond of making up interesting new punishments to fit the crime. When she decided that two overweight noblewomen were guilty of being greedy, she had them force-fed huge amounts of pastries until they almost choked to death on their own vomit. Few complained about the treatment: the empress always had their tongues pulled out first.
4. Empress Catherine I of Russia was a chronic alcoholic who shuffled through most of her reign in a drunken haze. She once survived an assassination attempt, too drunk to realize that anything had happened. While she was reviewing a Guards regiment, a bullet flew past her and killed an innocent bystander. The empress moved on without flinching.
5. Messalina, wife of the Roman emperor Claudius, claimed an all-time record for marital infidelity when she slept with 25 men in 24 hours. She often left the imperial palace at night in disguise and went to work at a local brothel, under the name Lycisca.

6. Queen Cleopatra tested the efficacy of her poisons by feeding them to her slaves.
7. Elizabeth de B'athory, the deranged late-sixteenth- and seventeenth-century lesbian Hungarian countess, believed she could reverse the ageing process by bathing in warm virgins' blood. In 1612, acting on countless rumours about her activities, troops stormed her castle and caught her literally red-handed. All her servants were executed and burned. The countess herself was sealed in her bedroom and left to die.
8. The Russian empress Elizabeth was extremely vain. She would not tolerate competition and no one else at court was ever allowed to wear her favourite colour, pink. The empress was naturally fair-haired, but had her hair dyed black to conform with the fashion of the day; when the fashion changed and she wanted to revert to blonde, she was unable to remove the dye from her hair and, in a fit of temper, shaved it all off. All her ladies-in-waiting were duly obliged to have their heads shaved, too.
9. Queen Maria Luisa of Spain had 24 childbirths and miscarriages, none of them attributable to her husband King Charles IV, who went through his entire marriage in blissful ignorance of his wife's countless adulterous relationships. The half-wit king even promoted his wife's regular lover – a sausage merchant half her age – to first minister of Spain.
10. Manuela, the widowed mother-in-law of France's emperor Louis Napoleon, was a major embarrassment to the French royal family. After a sex scandal had ended her career as head of the household to Queen Isabella of Spain, Manuela took to selling sexual favours to British ministers visiting Madrid. The main source of gossip,

however, were the country house orgies she regularly attended with young men half her age. She and several other middle-aged aristocratic women kidnapped young men who took their fancy and forced the captives to crawl around the floor naked on all fours, while the women straddled their backs and pretended they were knights jousting.

7
CRIME & PUNISHMENT

15 Original Observations made by Condemned Men

1. "At least I'll get some high-class education." – US murderer John W. Deering, facing the firing squad, after willing his body to the University of Utah.
2. "Pretty soon you're going to see a baked Appel." – George Appel, murderer of puns and of a New York policeman, as he was strapped into the electric chair in 1928.
3. "I am Jesus Christ." – Aaron Mitchell, cop-killer, awaiting death by gassing at San Quentin in 1967.
4. "Will that gas bother my asthma?" – Luis José Monge, at Colorado State Prison in 1967, awaiting death by gassing for the murders of his wife and three children.
5. "Warden, I'd like a little bicarb because I'm afraid I'm going to get gas in my stomach right now." – Charles de la Roi, sentenced to death by lethal gas in 1946 in California for the murder of a fellow prison inmate, bidding for the George Appel Worst Death Chamber Pun Award of 1946.
6. "Hurry it up, you Hoosier bastard. I could hang a dozen men while you're fooling around." – mass-murderer Carl Panzram, awaiting the gallows at Leavenworth prison in 1930.
7. "Just our luck . . . we haven't even got a decent day for it." – Frank Negran to his fellow murderer Alex Carrion as they awaited execution at Sing Sing in 1933.
8. "Damned if I care what you read." – murderer Alan

Adam, on being informed by the sheriff of Northampton, Massachusetts in 1881 that he was going to read aloud the execution warrant before Adam was hanged.

9. "Are you sure this thing is safe?" – the Rugeley poisoner Dr William Palmer, as he was escorted to the gallows trap door in 1855, after killing 14 people.
10. "I'd like to thank my family for loving me and taking care of me . . . and the rest of the world can kiss my ass." – Robert Alton Harris, gassed on 21 April 1992.
11. "I think I'd rather be fishing." – Jimmy Glass, electrocuted 12 June 1987.
12. "I'm still awake." – Robyn Leroy Parks, after his lethal injection on 10 March 1992.
13. "Commute me or execute me. Don't drag it out." – Jesse Bishop, gassed 22 October 1979.
14. "I guess nobody is going to call." – Edward Earl Johnson, gassed 20 May 1987.
15. "I want to make a complaint . . . the soup I had for supper tonight was too hot." – murderer Charles Fithina before his electrocution in New Jersey.

10 Most Optimistic Defences in a Criminal Law Court

1. Diana Smith from Kinsey, Alabama, pleaded guilty in December 1993 to tampering with a man's grave. The court heard that the 37-year-old woman had been charged with causing the man's death in 1990. She was merely digging up the casket in order to prove that he was faking it.
2. Mexican sisters Delfina and Maria Gonzalez were arrested and charged with murder in 1964 when police found the remains of at least 80 girls on the premises of their brothel. When asked for an explanation, one of the sisters volunteered: "Maybe the food didn't agree with them."
3. A court in Prince William County, Virginia, dropped charges of rape and sodomy against a 45-year-old schizophrenic after accepting evidence that one of the victim's multiple personalities had consented to have sex with one of the rapist's multiple personalities. The prosecution heard that the two had previously met in group therapy, and that many of their "different selves" had fallen in love and even talked of marriage.
4. In 1996 convicted Chicago paedophile Robert Ellison, 65, asked a judge for the immediate return of his child sex videos. He argued that he would surely molest more children if he could not relieve his urges through pornography. The judge opted to achieve a similar result by locking Ellison up.
5. Thirty-year-old Frederick Treesh was one of three men detained for terrorizing the Great Lakes area in North America with a series of spree killings during the summer of 1994. Treesh complained later: "Other than the two we

killed, the two we wounded, the woman we pistol-whipped, and the light bulbs we stuck in people's mouths, we didn't really hurt anybody."

6. Lawyers acting for Seattle death row inmate Mitchell Rupe appealed against his hanging because it would constitute "cruel and unusual punishment". They argued that 19-stone, 3-pound Rupe would be instantly decapitated by the pressure of his weight on the rope. The appeal failed and Rupe swung on 11 July 1994.
7. In 1996 in Providence, US, Anthony St Laurent admitted taking part in organized crime. On receiving a 10-month prison sentence, he informed the court that he was in point of fact innocent, and had only entered a guilty plea because an illness requiring 40–50 enemas a day would have made it difficult for him to sit through a very long trial.
8. In 1995 Baltimore police arrested Saladin Ishmael Taylor, 34, for the murder of a neighbour. A woman's body had been found lying next to a one-inch piece of Taylor's tongue, which had apparently been bitten off by the victim in their struggle. At his trial Taylor lisped that he had no knowledge of the murder. He admitted that he had recently lost part of his tongue in a street accident, but had no idea how it had ended up beside the woman's body.
9. Israel Zinhanga, 28, told a Zimbabwe court in 1996 that he had sex with a cow because he was afraid of contracting AIDS from a human partner.
10. In 1996 the US Supreme Court rejected the appeal of a convicted Arizona drug-user, who claimed he did not receive a fair trial because there were no fat people on the jury.

12 Crimes of *Passion*

1. Patricia Orionno was France's least competent murderess. In 1988 she decided to get rid of her husband because he made excessive sexual demands of her. She tried to kill him with sleeping tablets, but underestimated the dosage and only made him oversleep. She slashed his wrists, tried to gas him, then tried to smother him with a pillow. She was successful in her fifth attempt, stabbing him eight times. She was subsequently freed when the French judge ruled that it was a crime of passion.
2. When King John of England found out that his wife Isabella had taken a lover, he had him killed and his corpse strung up over Isabella's side of the bed.
3. Regina Chatien, 43, and Melvin Hoffman, 53, were each fined $1,000 for engaging in oral sex during a 1995 football game at the Los Angeles Dodger Stadium, while in attendance with their four children.
4. In July 1996 Gail Murphy, 47, of Brooklyn, New York, was arrested for shooting her husband dead because he had gone on a six-hour fishing trip while she was recovering from haemorrhoid surgery. A police investigator explained to the *New York Times*: "She felt that her husband didn't demonstrate that he cared for her on that particular day."
5. Jeffrey Watkins, 24, was convicted in 1994 of breaking into five New York mausoleums and stealing the skull of a woman who had been dead since 1933. Watkins confessed

that he had slept with remains inside coffins: "I feel safe with the dead, and I can trust them. I need their company to make me peaceful inside."

6. To see if he could get a reaction from his unfaithful wife, the Russian czar Peter the Great had the head of her suspected lover pickled in alcohol and placed in a jar at her bedside.
7. In 1994, when the wife of Polish adulterer Boris Paveharik found a pack of condoms in her husband's pocket, she filled them with ground pepper. After the next visit to his mistress Mr Paveharik was rushed to hospital suffering severe swelling and inflammation.
8. A 67-year-old American, Marland Maynard, was convicted of the manslaughter of his wife Maybel in 1995. The court heard that Maynard had returned home from work to find his wife in the act of attempting suicide with a handgun. When the gun jammed, Marland helped her reload it.
9. Three months after the burial of his fiancée, Roberto Carlos da Silva, 21, of Socorcaba, Brazil dug up her body, which was wearing a wedding dress, and had sex with it. He told the Estado news agency: "I was desperate and needed her."
10. Thai Buddhist monk Sayan Duriyalak was so outraged by the discovery that his 67-year-old abbot was violating his vow of chastity by having an affair with a 51-year-old nun that he attacked the couple with an axe while they made love, decapitating the abbot and seriously wounding the nun. Sayan told police that he had planned his attack to imitate an execution he had recently seen on a TV cop series.
11. In 1895 a New York doctor named Buchanan was charged with the murder of his wife. At his trial the prosecution set out to prove that in order to finance his gambling addiction, Buchanan had his wife heavily insured, then poisoned her

with morphine. They alleged that Buchanan had attempted to disguise the tell-tale sign of morphine poisoning – pinpoint pupils – by putting belladonna in her eyes to dilate them. To demonstrate their theory, a cat was put to death in the court room. The jury was convinced and Buchanan went to the electric chair at Sing Sing.

12. Texan John Celinski was fined £1,200 and sentenced to two years' probation in 1994 after he admitted microwaving two cats belonging to his ex-girlfriend. Celinski testified at his trial that he was jealous of her pets, Sugar Ray and Bonnie.

10 Most Bungled Executions

1. The most prolonged execution in French history occurred in 1626, when Count Henri de Chalais was condemned to death for his part in a royal assassination plot. When it was time for the count to be publicly beheaded with a sword, the regular executioner couldn't be found and an inexperienced replacement had to be drafted in at the last minute. The count's head was hacked off by the stand-in on the 29th stroke: he was still breathing at the 20th.
2. James Scott, the Duke of Monmouth and first-born illegitimate son of Charles II, was victim of Tower Hill's messiest execution on 15 July 1685. Although the handsome and popular duke complained loudly that the axeman's blade appeared to be very blunt, no one took much notice. In the event it was the fifth blow which finally severed his head from his shoulders just before he had a chance to say "I told you so". The crowd was appalled and the axeman narrowly escaped a lynching. It was belatedly discovered that the duke, although a person of great historical importance, had never actually had his portrait painted for posterity. His head was duly sewn back on, the joins covered up, and his portrait taken. He now hangs in the National Portrait Gallery.
3. In 1740 a 17-year-old rapist named William Duel was hanged to death, but emerged from a deep coma to find that his body had been donated to science and a surgeon's knife was already slicing into his stomach. Duel survived and his death sentence was subsequently commuted to transportation for life.
4. Two men have survived three hangings apiece. Murderer Joseph

Samuels was reprieved in 1803 after the rope broke twice on the first and second attempts, and the trapdoor failed to open on the third. A trapdoor mechanism also saved the life of convicted murderer John Lee in 1884. Even though it worked every time it was tested, it failed to open three times in the space of seven minutes. Lee was let off with life imprisonment.

5. America's most horribly bungled execution by electric chair was also one of the earliest. William Taylor was condemned to death in 1893 for killing a fellow inmate in Auburn Prison. As the first electric charge surged through his body, his legs went into spasm and tore the chair apart by his ankle strappings. The charge was switched off while running repairs were made to the chair. The switch was thrown again, but this time there was no current because the generator had burned out. Taylor was removed from the chair and given morphine in an attempt to deaden any pain he may have felt. By the time the power had been restored, Taylor was already dead; nevertheless, it was decided that the law required an electrocution, so he was strapped back into the chair and the current was passed through him for another 30 seconds.
6. In 1903 a young American, Frederick van Wormer, was sent to the electric chair for the murder of his uncle. Van Wormer was duly electrocuted and pronounced dead. In the autopsy room, as he was about to go under the scalpel, Van Wormer's eye was seen to flicker, and he moved a hand. The prison doctor was summoned, and confirmed that two full charges of current had failed to kill the prisoner. Van Wormer was carried back to the chair and several more currents were passed through him until his death was beyond dispute.
7. Murderer James Bullen was sent to the electric chair at Sing Sing in 1932. He recovered on the way to the cemetery, leaped out of the coffin and ran off. Unfortunately for Bullen he was caught and sent back to the chair.

8. The American cannibal and child-killer Albert Fish went to the electric chair at Sing Sing in 1936. The first electric charge failed, allegedly short-circuited by dozens of needles the old man had inserted into his own body. Doctors discovered a total of 29 needles in his genitals.
9. The electrocution of John Evans in Alabama state prison in 1983 required three surges of 1,900 volts each over a period of 14 minutes to finish him off. Eye-witnesses related that they saw Evans struggling for breath as smoke began to pour from the electrodes on his head and one of his legs. The autopsy on Evans's body revealed that he had endured fourth- and second-degree burns while he was still alive.
10. When 34-year-old American rubbish-van driver Billy White was executed in April 1992 by lethal injection in Huntsville prison, medical attendants spent 40 minutes trying to locate a vein, and it took another nine minutes for him to die.

10 Most Inspired Murder Motives

1. In 1979 two Brazilians, Waldir de Souza and Maria de Conceicao, murdered six children in Cantigulo, including a two-year-old boy. They later confessed that the killings were ritual sacrifices to ensure success in their new cement business.
2. François Gueneron was shot dead by his wife in 1995 because she could no longer tolerate his habitual flatulence. According to Mrs Catherine Gueneron, her husband, a 44-year-old French construction site manager, broke wind morning, noon and night for eight years. He finally received a pistol bullet in the chest from 35-year-old Catherine after breaking wind in her face in bed. She told Marseilles Judge Gilbert St Jacques: "I just snapped."
3. In 1993 a 36-year-old man from Peking, Ge Yunbao, admitted beating a six-year-old schoolboy to death and then leaving the child's severed head on a bus. Yunbao explained that he was annoyed at being passed over for promotion.
4. In October 1987 a Chinese pig-farmer, Chen Bohong of Liuzhou, was busy slaughtering a pig when he was interrupted by taxman Sun Taichang, who presented him with a bill. Chen was so irritated by the interruption that he stopped what he was doing and killed the taxman, instead.
5. The sensitive Russian Czar Paul, who was snub-nosed and bald, had a soldier scourged to death for referring to him as "baldy". The czar later had the words "snub-nosed" and "bald" banned on pain of death.

6. During the world population conference held in Cairo in 1994, the Egyptian newspaper *Al-Wajd* reported that a delegate had stabbed his wife to death because she refused go to bed with him.
7. A Liberian general, Gray Allison, was sentenced to death in August 1989 for the murder of a policeman. He explained that he needed the policeman's blood to perform a magic rite which would overthrow Liberia's dictator Samuel Doe.
8. Self-styled emperor of the former Central African Republic Jean Bokassa had 200 schoolchildren beaten to death by his imperial guard in the 1970s. Their crime was failure to comply with school uniform regulations.
9. In March 1984 a 16-year-old Malaysian boy was beheaded by a Chinese man in Kuala Lumpur, as a human sacrifice in an attempt to win the state lottery. The murder was in vain: in the event, it was a roll-over week.
10. In September 1994 in Messina, Italy, a patient who was being treated for paranoia shot his psychiatrist. The murderer commented later: "He never liked me."

10 Criminal Judges

1. Judge Roy Bean dispensed justice in Texas for 20 years, presiding from a saloon bar, the Jersey Lily, in the town of Langtry. Bean was renowned for his eccentric style, often interrupting trials to serve drinks to the court. Whenever he presided over a marriage ceremony he would finish with the line "may God have mercy on your soul". In 1882 he dismissed a murder charge brought against one of his regulars because "it served the deceased right for getting in front of the gun". The case against another regular drinker in the Jersey Lily was also dropped because the victim was Chinese. According to Bean's version of Texan law, there was "not a damn line here nowheres that makes it illegal to kill a Chinaman".
2. Sir George "Bloody" Jeffreys of Wem (1648–89) was Britain's most sadistic lord chief justice ever. He passed 331 death sentences and had hundreds more deported – arguably a fate worse than hanging. One of his most notorious sentences was conferred on Lady Alice de Lisle, whom he ordered to be roasted alive. The Church was outraged by the sentence and demanded clemency: Lady Alice had her sentence commuted on appeal and got away with a beheading. Jeffreys didn't allow a word of self-defence and always drove the prosecution through at high speed. The cause of this behaviour was his painful bladder-stone: he was compelled to urinate hourly and had to get through the trials as fast as possible to reach the lavatory.

3. The eccentric nineteenth-century earl Lord Monboddo, reputed to be "the most learned judge of his day", spent his life utterly convinced that babies were born with tails, and that there was a universal conspiracy of silence among midwives, who cut them off at birth. Monboddo's conviction wasn't swayed when he witnessed the births of his own children. He concluded that the crafty midwives had tricked him and destroyed the evidence.
4. Raynor Goddard was one of the most enthusiastic hangers and floggers to have held the post of lord chief justice. It has been claimed that he was sexually aroused by sentencing young men to death, and achieved orgasm while pronouncing the death sentence. It was Goddard who sentenced 19-year-old Derek Bentley to hang in 1953. Bentley had called "Let him have it, Chris", just before his friend shot a policeman. The defence claimed he was telling him to give up the gun.
5. In the middle of an important criminal trial in 1977, Judge Alan King-Hamilton solemnly told the jury that "the Australians are 4 for 1 wicket".
6. The seventeenth-century judicial system was inclined to give ugly people a raw deal: ugliness was seen as a sure sign of guilt. The French legal expert Henri Boguet declared that the repulsiveness of a man's face was enough to expose him to torture and make him confess his crimes. Some European medieval laws decreed that whenever two people were under suspicion for the same crime, the better-looking of the two was always the innocent one.
7. During a trial in 1986 Judge Michael Argyle complained to the jury that the lack of Test Match cricket on television was "enough to make an Orthodox Jew want to join the Nazi party".

8. Californian district attorney William Tingle once had three members of the jury removed from an attempted murder case because one was "grossly overweight", one had braided hair, which he considered "somewhat radical", and he disapproved of the third's "braids, obesity, size, and manner of dress".
9. The Persian king Cambyses II was found to have a finely tuned sense of poetic justice when one of his judges was found guilty of corruption. The king had him flayed alive, then had the judge's old seat reupholstered with his skin. As a final touch he appointed the dead judge's son as his successor, thus forcing the son literally to sit in judgement on his father.
10. In 1992 the Pennsylvanian judge Charles Guyer was sacked after a hidden video camera recorded him offering a novel form of plea-bargaining. He offered convicted men lighter sentences if they allowed him to shampoo their hair.

Hard Axe to Follow:
10 FAMOUS EXECUTIONERS

1. The chief executioners of Constantinople during the reign of the Ottomans excelled in diverse methods of despatching their victims. One of the preferred methods involved drowning by slow degrees; another involved forcing the victim to imbibe ground glass. The most prolific of them all was Souflikar, executioner during the reign of Mahomet IV. He preferred simple strangulation; he personally throttled about 5,000 people over a period of five years.
2. The psychopathic Duke of Alva, chief executioner to King Philip of Spain, was hired during the Holy Inquisition for his efficiency in wiping out heretics. His chosen method of execution was to seal the mouth of the victim with an iron gag, which allowed only the tongue to protrude. The tongue was branded with a hot iron so that it swelled and could not be withdrawn. The victim was then burned alive. At Antwerp the duke executed 8,000 people in one session. King Philip passed one of the most ambitious death sentences of all time in 1568, when he declared that the entire population of the Netherlands – approximately three million – were heretics and therefore should be executed. It was a tough nut to crack even for the Duke of Alva, but he did manage to kill 800 people during Holy Week.
3. Richard Brandon, son of the chief executioner Gregory Brandon, was destined to become England's most famous executioner. Known in the trade as "young Gregory", he

put in hours of practice on his axe technique as a youngster by decapitating cats and dogs, and boasted in later years that he only needed one blow of the axe to remove a victim's head. The climax of his distinguished career was the removal of King Charles I's head on 30 January 1649, although on the day Brandon was a reluctant executioner, and he and his assistant insisted on wearing masks and false beards to avoid any possible future repercussions. Five months later Brandon fell ill and died – "of remorse", it was said at the time, "at killing the king".

4. The innovative nineteenth-century English executioner William Marwood was responsible for a new method of hanging. Until Marwood's day, hanging in Britain usually meant a very short drop and slow strangulation at the end of a rope. The executioner often had to speed up the process by wrapping himself around the victim's legs, and recoveries from hangings were fairly commonplace. In 1871 Marwood perfected the long drop, a system which caused the victim to fall from six to 10 feet through a trapdoor. The drop caused fracture dislocation of the neck's vertebrae, severing the spinal cord and medulla, and so causing instant death and dramatically reducing the suffering endured by the hanged. Marwood liked to boast that unlike his predecessors, he did not "hang" his victims; he actually "executed" them. Marwood's system also had its problems, however, as the long drop often resulted in accidental decapitation.
5. London's eighteenth-century chief executioner John Thrift was considered the most incompetent man ever to have held that position. Thrift was a convicted murderer who was set free on condition that he did the government's dirty work as an axeman. He was desperately unsuited to the job: he was highly strung, unsure with the axe and liable to burst into tears at inappropriate moments, espe-

cially just before he removed a head. His most serious problem appeared to be that he couldn't stand the sight of blood. When he was called upon to execute the Jacobite rebel Lord Balmerino at the Tower of London in 1745, he fainted, then lay on the ground sobbing while onlookers tried to persuade him to get on with it. When Thrift finally took up his axe, he took five blows to sever Lord Balmerino's head. Thrift never quite got the hang of it, yet he somehow managed to blunder and hack his way through a 17-year career. He was widely hated by the public for his clumsiness, and when he died in 1752 a jeering mob pelted his coffin and his pall-bearers with stones and the rotting bodies of dead cats.

6. The most famous executioner of the French Revolution was the chief executioner of Paris, Charles Henri-Sanson, the most prolific member of an extraordinary family, who provided the nation with six generations of public executioners from 1635 to 1889. Sanson became so adept at his job, thanks to endless practice on the necks of French aristocrats, that he was able to despatch 12 victims in 13 minutes. At the height of the reign of terror he removed the heads of 300 men and women in three days. His guillotine in the Place de la Révolution was so busy that residents in a nearby street complained that the stench of blood from the street stones was a health hazard and lowered the value of their houses. On 16 October 1793, 200,000 people turned out to watch Marie Antoinette lose her head. They were all kept waiting while Sanson untied her hands, so that she could empty her bowels in a corner behind a wall.
7. The Nantes lawyer and French revolutionary Jean-Baptiste Carrier considered the guillotine too slow and inefficient. He preferred to have his victims packed into barges, towed into the River Loire and drowned. Couples were stripped

naked and tied face to face, while Carrier's henchmen stood on the river banks with axes to cut down anyone who escaped. The water became so polluted with human corpses that fishing was banned. Carrier also discovered that the guillotine was an unsatisfactory method of beheading infants. The heads of tiny children were chopped in half because their necks made too small a target for the blade: one executioner collapsed and died from a heart-attack after beheading four little sisters. Instead Carrier had 500 children rounded up in a field and shot and cudgelled to death.

8. Britain's last and most famous official executioner, Albert Pierrepoint, terminated the lives of 450 murderers and traitors during his 25-year career. After resigning he wrote: "I do not now believe that any one of the hundreds of executions I have carried out has in any way acted as a deterrent against future murder. Capital punishment, in my view, achieved nothing except revenge." Pierrepoint's fee for executing Ruth Ellis, the last woman to be hanged in Britain, was 15 guineas (£15.75).
9. The most practised hangman of the twentieth century was John C. Woods of San Antonio, US. He hanged 347 men and women, including 10 Nazi leaders condemned to death at the Nuremburg trials. Woods was heavily criticized for bungling the war criminals' executions: it was alleged that the prisoners' necks had not been properly broken.
10. Edwin T. Davis was the world's first official state electrocutioner. Davis was a professional electrician who supplemented his income from 1890 to 1914 by sending 240 people to their deaths in the electric chair. He was official executioner for three states – New York, New Jersey and Massachusetts – travelling from prison to prison wearing his trademark black felt hat. Davis was the designer of the

original electric chair and helped make many refinements to the system during his career. He held patents on some of the equipment. Before every execution he tested the apparatus on chunks of beef. He attached sponge pads to the meat, inserted the wires and switched on the current: as soon as the beef began to roast he knew the chair was in full working order. Davis maintained to his death that he opposed capital punishment.

10 Hanging Offences in Nineteenth-Century Britain

1. Associating with gypsies.
2. Setting fire to a hayrick.
3. Writing on Westminster Bridge.
4. Impersonating a pensioner of Greenwich Hospital.
5. Writing a threatening letter.
6. Appearing on the highway with a sooty face.
7. Damaging a fish pond.
8. Cutting down a tree.
9. Secreting notes in a post office.
10. Stealing a spoon.

8 Royal Assassinations

1. Czar Peter III (1728–62). Just six months after his accession his reign was terminated by a palace coup, organized by imperial guards on behalf of his wife, the new empress Catherine the Great. She ordered that her husband be locked up, but after a few weeks he died in custody. An official announcement was made that the erratic and unstable ex-czar had died of an acute attack of colic during one of his frequent bouts of haemorrhoids.
2. Czar Paul I of Russia (1754–1801). Late one evening he answered a knock on his bedroom door and was confronted by a small group of officers, who confronted him with a proclamation of abdication, which the czar was asked to sign. There was a scuffle, and minutes later Paul lay dead. He had been strangled, but the Russian people were informed that their czar had died of an "attack of apoplexy".
3. Czar Alexander II of Russia (1818–81). The czar's carriage was hit by a grenade, thrown by a revolutionary assassin as it raced along the riverside embankment in St Petersburg. The czar alighted from the carriage unharmed, but a second assassin, standing six feet away, lobbed another grenade between the czar's legs. The bomb exploded, killing them both.
4. Czar Nicholas II of Russia (1868–1918). On the evening of 16 July Czar Nicholas II, his family and servants were

being held by Bolshevik revolutionaries in a building in Ekaterinburg, about 800 miles from Moscow. Just before midnight they were summoned to a basement room and arranged in two rows before a death squad led by Commander Jacob Yorovsky. A decree of execution was read out to them, and they were shot dead. Their bodies were subsequently burned, then tossed down a mineshaft.

5. Empress Elizabeth of Austria (1837–98). On 10 September Emperor Franz Ferdinand's wife was in Geneva, where she was about to catch a steamer. As she walked the short distance from her hotel to the quayside, a 26-year-old Italian builder's labourer, Luigi Lenchini, stabbed her through her breast. The killer later confessed that he had nothing at all against the empress, and had actually set out to kill King Umberto I of Italy, but hadn't been able to afford the extra 50 lire he needed to travel to Rome.
6. King Henry III of France (1574–89). The king was stabbed to death by a Dominican friar, Jacques Clément, egged on by the pope, who had excommunicated the French king, branding him "an assassin, a heretic and an infidel".
7. King Alexander and Queen Drago of Serbia. In 1903 a group of army officers burst into the royal palace, sprayed the king and queen with bullets, hacked them to pieces with swords, bashed their skulls in with rifle butts and tossed the corpses out of the window into the gardens below. A few of the queen's relatives who got in the way were also slaughtered for good measure.
8. Emperor Maximilian I of Mexico (1832–67). The short reign of the former Habsburg duke and brother of

Austria's emperor Franz Josef was terminated by a firing squad of Mexican bandits on a hillside in 1867. Parts of his body were auctioned off to souvenir-hunters. Maximilian begged his executioners to shoot him cleanly so that he could die with dignity; however, they were poor shots, and their bullets blew most of his face off.

10 Capital Oddities

1. When murderer Albert Clozza was sent to the electric chair in Virginia, in 1991 the surge of current caused his eyeballs to pop out onto his cheeks.
2. The biggest ever mass execution in US history occurred on Boxing Day, 1862. The US army hanged 38 Sioux warriors for their part in the massacre of 800 settlers.
3. The details of precisely what the Holy Inquisition could and could not do to extract a confession were spelt out in *The Book of Death*, which was on display in the Casa Santa in Rome until the nineteenth century. There is no record of an Inquisition acquittal. The accused was not told what he or she was charged with, and was actually forbidden to ask, nor was anyone permitted a defence council or allowed to call defence witnesses.
4. Although common criminals were hanged in England in the sixteenth century, heretics were burned at the stake, so that the flames could cleanse their souls. Lucky victims were allowed to hang a small bag of gunpowder around their necks to speed death.
5. In Britain witches were never burned to death, as they often were abroad. There were other crimes for which a woman could be burned at the stake: petty treason or forgery, for example. The last female to be judicially burned to death in Britain was a woman named Murphy, convicted with a gang of forgers in London in 1789.

The male members of the gang were simply hanged. The law was repealed the following year.

6. The authorized method of execution during the reign of the Roman emperor Tiberius was strangulation. There was also a law which forbade the strangling of virgins, but the resourceful Tiberius found a loophole: he ordered that virgins should first be defiled by the executioner.
7. When California's notorious San Quintin gas chamber was installed in the 1930s it was tested on live pigs. The city authorities were so proud of their "humane" new system that, in a desperately miscalculated exercise in public relations, they invited newspaper reporters to witness their first disposal of a human being. The reporters were appalled by what they saw: one described it as "more savage than being hanged, drawn and quartered".
8. A novel variation on hanging, involving a large counterweight which broke the criminal's neck by flinging the victim 12 feet in the air, was was widely practised in the US in the early part of the twentieth century.
9. In May 1994 a prison in Varner, Arkansas, began a policy of executing two death row inmates at a time, because multiple executions saved money on overtime pay for employees, and were "less stressful". A prison official explained: "Nobody wants to get up in the morning and go kill somebody."
10. The longest anyone has ever survived on death row is 34 years. The Kentuckian Henry Anderson was convicted for murder in 1958 and sentenced to death in 1960. Although the state death penalty law was repealed in 1972, Anderson refused to have his sentence commuted because he said it would be an admission of guilt. In April 1994, aged 79, he died of cancer at the Kentucky State Reformatory.

The World's 20 Most Prolific Mass **Murderers** and Serial **Killers**

1. Behram (India): killed 931. Behram was a member of the killer cult Thuggee, an exclusive order which required members to strangle a minimum of one innocent victim a year. At his trial he was convicted of using a strip of cloth to strangle to 931 people over a 50-year period.
2. Teofilo "Sparks" Rojas (Columbia): killed 592. The bandit leader is known to have killed almost 600 people between 1948 and his death in an ambush in 1963.
3. Herman Webster Mudgett, a.k.a. Dr H.H. Holmes (US): killed 200+. Mudgett began his criminal career as a New Hampshire medical student, by stealing corpses from the University of Michigan and using them to collect insurance money from policies taken out under fictitious names. He moved to Chicago, and under the alias Dr Holmes started a successful drugstore empire. During the Chicago Exposition in 1893 Mudgett seduced, drugged and murdered a succession of young girls in his 100-room mansion in 43rd Street, which was subsequently dubbed the "Torture Castle". He disposed of his victims' bodies by burning and dissolving the corpses in acid and lime, occasionally saving body parts for further experimentation in his upstairs

laboratory. When police grew suspicious about his activities, Mudgett set fire to the building and fled. Chicago police searched the charred premises and found the remains of about 200 corpses, but admitted that there may have been hundreds more. Mudgett was caught and hanged on 7 May 1896.

4. Gilles de Rais (France): killed 140+. The fifteenth-century Frenchman was an ally of Joan of Arc during the Hundred Years' War. He became a national hero and was accorded the title Marshal of France by King Charles VII. He later settled in Brittany, where he turned to torturing, raping and killing young boys. De Rais also practised black magic and alchemy. His reign of terror ended when the Duke of Brittany dug up the mutilated remains of 50 boys in his castle. De Rais confessed to 140 killings but it is believed that the body count could have been as high as 300. In 1440, De Rais was simultaneously burned and hanged along with his two servant accomplices.
5. Sawney (Sandy) Beane (Scotland): killed 100+. A radical experiment in the "good life" was effected by Britain's most prolific mass murderer, born in the fifteenth century in East Lothian, a few miles from Edinburgh. As a young man Beane eloped with his new bride and set up home in a cave in a deserted part of Galloway, on the wild west coast of Scotland. There the couple had eight sons and six daughters, who incestually increased the Beane family with the addition of 18 grandsons and 14 granddaughters. At first Sawney Beane provided for his growing clan by stealing sheep, but he soon found that the family that slays together, stays together. Soon they were all murdering passing travellers and took to

cannibalism as the best method of filling their stomachs and disposing of the evidence. In 1435 the Scottish King, James I, led a posse of 400 men to flush out Beane and his family. They caught several members of the family red-handed, attacking a man and killing his wife. When they finally discovered the Beane lair they found evidence of hundreds of murders, including a well-stocked larder containing dried, pickled and salted human body parts. Sawney Beane and the adult members of his family were put to death following a show trial at Leith. The men had their hands, feet and sexual organs cut off and were left to bleed to death. Their wives were forced to watch, then burned at the stake.

6. Julio Gonzalez (US): killed 87. Cuban-born Gonzalez went to live in the US in 1980. Ten years later he had a fit of jealousy because his girlfriend Lydia was dancing at a party with someone else. Gonzalez bought a can of petrol and set fire to the Bronx's Happy Land Social Club, killing almost everyone inside. Only six people survived, including his ex-girlfriend, lucky Lydia.
7. Bruno Ludke (Germany): killed 85+. The 35-year-old German was apprehended in 1943 after he had strangled and knifed to death at least 85 women over a period of about 17 years. His arrest was never reported to the German public: Ludke was an embarrassment to the Nazi authorities, since several apparently innocent men had already been tried and executed for his crimes. He was sterilized and confined to a Vienna hospital, where he died in 1945, the victim of a Nazi medical experiment.
8. Liao Chang-Shin (China): killed 79+. Between April and July 1945 more than 100 people mysteriously disap-

peared from the small Chinese town of Changstow, a port on the Yangtze River. The local innkeeper subsequently confessed to robbing and killing 79 of his guests, averaging about a murder a day. He and an accomplice, Hsui Chang-Shan, were executed.

9. Woo Bom Kong (South Korea): killed 58. On 28 April 1982, a 27-year-old policeman became the world's worst-ever spree murderer. Violently drunk after a row with his common-law wife, he raided his local police department armoury, helping himself to 180 rounds of ammunition, two rifles and several hand-grenades. His rampage took him through five villages, where he randomly killed passers by, while his fellow police officers pursued him with orders to shoot to kill. The eight-hour massacre ended when Woo Bom Kong exploded a grenade, killing himself and three nearby peasants.

10=. Andrei Chikatilo (Russia): killed 53+. The "Rostov Ripper" was a grandfather and former schoolteacher. He went to his execution in 1994 after sexually assaulting, killing, butchering and then eating at least 53 people, many of them children he had taught at school, between 1978 and 1990. He stalked most of his victims in train and bus stations and had a penchant for disembowelment and mutilation. His trial was the Soviet public's first experience of a cannibal serial killer.

10=. Pedro Lopez (Colombia): killed 53+. Between 1967 and 1980 the "Monster of the Andes" raped and strangled young girls between the ages of eight and 12 across three countries – Ecuador, Colombia and Peru. When he was 18 years old he was gang-raped in prison and retaliated by killing three of his assailants. After his release he started killing young girls, at one stage averaging about three murders a week. His killing spree should have been terminated early on, when he was caught trying to abduct a nine-year-old girl, but the Peruvian authorities elected not to prosecute because it was easier to have him deported. He resurfaced in Ecuador, where he was finally arrested while attempting to kidnap a 12-year-old. Lopez led the police to 53 graves, but claimed a total of 310 murders.

12. Anatoly Onoprienko (Ukraine): killed 52. The 37-year-old former forestry student, a native of Zhitomir, was known as "The Terminator". A manhunt was launched across Ukraine in 1996 after eight families were brutally murdered in their homes. Most of the victims were in remote villages in the Lvov region, near the border with Poland. There were so many killings in one area that army troops were sent to patrol the streets. When Onoprienko was picked up and placed in custody he immediately confessed to eight killings between 1989 and 1995. He later admitted killing 52 victims in a six-year killing spree, claiming the murders were ordered by "inner voices" in his head.
13. Martin Rivera Benitez (Mexico): killed 50+. This professional assassin, known as "Big Soul", plied his trade in Mexico from 1969 to 1972. To prove that he had done his job properly he would present his employers with the heads of his victims. The police subsequently discovered a dozen headless corpses buried in woods near his home, although the number he actually killed was at least 50. Benitez later claimed he was so much in demand that queues would form outside his house. He

went to his death unrepentant about killing for money. "If I hadn't done it," he explained, "someone else would."

14. Martin Bryant (Australia): killed 35. On 28 April 1996, Bryant, a 28-year-old with a history of mental instability, armed himself with a surfboard and two semi-automatic rifles and went on an 18-hour rampage in the quiet tourist resort of Port Arthur, in the south-eastern corner of Tasmania. He began his killing spree in the Broken Arrow Café, killing 20 people as they ate lunch, then set off through the resort, randomly shooting dead another 12 people, including a mother and her two infant daughters. He finally took refuge in a guest house with three hostages and was surrounded by 200 police officers. During the following 12-hour siege an Australian journalist managed to contact Bryant by phone. He told her: "I can't talk now, I'm having too much fun." Bryant was captured when he fled from the blazing building with his clothes on fire.
15. Donald Harvey (US): killed 34+. The male nurse and amateur Satanist liked to joke with his fellow hospital staff about "getting rid of patients." He murdered from the early seventies to 1987, when he was finally caught, and later claimed that the deaths were mercy killings, although his victims were often horribly poisoned. He also killed a neighbour out of spite, by lacing her drink with hepatitis, and on another occasion poisoned his male lover's family, killing the mother. He was convicted of 34 murders, but it is thought that he was probably responsible for at least 87 deaths.
16. John Wayne Gacy Jr (US): killed 34. With one previous conviction for homosexual rape in Iowa, Gacy moved to

Chicago in the 1970s and took to sexually molesting young boys and men at gunpoint, before murdering them and burying the bodies. In his spare time he dressed in a home-made clown outfit and entertained small children. Between 1976 and 1980 he killed 34 times, his victims ranging from nine-year-olds to adult. When police became suspicious of his activities after checking on his earlier conviction, they set up a 24-hour surveillance on his home. Gacy, emboldened by his apparent ability to murder at will without detection, actually invited two police officers in to his home for breakfast. As they sat down to eat they became aware of a peculiar smell, which led them to the discovery of 29 bodies in the crawl space underneath Gacy's house. In prison Gacy began a new career as an artist, painting mostly colourful clown pictures, which have since been shown in galleries across the US. He was executed by lethal injection in 1994.

17. Carl Denke (Germany): killed 30+. Denke, landlord of an inn at Munsterberg, Silesia, was an outwardly respectable middle-class churchgoer who offered free shelter to homeless vagrants passing through the town. No one suspected that he also ate most of his guests. In 1924 one of Denke's boarders went to the local police station covered in blood, complaining that his landlord had hit him from behind with an axe. A search of the premises led to the discovery of vats of bones and pickled flesh. While Denke was in police custody he hanged himself with his braces.
18. Patrick W. Kearney (US): killed 28+. The Californian freeway killer left his dismembered victims neatly wrapped in trash bags along the Californian high-

ways. Kearney and his live-in lover, David Hill, lived in Redondo Beach, where they began the series of "Trash Bag Murders" in 1975. In 1977 the two men walked into the sheriff's office in Riverside, saw a wanted poster of themselves and surrendered. Hill was subsequently released for lack of evidence. Kearney took all the blame, confessing that killing "excited him and gave him a feeling of dominance".

19. Fritz Haarmann (Germany): killed 27+. Haarmann and his lover Hans Grans stalked the train stations of post-World War I Hanover searching for young boys. They later sold the flesh and clothing of their victims. Their trade was first discovered in 1924 when bones from 27 bodies were dredged out of the Leine River and a coat from one of the missing boys was traced back to Haarmann's flat. He took delight in the attention he received during the trial and boasted of having killed up to 40 people. He was decapitated on 15 April 1925. Grans, who was not directly implicated in the killings, received a 12-year sentence for receiving stolen goods.
20. Dean Corll (US): killed 27. The portly Texan known as "the Candyman" killed young boys in the comfort of his own home. Corll's technique involved inviting victims into his house to sniff glue, then sexually molesting them when they passed out. In August 1973, one of his teenage guests, Elmer Wayne Henley, shot and killed Corll. Police discovered 17 bodies under the floor of a boat house rented by Corll, plus a bag of severed genitalia.

10 All-Time Worst Murderesses

1. Belle Gunness (US): killed 100+. Born in Norway, Gunness emigrated to the US in 1883 aged 24, and settled in Chicago. Her first victim was probably her husband, a Swede named Albert Sorenson, who died mysteriously in 1900 while heavily insured. Gunness cashed in on his policy the day after his death and used the money to purchase a large farm in La Porte, Indiana. It was there that, according to a farm hand, "She killed people the way you and me kill rabbits." Over a period of about five years she advertized for husbands in the personal columns of small provincial newspapers across the US. Middle-aged men with large bank accounts replied to her advertisements by the score, only to be subdued with chloroform, topped with an axe, then placed in the private cemetery under her cement farmhouse floor. In 1908 Gunness probably faked her death in a farmhouse blaze to escape the net that she feared was closing in on her. Police found the headless corpse of an unidentifiable female and the charred remains of Gunness's three infant children. They later discovered more than 100 corpses buried in the farmstead and surrounding fields. The identity of the headless woman was never established and there were many subsequent "sightings" of Belle Gunness all over America.
2. Delfina and Maria Gonzalez (US): killed 80+. The Mexican sisters ran a brothel, in which most of the prostitutes were enslaved and tortured. Whenever the girls in their employ attempted to escape, or became ill or pregnant, they would

vanish without trace. In 1964 the sisters were arrested, and police found the remains of at least 80 girls on the premises.

3. Suzanne Fazekas (Hungary): killed 40+. A midwife living in the isolated village of Nagyrev, south-east of Budapest, assisted in the deaths of up to 50 men between 1911 and 1929, by providing local women with the means to dispose of unwanted husbands without detection. She poisoned her victims with arsenic, which she acquired by boiling large quantities of fly paper, and persuaded her cousin (who happened to be the official responsible for signing death certificates) to falsify the cause of death. Over a period of nearly 20 years it was noted that the small village of Nagyrev consumed more fly paper than the rest of the whole of Hungary. When the police finally came for her, Suzanne Fazekas drank her own poison rather than submit to arrest.
4. Jane Toppan (US): killed 30+. Toppan was born in Boston in 1854 and raised by her father, who was subsequently certified insane and placed in asylum, after being discovered attempting to sew his eyelids together. She was adopted and went on to find employment in a series of nursing homes, systematically murdering the patients in her care by poisoning them with morphine or atropine. Jane Toppan was convicted of 30 murders, although the true figure was probably nearer 100. She was sent to the Taunton State Asylum for the Criminally Insane, where she died, aged 84.
5. Mary Anne Cotton (England): killed 15+. Born in 1832 in a Durham pit village, the psychopathic Ms Cotton killed at least 15, probably 21 people, including her mother, three husbands, eight of her children and four step-children. Her badly bungled hanging in March 1873 took several minutes to complete.

6. Genene Jones (US): killed 12. The 31-year-old "Death Nurse" of Kerrville Hospital, Texas killed 12 children, mostly by administering the powerful muscle relaxant Anectine. In February 1984 she was sentenced to 99 years in prison.
7. Nannie Doss (US): killed 11. "Arsenic Annie" of Tulsa, Oklahamo was apprehended in 1954 after killing her fifth husband Samuel by feeding him stewed prunes laced with enough poison to kill 20 healthy adults. She broke down and confessed to 10 other murders, including her mother, three husbands, two infant children, two sisters and a nephew of a previous husband. She died of leukemia aged 60 while serving a life sentence.
8. Marie Alexander Becker (Belgium): killed 10+. The middle-aged housewife from Liège killed at least 10, maybe 20 times before her arrest. She poisoned her victims with digitalis, which she administered in cups of tea in the back room of her small dress shop. While her victims were drugged and dying, she would relieve them of their money and valuables, and was then usually able to smuggle them home, where they would later die of unknown causes. She regularly attended the funerals of the people she killed, and was observed kneeling at the gravesides, weeping hysterically. Becker died in prison serving a life sentence.
9. Rosemary West (England): killed 10+. West and her husband Frederick combined to make the most extraordinary homicidal double act in criminal history. In 1994 police dug up their home and garden at 25 Cromwell Street, Gloucester and discovered bodies which had been buried over a period of 23 years, including those of two of their daughters. Fred West hanged himself in his cell on New Year's Day 1995, after telling police that there were 20 more undiscovered bodies and that his wife Rosemary and

his brother John were among those responsible. In December 1996 Fred West's younger brother John, a 54-year-old retired dustman and father of four, also hanged himself in his garage, hours before a jury had the chance to convict him on charges of raping his own niece on more than 300 occasions.

10. Amelia Dyer (England): killed 7+. It is a distinct possibility that this former Salvation Army worker from Bristol may have been the UK's deadliest ever serial killer. In the 1870s she worked as a midwife, supplementing her income with the illegal Victorian trade of "baby-farming", a convention whereby the illegitimate or inconvenient babies of middle-class women would be farmed out to working-class foster mothers for anything up to a few years at a time. Dyer's handling fee was usually £10 per child. In 1895 police dragged the Thames near Richmond and found the bodies of seven infants, all parcelled, taped and weighed down with bricks. They were all children who had been "farmed" by Amelia Dyer. She never revealed how many she had killed, but her carefully detailed accounts showed that she had handled scores of children over a period of 20 years, none of which could be traced. Her jury took five minutes to declare her "guilty – not insane", and she was hanged at Newgate prison on 10 June 1896.

10 British Murderers who took More Lives than Jack the Ripper

1. Sawney (Sandy) Beane (100+). See page 384.
2. Thomas Watt Hamilton (17). At about 9.30AM on 13 March 1996, 43-year-old Watt, a disgraced ex-scoutmaster with an obsession for boys and guns, walked into a primary school gymnasium in Dunblane, central Scotland, armed with four handguns and over 600 rounds of ammunition. In less than three minutes he shot and killed 16 children aged between five and six and their teacher, before turning a gun on himself. Watt harboured a 20-year grudge against the local community for labelling him a child molester.
3. Michael Ryan (16). On 19 August 1987, Ryan, an unemployed labourer, strolled through the small town of Hungerford, Berkshire, wearing combat fatigues and an ammunition belt, and carrying an AK-47 automatic rifle. In 10 minutes he killed 16 people and wounded 14 others. Ryan was subsequently cornered in a primary school where, seven hours after his first killing, he shot himself through the head with a 9 mm pistol. No explanation was ever found for the murders.
4. Mary Anne Cotton (15+). See page 392.
5. Dennis Andrew Nilsen (15). A former Metropolitan police officer, Nilsen was a homosexual with a death fixation. Over a period of five years he picked up 15 young men in gay bars across London and invited them back to his flat, where he strangled them. He hid some of the bodies under his floorboards, but most were dumped in the local sewer, thereby drawing attention to his crime by rendering the inhabitants of Muswell Hill incapable of flushing their toilets. He was sentenced to life imprisonment on 4 November 1983.
6. Peter William Sutcliffe (13). The "Yorkshire Ripper" sparked off

the biggest murder manhunt in British history between July 1975 and November 1980, when he raped and murdered 13 women. Most of his victims were prostitutes, bludgeoned to death with a hammer or strangled, in an area between Leeds, Bradford and West Yorkshire dubbed the "triangle of terror". Sutcliffe was eventually discovered during a routine police check while he was having sex with a prostitute in a parked car in Sheffield. He was tried at the Old Bailey in May 1981 and currently serves life imprisonment.

7. Frederick West (13). See page 393.
8. Rosemary West (10). See page 393.
9. Amelia Dyer 7+. See page 394.
10. John Reginald Halliday Christie (6+). The outwardly meek and bespectacled occupant of 10 Rillington Place, Notting Hill, London was a part-time necrophiliac who lured prostitutes into his home while his wife was away. He gassed them, strangled them while they were unconscious, then raped their corpses. His final victim was his wife, Ethel. Their bodies were later discovered hidden behind interior walls, under the floorboards and buried in the garden. He was hanged at Pentonville Prison on 15 July 1953. It is likely that two additional murders, attributed to a lodger, Timothy John Evans, may also have been committed by Christie.

8
AD NAUSEAM

12 Instant Dismissals

1. In 1994, 26-year-old stripper, Lisa Evans, filed an appeal for unfair dismissal against the owners of a nightclub where she had worked in a nude peepshow booth in Edmonton, Alberta. Management said customers had complained that the 19 stone, 4-pound stripper was difficult to fantasize over.
2. Madras train announcer Rajiv Kamir was fired in September 1996 for breaking wind over the PA system to the opening of Beethoven's Fifth. A railway spokesman noted: "It was a disgusting deviation from the timetable."
3. The fifteenth-century German emperor Wenceslas, a violent and unstable drunk, had his cook roasted on a spit when his normally exemplary meals fell below standard. On another occasion he was out hunting when he came across a passing monk and shot him dead: Wenceslas explained that monks had better things to do than wander about in woods.
4. Exotic dancer Pamela Harrison was dismissed by the Kat Tales club in Stuart, Florida in 1996. Fellow dancers complained that she was a health hazard because she wore her colostomy bag tucked into her G-string during her performances.
5. The French king Louis XV understood nothing about money. When he heard that the workers were starving he sympathetically sacked 80 gardeners.
6. In 1996 the county coroner in Tacoma, Washington was removed from his post, following complaints that he had encouraged his employees to make sexually explicit jokes about corpses, and that he allowed them to circulate photographs of the private parts of deceased prominent local personages.

7. John Rossi was fired from his job at Kragen Auto Parts in California in 1993 because he was obese. Apparently, during his 10 years with the company, his weight veered somewhere between 28 and 35 stones. He successfully sued and was awarded $1 million for emotional distress and lost compensation and benefits, after proving that his weight problem was a physical disability caused by a physiological disorder.
8. King Gustavus I of Sweden hacked to death his royal goldsmith because he took a day off without permission.
9. In 1994 the licence of US neurosurgeon Dr Raymond Sattle was removed from his post after he left a patient alone on the operating table with his brain exposed for half an hour, while he went out for his lunch break. The North Carolina Board of Medical Examiners heard that Dr Sattle also frequently forgot the names of his surgical equipment during operations, allowed an untrained nurse to drill holes in a patient's head, and had intravenous fluids pumped into his own veins while he was operating, to help him stay on his feet.
10. Henry VIII invented a new method of execution for Richard Rosse, cook to the Bishop of Rochester, who had poisoned the soup at a formal banquet and killed 17 people over dinner. The king had him boiled to death in one of his own stockpots.
11. Forty-year-old Milton Ross was fired from his desk job in St Joseph, Montana in 1994 after a video camera recorded him urinating into the office coffee pot. The video trap was set after his colleagues noted that their morning coffee seemed "off".
12. Susan Franano, general manager of the Kansas City Symphony Orchestra, sacked oboist Ken Lawrence in

1993 after he made a "facetious response" to a complaint about him. It appears that during a rehearsal for *Nutcracker*, Lawrence had broken wind in a loud manner, "creating an overpowering smell".

12 Extraordinary Origins

1. Dr Harvey Kellogg intended his first breakfast cereal product to be an antidote to masturbation.
2. In Britain and the US opium was originally recommended as a cure for cholera, dysentery, toothache, flatulence, the menopause and mental illness, and was once the basis for many patent baby-soothing remedies.
3. Dr Klaus Martens designed the Dr Martens boot in the 1940s as a "comfort aid" for elderly German women with foot trouble.
4. When Sir Walter Raleigh brought tobacco and potatoes back with him from the New World they received a mixed reception. It was generally agreed that spuds were a health hazard leading to scrofula, consumption, flatulence and unnatural carnal lust; tobacco, on the other hand, was quite harmless.
5. Digestive biscuits were originally made as an aid to control flatulence.
6. In 1931 Earle Cleveland Haas invented Dr Haas's Catamenial Device. Later the name was changed to Tampax.
7. The first tomato ketchup was sold in the US as a patent medicine.
8. Vaseline was invented in 1859 in Brooklyn, New York by a young chemist named Robert Chesebrough. It was to be used for dressing cuts and bruises, removing stains from furniture, polishing wood surfaces, restoring leather and preventing rust. Chesebrough also recommended a spoonful every day for good health: he ate a spoonful every morning and died aged 96.

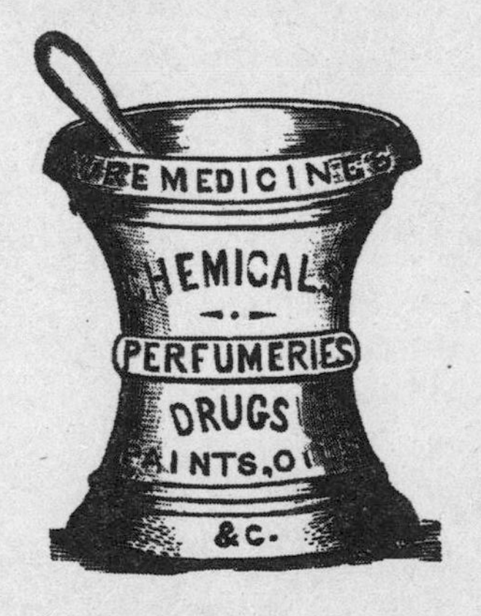

9. Marmite was originally prescribed in the Middle East as a cure for Beri

Beri. A 1951 British army medical report confirmed that Marmite was an effective treatment for scrotal dermatitis.

10. Salversan, the first effective treatment for syphilis, was invented by the admirably persistent Paul Ehrlich in 1910. It was popularly known as Treatment 606 because it was Ehrlich's 606th attempt to find a cure.
11. Atlanta pharmacist John Pemberton first stumbled across the original recipe for Coca-Cola in 1886. At the time he was working on a series of patent medicines and hair restorers, including Triplex Liver Pills, Indian Queen Hair Dye and Globe of Flower Cough Syrup.
12. Bayer, the company known for manufacturing aspirin, created Heroin as a brand name for their patent cough medicine. The exciting new wonder drug, first made in 1898 from synthesized morphine, was the subject of an intense advertizing campaign at the turn of the century. Heroin was also used to "cure" morphine addiction, to send babies with colic to sleep, and as a general pain-killer. By 1920 the streets of New York City had far fewer hacking coughs, but an estimated 300,000 heroin addicts.

15 Heroic PR Campaigns

1. After the world's media descended on 10 Cromwell Street, Gloucester in 1994, following the discovery of bodies in Frederick and Rosemary West's "garden of death", city fathers decided it was necessary to launch an advertizing campaign to improve Gloucester's image. The Touchpaper agency came up with the winning slogan: "Gloucester – easy to get to, hard to leave."
2. The Ramses brand of condom in the US is named after the great pharoah Ramses II, a man who fathered over 160 children. In the late nineteenth century British condoms were illustrated with a portrait of Queen Victoria: she was a mother of nine.
3. The US motor giants Ford suffered a setback when their new Pinto went on sale in Brazil. No one had told them that Pinto was Portuguese slang for "small male genitals".
4. Israel's notoriously reckless drivers kill about 500 people a year. In 1994 a Tel Aviv advertizing agency erected posters around the city chastizing Israeli drivers with the message: "Research proves drivers who get rowdy on the road have small penises."
5. In November 1994 Holland's National Liver and Intestine Foundation, which supports research on digestive problems, launched a publicity campaign. It encouraged people to break wind 15 times a day to ease intestinal discomfort.
6. Parker Pens translated the slogan for its ink "Avoid Embarrassment – Use Quink" into Spanish as "Evite Embarazos – Use Quink", which also means "Avoid Pregnancy – Use Quink."
7. When the US baby-food-manufacturer Gerber first started selling their products in Africa, they used the same packa-

ging as in the US, with a cute baby on the label. Gerber were perplexed when they failed to get anywhere near their projected sales figures, until someone pointed out to them that it is common practice in Africa to put pictures of the contents on food package labels.

8. Coca-Cola first launched their product in China in the 1920s, unaware that their famous brand name translated literally as "bite the wax tadpole". It was hurriedly changed to something which translated roughly as "happiness in the mouth". When Pepsi Cola was first launched in China in the 1970s the company's marketing men opted to play safe with their award-winning slogan "Come alive with Pepsi." Predictably, however, it did not translate quite as intended, and the product was introduced to a quarter of the world's population with the line: "Pepsi brings your ancestors back from the grave."
9. A men's underwear advertisement on billboards in Tel Aviv featured a photo of the late Israeli prime minister Golda Meir, and the slogan: "Eventually we remember those who had balls."
10. The Johnson Company once attempted to market their wax-cleaning product Pledge in the Netherlands. In Dutch, "pledge" means "Piss".
11. Less successful attempts by Japanese companies to sell their products to the West include a beef jerky called Homo Sausage, a lawn fertilizer called Green Piles, and a paper tissue called Last Climax.
12. Before the BSE crisis in 1996 the German confectionery company Katjes Sassin launched a new brand of sweets called Verückte Kühe – "Mad Cow".
13. US chicken magnate Frank Perdue's ad campaign was based around the slogan: "It takes a tough man to make a tender

chicken." The Spanish translation came out as: "It takes a sexually stimulated man to make a chicken affectionate."

14. The slogan used by US brewers Coors, "Turn it Loose," translated into Spanish as "Suffer From Diarrhoea."
15. When the president of Haiti, "Papa Doc" Duvalier, discovered that tourism in his country was down by 70 per cent, he found himself torn between his country's need for revenue and his deep mistrust of foreigners. Papa Doc hit upon a compromise. He launched a publicity drive to tempt the visitors back, then had the corpse of a dissident flown into the capital, Port-au-Prince, where it was left to rot in public. It was strategically placed by an exit from the airport, next to a sign which read "Welcome to Haiti".

10 Professions In Need of a Union

1. Henry VIII employed a Groom of the Stool, who was required to wipe the royal anus.
2. The ancient Egyptian pharoahs employed human fly traps, who were smeared with asses' milk and made to stand in a corner of the room.
3. The diamond company De Beers once employed security guards to undertake fingertip searches through the faeces of their fellow employees, to make sure they weren't taking their work home with them.
4. In the court of Imperial China, human wet nurses were trained to suckle the royal Pekinese puppies.
5. In 1895 a dispute over trading rights resulted in an attack by more than a thousand angry tribesmen, led by King Koko, on the British-owned Niger Company in Akassa. The native chiefs later sent a letter to Britain, addressed to the Prince of Wales, expressing their deep regrets for having taken the law into their own hands, and especially for having eaten his employees.
6. The ancient Egyptians were martyrs to their bowels: believing that all diseases were diet-related, they binged on laxatives and purged themselves for three days at a time. The court official who supplied the enema to the pharaoh was given the title Shepherd to the Royal Anus.
7. Because the average weight of a Japanese Sumo wrestler is about 22 stone, and many of them are too fat to wipe their own backsides, novice wrestlers are expected to do it for them. Six out of every 10 novices vanish from their

workplace in the first year of apprenticeship.

8. In eighteenth-century London, long before the invention of the public convenience, it was possible to make an honest living from ownership of a long cloak and a bucket. You simply walked the streets until you found a desperate client, then for an agreed fee wrapped the cloak around him and looked the other way while your client relieved himself.
9. In 1911 the Japanese emperor was delayed for twenty minutes when his train jumped the joints. A station master accepted responsibility and disembowelled himself.
10. The world's most difficult stand-up comic routine was performed by the eunuch dwarfs in the court of the Ottoman sultans. The dwarfs were required to keep the royal womenfolk amused while they gave birth.

10 Unsung Siblings

1. Paula Hitler, younger sister of Adolf.
2. Maria Goebbels, younger sister of Josef.
3. Gebhard Himmler, elder brother of Heinrich.
4. Hannah Arnold, younger sister of Benedict.
5. Henriette Marx, younger sister of Karl.
6. Feodor the not even remotely Terrible, younger brother of Ivan.
7. Pierre d'Arc, flame-proof younger brother of Joan.
8. Mlahlwa Mandela, older brother of Nelson.
9. Alexander Trotsky, older brother of Leon.
10. Xianlie Xiaoping, Deng's big sister.

16 Litigious People

1. In 1994 Bernadette French, a 36-year-old manic depressive, successfully sued the Wilmington Hospital in Delaware, US, for $1.1 million. A judge ruled that hospital staff had been negligent in allowing her to gouge her own eyes out.
2. A 54-year-old truck driver filed a $10 million lawsuit in Gallatin, Tennessee in April 1996 after he received a defective penile implant. The complainant said he suffered blisters, bruising, infection and embarrassment. His attorney added: "He could be just walking down the street, and it would erect on its own."
3. Robert Jones of Berkshire filed an insurance claim in 1994 against an electricity company for the loss of his parrot. The recently deceased Polly, killed by Jones's dog, had been kept in the family freezer for posterity, but during a power cut had thawed and decomposed.
4. In 1994 a jilted Spaniard broke into his ex-girlfriend's car in Barcelona and blew his brains out with a gun. Vehicle-owner Maria Valdez later sued his family for ruining the interior of her car.
5. Thirty-two-year-old Ernesto Mota suffered brain damage when he swallowed the entire contents of a bag of cocaine in a Chicago police station, so that it could not be used against him as evidence. He sued for the police for $7 million damages because they failed to stop him from doing it.
6. In Albuquerque, New Mexico, George Diesel and his wife sued both Foley's department store and the Levi Strauss Company. According to Mr Diesel, as he was pulling on his Levi 501s for the very first time a faulty fly

button rivet tore into his penis, causing him severe pain. Mrs Diesel also sued for the loss of her husband's services.

7. In 1993 Ohio prison inmates Pau Goist and Craig Anthony filed a lawsuit against the company General Foods. They complained that the company failed to tell them that Maxwell House coffee is addictive, and demanded compensation for the headaches and insomnia they suffered in prison.
8. Vicki Daily of Jackson, Wyoming filed a lawsuit in July 1993 against the widow of the man she had earlier run over and killed in her pick-up truck. Ms Daily demanded compensation from the widow for the "grave and crippling psychological injuries" she suffered while watching the 56-year-old man die.
9. In December 1993 a New York appeals court rejected housewife Edna Hobbs's lawsuit against a company that sold a time-saving kitchen device called The Clapper. The complainant said that in order to turn her appliances on, she clapped until her hands bled. The judge found that Mrs Hobbs had merely failed to adjust the sensitivity controls.
10. In 1994 a handicapped French woman, Yvette LeMons, sued the owner of her rented Toulouse flat for $25,000. Lawyers acting for Miss LeMons said the apartment owner had allowed termites to enter the premises, which had then eaten her wooden leg, causing her to fall down and break her arm.
11. An American, Joel Ford, filed a $45 million lawsuit against the Oxford University Press, publishers of the principal edition of the Bible, on the grounds that it is "based on hearsay" and "oppresses blacks and gays".

Ford dropped his action a few weeks later because, he said, he had received death threats.

12. Texan nurse Bobbie Heaney sued Dr William McIntosh in 1994. She complained that during a squabble in the hospital delivery room, Dr McIntosh had deliberately squirted her in the face with blood from an umbilical cord.
13. Loresa Goodly filed a lawsuit for injuries she incurred while receiving the Holy Spirit at a church revival meeting, when she passed out on the floor. A few moments later another woman received the Holy Spirit and fell on top of her, breaking three of Ms Goodly's ribs.
14. An Israeli woman in Haifa sued the popular television weatherman Danny Rup, seeking $1,000 after he predicted sunshine for a day that turned out wet and windy. The woman claimed that because of Rup's forecast she left home lightly dressed and as a result caught flu, causing her to miss four days' work and spend $38 on medication.
15. In 1964, a jury awarded $50,000 to a woman who claimed a cable car accident in San Francisco had made her into a nymphomaniac.
16. In 1997 Mrs Clarence Freeman Jr sued a Los Angeles undertaker's firm for allegedly putting her 6 ft 9 ins tall deceased husband into too small a coffin "bent like a pretzel". His widow complained, "He can't rest in peace comfortably."

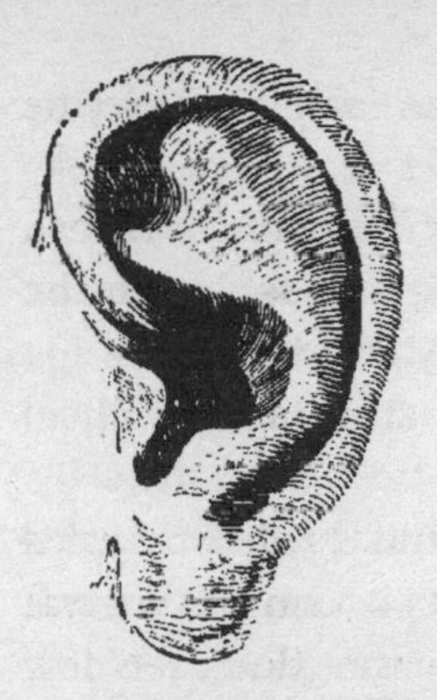

You Shouldn't Have: 12 Original Gifts

1. In 1995 Lord Erskine of Rerrick bequeathed his testicles to the Bank of Scotland, which had declared him bankrupt, because it had "no balls".
2. At Christmas 1888 Vincent van Gogh called at a Paris brothel known as the House of Tolerance with a present for one of the girls, whose name was Rachel, and told her "keep it and treasure it". It was his ear.
3. Moulay Ismael, the sultan of Morocco from 1672 to 1727, gave samples of his bowel movements to ladies of the court as a mark of special favour.
4. On Queen Isabel of Spain's birthday, Pope Pius IX gave her the embalmed corpse of Saint Felix.
5. Edward VII owned a golf bag made from an elephant's penis. It was a gift from an admirer, an Indian maharajah.
6. Warriors of the cannibal Brazilian Cubeo tribe always gave their wives the penis and scrotum of defeated victims. The wives were expected to eat them, and thus became fertile.
7. Pills made from the toxic metal antimony were highly esteemed in medieval times as great bowel-regulators. The pill irritated the intestinal tract, causing loose motions, and would pass through the body unharmed, enabling them to be handed down from father to son and from mother to daughter as precious family heirlooms.
8. The 1897 Sears, Roebuck & Co. mail order catalogue offered a selection of hypodermic syringe kits for shooting up heroin.
9. The most generous last will and testaments of all were left by Ecuadoran Indian endo-cannibals – i.e. cannibals who eat and are

eaten by members of their own family. Their wills gave express details of which body parts were to be eaten by which lucky relative. When the will had been read, the funeral became a banquet, as the corpse was roasted, cut into pieces and consumed by grieving relatives. The head was generally kept until it was ripe with maggots, then the brains were eaten with spices.

10. When Albert Einstein died in 1955 his body was cremated, but his brain was preserved in a glass jar. It was Albert's dying wish that his best bit should be given to science so that post-mortem analysis should shed new light on the rare gift of human genius. It didn't.
11. Hannah Beswick of Cheetwood Hall, Lancashire lived with a constant fear of being buried alive. When she eventually expired in 1758 aged 77, she left £25,000 to her doctor with instructions that he regularly inspect her corpse for signs of life. Her body was embalmed and crammed inside a grandfather clock with a velvet curtain tastefully draped across the glass viewing panel. One hundred and ten years after her demise, the trustees of her estate agreed that Hannah Beswick's state of health was finally beyond dispute, and she was granted a decent burial.
12. In 1910 Olav Olavson, desperate for cash, willed all rights to his body to the Karolinska Institute for Medical Research. The following year he had an unexpected and massive windfall and tried to buy himself back. The Institute refused to sell, and went to court to verify its claim. As Olav had since had two teeth pulled without seeking their permission, the Institute was even awarded damages.

12 Gruesome Collectibles

1. The fridge in which serial killer Jeffrey Dahmer, "the Milwaukee Cannibal", stored his victims' skulls was auctioned in 1996 to settle claims made by the families of some of his victims. Dahmer was beaten to death in prison in November 1994 while serving life for the sexual assault and murder of 17 young men and boys.
2. The stuffed carcass of Toto, the dog who starred with Judy Garland in the 1939 film *Wizard of Oz*, fetched £2,300 at auction in 1996.
3. In 1992 the blood-stained toe tag from the corpse of Lee Harvey Oswald, together with a lock of his hair, were auctioned in New York. The items were allegedly removed from Oswald by the ambulance driver as he drove him to the Dallas morgue.
4. A Texan mechanic sparked a major police murder hunt in 1996 when he opened the glove compartment of the car he was repairing and discovered a human hand. The car's owner, Alison Hastings, later explained that she kept it as a memento from her grandfather, a university anatomy professor who owned 75 similar specimens.
5. A toilet seat allegedly belonging to Adolf Hitler was put up for auction in Los Angeles, California, in 1968. The seller, Guy Harris, a former American fighter pilot, claimed he rescued it from Hitler's bunker in 1945 – the only item he could find that had not already been scavenged by Russian troops.
6. The legendary bank robbers Bonnie and Clyde were

enjoying bacon and tomato sandwiches in their car when they were ambushed by a posse of patrolmen and perforated by 77 bullets, splattering bits of brain all over the upholstery. The car and its contents were swooped on by local trophy-hunters, who even cut off locks of Bonnie Parker's hair. One man was apprehended by a coroner as he was attempting to saw off one of Clyde Barrow's ears.

7. The surgeon John Hunter, the unrivalled expert of eighteenth-century anatomy, was a tireless collector of anatomical artefacts, including embalmed foetuses, corpses and human and animal skeletons. Over a period of 30 years he amassed about 65,000 items. His uncomplaining wife Anne is said to have registered a protest only once, and that was when he brought home a stuffed giraffe which was too tall to fit inside his house. Hunter shortened it by hacking the legs off below the knee, and placed it in his hall. When he died he bequeathed the lot to the Company of Surgeons in London. In May 1941 the building in Lincoln's Inn took a direct hit from a German bomber, and now only 3,600 specimens remain.
8. Lincoln's Inn was also the home of the finest collection of bladder stones ever assembled by one man. It was the pride and joy of the surgeon Sir Henry Thompson, urologist to the crowned heads of Europe. When Sir Henry died he bequeathed all 1,000 of his bladder stones, including a couple removed from Leopold I King of the Belgians and the French emperor Napoleon III, to the Royal College of Surgeons in London.
9. The world's most collectible piece of human ordure is a nine-inch stool known as the Lloyds Bank Turd. The unique Viking turd, so called because it was found in an archaeological dig under a Lloyds bank, is insured for

£20,000. It is highly valued because of its near perfect condition – a rarity amongst 1,000-year-old turds.

10. Ron Sherwin of St Ives, Cornwall, has the world's only known collection of airline sick bags.
11. Maori tribesmen often preserved the elaborately tattooed heads of their deceased relatives as "auto-icons" to keep alive the memory of the dead. The heads would be steamed several times in an oven, smoked dry, and their hair carefully combed into a top-knot. In 1770 the British explorer Sir Joseph Banks acquired the first specimen Maori head ever seen in Europe, and heads suddenly became collectible items. The Maoris quickly overcame their initial objections to selling off the heads of their loved ones when they discovered that British museums and private collectors were prepared to pay generously for good quality, highly decorated specimens. As heads became scarce, unscrupulous Maori dealers would supply the heads of recently deceased slaves: few Europeans could tell the difference. By this time the greedy dealers were only one short step away from depriving living Maoris of their heads. In 1832 the gruesome practice had reached such horrific proportions that the head trade was finally made illegal.
12. The wealthy nineteenth-century naturalist and explorer Charles Waterton was noted for anti-social behaviour, which earned him affectionate respect as one of England's great eccentrics. Waterton loved to exhibit his prized collection of stuffed animals around his home, but found orthodox taxidermy too boring. He kept himself amused by grafting parts of different animals onto each other, and once surprised his dinner guests by displaying the partially dissected corpse of a gorilla on his dining table.

10 Odd Losses

1. In October 1993 the US Air Force confessed that it had again lost an $18 million F-16 fighter plane, because the pilot was unable to control the aircraft while using his "piddle pack" during in-flight urination. The earlier F-16 crash had been in March 1991.
2. Sixty-four-year-old widow Jean Carberry was distraught when, in October 1996, she accidentally put her husband Dennis's ashes out for the bin-men, but resolved to become re-united with him by searching through hundreds of tons of rubbish on the council tip. "I'd recognize him straight away," she explained hopefully. "He was in a green Barnardo's plastic bag . . . Dennis was a bloke in a million."
3. A German whose tongue was cut off during a drunken brawl at a party in Leipzig in 1994 scoured the floor for it in the hope of having it sewn back on. The 45-year-old gave up his search when someone commented that they had seen it eaten by a cat.
4. In 1973 the New York City Police Department admitted that they had lost about 400 pounds of heroin and cocaine, with a combined estimated street value of $73 million.
5. At the height of the Cold War the CIA spent thousands of dollars on a covert operation which involved the theft of a specimen of urine, passed by a member of the Politburo, from a laboratory in Vienna. The CIA regarded it as a great coup. They deduced from the sample, incorrectly as it turned out, that the Russian was seriously ill with kidney disease and didn't have long to live.
6. In 1989 thieves made off with £6,000 worth of frozen bull semen from a university in California. In spite of a £1,000 reward, it was never recovered.
7. In August 1994 Robert Carruthers, 33 years old and homeless,

spent the night in a Brighton shop doorway and woke to find that thieves had stolen his false right leg.

8. A severe national toilet paper shortage in Cuba in 1994 led to the ransacking of a library, where rare books were stolen and torn apart. An official explained that most Cubans had long since used up their telephone books and old magazines.
9. In 1994 Dutch newspapers reported that 10 people in Alphen Aan de Rijn had fallen victim to a denture thief. A telephone caller would persuade victims to leave their dentures in a bag outside the door at night to be collected, refurbished and returned the next morning.
10. In addition to the 1,200 pairs of shoes that the Philippine government confiscated from Imelda Marcos, they also swiped her only bulletproof bra.

10 Strange Discoveries

1. During a drugs raid on a house party in Kansas in 1994 police officers found a mummified female head in a box marked "Eight-Piece Party Cook Kit." The head was wrapped in a white lab smock, had blond hair and eyebrows, and its brain had been removed. The owner, 51-year-old Donald Donohue, said that it had been a gift from a medical student.
2. In 1994 police in Nairobi, Kenya discovered 600 human heads in an abandoned warehouse. It was their first major break since discovering 600 decapitated bodies two years earlier.
3. In November 1994 a Cardiff ice hockey team on a visit to Minsk complained about the smell in the local hotel restaurant. Management later discovered a corpse under the floor.
4. Police and paramedics sparked off an emergency dash across New York City in 1994 after the apparent discovery of a three-month-old human foetus in a paper bag in the ladies' lavatory of Macy's department store. A police spokesman later revealed that a more detailed medical examination had revealed the contents of the bag to be spaghetti in red sauce.
5. The body of an elderly Swedish woman who died in 1990 lay undiscovered in her Stockholm apartment for more than three years while computers received her pension and automatically paid her bills. The woman's last opened mail was dated 11 May 1990, indicating that she had died at the age of 72.

6. The world record for an undetected death in the home is seven years. In April 1996, 54-year-old Gabriella Villa

was discovered in Monza, Italy, seven years after her death by natural causes. Neighbours said they assumed that she had simply moved house.

7. In Sweden in 1994 a man with impaired hearing made a complete recovery after doctors removed a 47-year-old bus ticket from his ear.
8. Genuine items deposited in London Transport's Lost Property Office include a box of false eyeballs, an urn containing the ashes of a recently cremated male, a stuffed bird, a false leg, a bottle of prize bull sperm, half a theatrical prop coffin, a stolen park bench, and a box containing a pair of breast implants.
9. In 1994 the US Ripley's Believe It or Not! museums staged a contest to find the world's largest hairball. The winning hairball, from over 300 entries, was 33 inches in circumference. Sadly, Ripley's subsequently discovered that the Finney County Historical Society Museum in Garden City, Kansas had upstaged them by discovering a hairball measuring 37 inches.
10. When Richard Ramirez, the notorious US mass murderer known as "Night Stalker", failed a metal detector test at San Francisco County Jail, X-rays detected a variety of items in his rectum, including a small handcuff key, an empty syringe, the cap of a pen, and a small piece of cellophane on which was printed the words "I like chocolate."

10 Members of the Animal Kingdom Least Likely to Star in a Disney Cartoon Film

1. The candiru is a tiny catfish which lives as a parasite in bigger fish in the Amazon, and is attracted to the smell of human urine in water. Unfortunately, it often mistakes male humans for big fish, and it will enter the swimmer's body through his anal passage, burrow its way into the penis and stick out a set of spikes. The pain is excruciating: the victim is best advised get to a hospital quickly, before the bladder bursts, and ask a surgeon to cut off his penis.
2. When toads vomit, their emetic reflexes are so strong that they bring up not only the stomach contents, but the stomach itself, which then hangs from the toad's mouth. The toad then wipes away the remaining sick before re-swallowing the stomach.
3. The six-inch New Zealand flatworm *Artioposthia triangulata* feeds by spewing an enzyme over the victim's body, which first drugs it then turns it into soup. When it gives birth its back splits open and a small egg drops out. The official advice for killing one is to cover it in salt or stamp on it very hard.
4. Nature's most ruthless rapist is a parasitic wasp, whose natural habitat is the inside of a green vegetable bug. As soon as the tiny parasite is born it waits beside the unhatched female eggs of its sisters so that it can rape them the moment they are hatched.
5. Thanks to a high-fibre diet of bamboo, which keeps it

chewing for up to 14 hours non-stop, the giant panda has to defecate about 48 times a day.

6. When mountain gorillas fancy a hot meal on a cold day, instead of the usual salad, they often eat their own faeces.
7. The ladybird is the only insect known to suffer from a sexually transmitted venereal disease. The infection takes the form of a highly unpleasant form of lice, which is passed on during the ladybird's three-hour orgies.
8. Owing to an oversight by mother nature, the female bedbug is born without a sex organ. The male bedbug has a pointed penis, with which he drills a hole in his partner's gut and deposits his sperm in her bloodstream. When the female bedbug can't find any human blood to feed on she will happily dine on her male partner's semen.
9. The process by which the flea *Xenopsylla cheopsis* transfers bubonic plague from the black rat to humans is particularly unpleasant. The plague bacillus is carried in the rat's blood, where it rapidly multiplies. The flea feeds on the rat's blood, and the bacteria then form a solid mass inside the flea's stomach. The flea becomes "blocked" and suffers acute hunger. When it tries to feed again on a warm-blooded human, its gullet is stretched to the limit and infected blood is regurgitated back into the open wound. When a flea feeds it automatically defecates, depositing bacteria in its faeces. The victim, irritated by the flea bite, scratches the wound, thus spreading the bacteria-infested flea faeces.
10. When a sea cucumber becomes alarmed, or suffers from indigestion, it disembowels itself, ejecting its reproductive, respiratory organs and its entrails through its anus.

10 Heroic Business Opportunists

1. A Swedish court convicted a 34-year-old taxi driver of overcharging a 49-year-old woman after he left the meter running while he had sex with her. According to the *Aftonbladet* newspaper, the driver billed the woman the equivalent of about £5,000 for 25 occasions of "sexual services". The bill included 25 per cent sales tax, plus charges for trips, hotel and telephone calls.
2. The Russian psychologist Petrovitch Pavlov, best known for proving that dogs could be conditioned to salivate at the sound of a bell, attempted to cash in on his discovery by collecting large quantities of doggy phlegm and selling it bottled as an appetite stimulant. There were few takers.
3. Three hospital workers in Zimbabwe were arrested in 1994 and charged with stealing human hearts from the mortuary and selling them to witch doctors. The hearts, worth around £90 each (four times the local average monthly wage), were made into fashionable good luck charms for wealthy businessmen.
4. In 1994 six hospital orderlies in Calcutta, India were found guilty of making more than £150,000 over a five-year period by stealing the eyes from dead and dying patients and selling them to eye banks.
5. In 1996 the US mass murderer Charles Manson released his first exercise video. Manson's smiling promoter Fred Zalemond explained: "Charles regrets the lives he took. Now he's saving lives by protecting people from heart attacks and strokes."
6. A morgue in Brisbane, Australia, routinely sold organs from corpses without seeking permission from the families of the deceased. A former morgue attendant confessed that in 1993 the facility had sold pituitary glands for about 50 cents each in order to fund the staff Christmas party.

7. While serving a life sentence in Saskatchewan, Canada, for the rape and murder of eight girls and three boys, Clifford Olson registered copyright on his proposed video offering psychological insights into murder. It was snappily entitled *Motivational Sexual Homicide Patterns of Serial Child Killer Clifford Robert Olson.*
8. In 1996 the first-ever Ku Klux Klan museum and shop, called The Redneck Shop, opened in Laurens, South Carolina. Commenting on the negative reaction to his new enterprise, owner John Howard complained: "The only people I've had a problem with . . . have been blacks. I didn't know blacks here were so prejudiced."
9. In 1986 a couple from Winnipeg, Manitoba opened the world's one and only toilet theme restaurant, The Outhouse. It was closed down by health inspectors within a few weeks.
10. In 1911 a mail order con in the US netted hundreds of thousands of dollars with the promise of a miracle cure that could turn blacks into whites. The most outrageous American mail order con of all time, however, began in 1946 and lasted for a decade. William Johnson, a semi-literate miner from Kentucky, decided to cash in on a rumour sweeping America that Adolf Hitler had been smuggled out of Europe after World War II and was alive and well and living in North America. Johnson posed as Hitler, who was now settled in Kentucky with some of his Nazi chiefs of staff and planning to take over the US. He made a public appeal for cash to help his cause, and right-wing Americans and fascists of German extraction sent him a steady stream of postal orders, as he elaborated on his dastardly plans for space ships, "invisible ships" and underground hordes of ammunition. The fact that he often signed himself "The Furrier" instead of "The Führer" didn't stop the American public from sending him tens of thousands of dollars.

10 Embarrassing Elections

1. In Oklahoma in 1990 Frank Ogden III enjoyed a landslide local election victory over Josh Evans. Evans lost despite having run on a campaign of being an "able lawyer and a living person". He was convinced that this would give him an advantage over Ogden, who had died three months before polling day.
2. In 1991 Texan state legislator Larry Evans was discovered dead in his Austin apartment. His demise caused some embarrassment when it became clear that although he had obviously been deceased for some time, according to House records he had voted on at least one measure that very day.
3. In 1868 Thaddeus Stevens, a popular Republican congressional candidate from Pennsylvania, died aged 76. His party decided to go ahead and nominate him as a candidate for the House of Representatives anyway, as a belated tribute to "our most able and distinguished champion of justice". The corpse was duly elected with a large majority over its Democrat rival eight weeks later.
4. Although US Vice-President James Sharman died of uraemic poisoning a few days before election day in 1912, he still managed to win almost three and a half million votes. The incumbent ticket of Taft and Sherman came in third, and Sharman's eight electoral votes for Vice-President were cast for Nicholas M. Butler.
5. In 1974 a town in Western Australia accidentally re-elected a mayor whose death had originally caused the election. The town clerk was forced to admit later that this had been "a bad mistake".

6. In 1975 Philadelphian Frank O'Donnell was elected to serve on the city council despite dying of a heart attack a week before election day. A city council spokesman explained: "It seemed appropriate to remove his name from the ballot but there just wasn't enough time."
7. In 1982 Texan Democrat John Wilson was elected to the Senate with 66 per cent of the vote. Senator Wilson had been dead for two months but his name could not be removed from the ballot sheet for "technical reasons".
8. In 1928 the incumbent president of Liberia, Charles King, enjoyed a landslide electoral victory, beating his rival Thomas Faulkner by 600,000 votes. At the time Liberia had only 15,000 registered voters.
9. In July 1996 the former mayor of the 1980s cult-dominated US town of Rajneeshpuram, Oregon, admitted vote-rigging by using various schemes to keep the non-cult townspeople away from the ballot box during local elections. His methods included making them sick by tampering with the food at a restaurant and by coating courthouse doorknobs with a chemical irritant as election day approached.
10. Candidate Hamish Nixon ran for New Zealand's parliament in 1996 under the slogan "Nixon – The Name You Can Trust". Mr Nixon said: "I can't understand why people laugh when I talk about the need for trust and integrity in politics. It's as if they know something I don't."

9 Royal Obsessions

1. King George IV had a unique system for recording the number of women he slept with. He would ask each lover for a lock of hair, which he then placed in an envelope and labelled. When he died his brothers went through his personal belongings and found 7,000 envelopes containing enough hair to stuff a sofa, and hundreds of women's gloves.
2. Prussia's eccentric king Frederick William I was obsessed with creating a regiment of very tall men. He established a regiment of freakishly tall grenadiers known as the Potsdam Giant Guards. The minimum height requirement for the Potsdam regiment was six feet, although most were over seven feet and the tallest were almost nine feet tall. All of them wore special pointed headgear which sometimes reached a height of 10 feet. Height was the only criterion: many of them were mentally retarded.
3. Queen Victoria collected dead flowers taken from the graves of deceased royals. She began her collection with some that grew on her late husband Albert's last resting place, and it just sort of took off from there.
4. Many of the Hohenzollern kings of Prussia were military uniform fetishists, none more fanatical than Kaiser Wilhelm II. He had over 400 uniforms stashed away in his mahogany wardrobes. In the first 17 years of his

reign the Kaiser redesigned the uniforms of his German army officers 37 times; a squad of tailors was on permanent standby in the palace. He had uniforms for attending galas, uniforms to greet every one of his regiments, uniforms with which to greet other heads of state, uniforms for eating out, even "informal" uniforms for staying in. It was said that he had an admiral's uniform which he only ever wore to see performances of *The Flying Dutchman*.

5. Russia's czar Peter the Great had a fascination with freaks of nature, mostly human, and established a bizarre private collection, known as the Museum of Curiosities. The items, individually pickled in jars of alcohol, included a man without genitals, a two-headed child, a five-footed sheep, a deformed human foetus, the organs of a hermaphrodite, "the hand of a man who died by excessive drinking" and the corpses of Siamese Twins. One of the star exhibits was a large pickled phallus, donated to the museum by Prussia's King Frederick William. It also contained two human heads, one belonging to a man he suspected of being his wife's lover, and the other of a lady-in-waiting he had had executed. The museum's original curator, a badly deformed dwarf, was eventually also pickled and put on display when he died.
6. King Edward VII faithfully recorded the height and weight of everyone who ever visited his home at Sandringham.
7. Whereas King George V was content to collect stamps, his wife Queen Mary was the only known royal kleptomaniac. She was a prolific collector, especially of ornaments, family portraits and miniatures, and during her

lifetime she amassed a huge and eccentric private collection. What made hers different from other royal collections was the method she employed to put it together. On her frequent visits to London's antique-dealers, and occasionally on visits to the homes of wealthy friends, the queen was prone to taking what she wanted without paying for it, often slipping small items into her handbag. Buckingham Palace became aware of Queen Mary's problem when some of her victims complained about the thefts, and the queen's ladies-in-waiting were quietly instructed to keep a close eye on her. From then on, whatever Queen Mary stole was usually retrieved by an aide and mailed back to the original owner with a covering letter explaining that there had been a "mistake". When stories about Queen Mary's compulsive theft leaked out, the palace explained it as "her natural keenness to save anything worthwhile for the nation".

8. Egypt's king Menaphta, who defeated the Libyans in 1300 BC, collected as battle trophies the penises of all his slain enemies.
9. Prince Charles once claimed he had a collection of toilet seats.

10 FIRSTS

1. Buzz Aldrin was the first man to defecate on the moon.
2. Ronald Reagan was the first president to have his nasal polyps discussed on live TV.
3. On 1 July 1966 Mao Tse-Tung became the first senile septuagenarian to claim a world swimming record. The 72-year-old Chinese leader was reported to have smashed the existing record when he swam 10 miles of the River Yangtze in under an hour. His doctor now thinks it safe to point out that as Mao was too fat to sink or swim, the only way he night have completed even part of the journey (which is highly unlikely) was to have been swept along by the strong river current, unable to get out.
4. George Bush was the first president to be seen throwing up on live TV.
5. Theatre critic Kenneth Tynan became the first man to use the F-word on British television on 13 November 1965. It caused howls of outrage across the country and even in the House of Commons, where prime minister Harold Wilson was obliged to pass comment.
6. Shakespeare was the first writer to use the word "bog".
7. Before he became the first to lose his head, Louis XVI was also the first French king to use a knife and fork, take a regular bath and brush his teeth.
8. The first toilet paper, manufactured in the 1850s, was an unmentionable item, euphemistically referred to by the Victorian advertizing profession as "curl papers for hair-dressing". Britain's first soft toilet paper, which appeared in 1947, was available only from Harrods.
9. The first frontal leucotomy was experienced by the US quarryman Phineas Gage in 1848. After a quarry explosion, Gage was left with a three-foot crowbar sticking out of his forehead. Although a doctor was able to put his fingers

inside Gage's skull, the quarryman regained consciousness in minutes and lived on for another 12 years. The only noted long-term effect was a marked change in his personality.

10. The first man to design and make a parachute was the Frenchman Louis Sebastian Lenormand, in the late eighteenth century. He did not test it himself: he preferred to drop domestic animals from the the top of the tower of Montpelier Observatory.

10 FORMER OCCUPATIONS

1. Genghis Khan: goatherd.
2. Nostradamus: wrote about jam-making.
3. Al Capone: used furniture-dealer.
4. Josef Goebbels: accountant.
5. Heinrich Himmler: clerk in an agricultural fertilizer company.
6. Vladimir Ilyich Ulyanov (Lenin): lawyer.
7. Iosif Vissarionovich Dzhugashvili (Joe Stalin): trainee priest.
8. Ronnie and Reggie Kray: agents for Alvin Stardust.
9. Pol Pot: Buddhist monk.
10. US president Gerald R. Ford: male model.

10 Lavatorial Euphemisms

1. Jakes (England, sixteenth century).
2. Necessary house (England, seventeenth century).
3. Cackatorium (England, eighteenth century).
4. Boghouse (England, nineteenth century).
5. Dunny, diddy, toot, brasco (Australia, twentieth century).
6. *Bagno* ("bath"), *cabinetto* ("cabinet") (Italy, twentieth century).
7. *Ubornaya* ("adornment place") (Russia, twentieth century).
8. *Abort* ("away place"), *stlles örtchen* ("silent little place"), *donnerbalken* ("thunder board"), *plumsklo* ("plop closet") (Germany, twentieth century).
9. *Pissoir* (France, twentieth century).
10. *Bestekamer* ("best room") (Holland, twentieth century).

10 Occupational *Hazards*

1. The only recorded death of an obstetrician during childbirth occurred in February 1996. Finnish Dr Arvo Nikula was holding upside-down the newborn baby he had helped deliver when it kicked him in the right temple, triggering a fatal haemorrhage.
2. Swedish medical research teams claim to have established that office workers risk damaging their health by inhaling the noxious fumes emitted by their flatulent colleagues – i.e. passive farting. High concentrations of human methane can lead to a variety of serious health problems, including heart disease and serious respiratory problems.
3. The US author Gavin Whitsett was mugged and badly beaten in Evansville, Indiana in 1994. He is chiefly known for a surprise bestseller which urges his fellow Americans to indulge in random and spontaneous acts of kindness.
4. In May 1994 a French clown called Yves Abouchar died during his circus act, the first clown ever to have choked to death while receiving a custard pie in the face.
5. In 1994 French policeman Pierre Lemieux lost the sight in his right eye after a motorist accidentally spat a peanut into it. Jacques LeMans, who told Paris magistrates that he had his mouth full when he was stopped for speeding and questioned by officer Lemieux, explained: "I just wanted to clear my mouth so I could speak respectfully."
6. From 1956 to 1963 between a quarter and half a million US military personnel were deliberately exposed to fallout from atomic test bombs, mostly without any form of protective clothing or equipment, "for troop training purposes". The US Air Force Brigadier General A.R.

Leudecke even complained because his men weren't allowed to stand close enough to the blast.

7. When a team of palace surgeons failed to restore the eyesight of Bohemia's blind King John, he had them all drowned in the Danube.
8. In 1994 a 24-year-old Pakistani textile worker, Ahmed Bulwarj, was knitted to death when he fell head-first into a factory machine used to make cotton fabric. Before his body could be retrieved it had been punctured many hundreds of times by moving knitting needles.
9. Anesthesia by nitrous oxide – "laughing gas" – was discovered in 1884 by Horace Wells, a young dentist living in Connecticut. Wells didn't live long enough to enjoy the full rewards of his marvellous discovery. He became a hopeless chloroform junkie, and one day while high on the drug he ran into the street and doused two passing prostitutes with acid. Wells killed himself before his case came to trial.
10. In April 1983 Mike Stewart, President of the Auto Convoy Company, Dallas, Texas, was standing on the back of a flatbed truck when it passed under a low-level bridge, killing him instantly. At the time he was presenting a piece to camera for a TV item about the dangers of low-level bridges.

10 Nationalities yet to have been Insulted by Prince Philip, the Duke of Edinburgh*

1. Germans.
2. Greeks.
3. Danes.
4. Argentinians.
5. Russians.
6. Mongolians.
7. Japanese.
8. Fins.
9. Spaniards.
10. Sudanese.

* Chinese: he advised a British student in Beijing: "Don't stay here too long or you'll go back with slitty eyes" and described Peking as "ghastly".

Chileans: at an official function he was introduced to Dr Allende, soon to become Chile's president. The duke picked fault with Dr Allende's attire, which comprised an ordinary suit instead of the required white tie and tails. Allende explained that his people were very poor and that as their representative it would be inappropriate of him to dress expensively. Philip replied: "If they told you to wear a bathing costume, I suppose you'd have come dressed in one."

Canadians: "We don't come here for our health, you know."

British women: "You know, British women can't cook."

The Dutch: "What a po-faced lot the Dutch are."

The French: "Isn't it a pity Louis XVI was sent to the guillotine?"

Jews: on a tour of South America he told the fascist dictator of Paraguay, General Alfredo Strossner, a protector of surviving Nazi war criminals, "It's a pleasant change to be in a country that isn't ruled by its people."

Panamanians: on a trip to Panama he shouted at his official police escort who had sounded a siren: "Switch that bloody thing off, you silly fucker."

Hungarians: "Most of them are pot-bellied."

Scots: "They drink too much."

15 Rules of ETIQUETTE

1. In the nineteenth century sailors in the Royal Navy were forbidden to eat with forks, because they were considered "cissy".
2. It is traditional for Russian cosmonauts to urinate on a tyre of the bus that takes them to the launch pad, a custom initiated by Yuri Gagarin himself.
3. According to British royal etiquette, any man suffering from ringworm is exempt from the rule which obliges all men to remove their hats in the presence of the monarch.
4. In Nepal, Narikot wives are obliged to wash their husbands' feet, then drink the dirty water as a token of their devotion.
5. The typical greeting of Masai tribesmen is to spit at each other.
6. In sixteenth-century England it was customary for men to greet female guests by fondling their breasts, provided they were related.
7. Until about 100 years ago it was commonplace for wealthy Egyptian men on their wedding night to pay a servant to consummate the marriage for them: hence the old Arab saying: "A woman for duty, a boy for pleasure, but a melon for ecstasy."
8. According to ancient Jewish law, bad breath is grounds for divorce.
9. Fijian cannibals usually ate with their hands, but as a token of respect for the dead they used a ritual wooden fork for eating people.
10. In accordance with the ancient Indian laws of Manu, any citizen who broke wind in front of the monarch was liable to have his posterior amputated.
11. Tokyo has had 24 recorded instances of people who have been

killed or received serious skull fractures while bowing to each other with the traditional Japanese greeting.

12. In some Latin and Mediterranean countries, loud public belching is a sign of appreciation after a good meal.
13. Tibetans used to grow the fingernail long on the little finger of the left hand, so that they can use it to pick their ears and noses clean.
14. Russia's first-ever book of etiquette was published in 1718 by the Romanov empress Anne, a female psychopath who nevertheless had revolutionary ideas about good manners and wanted to keep up with European standards of good taste. Entitled *The Honest Mirror of Youth*, the slim volume advised discerning Russians how to use a knife and fork, when not to spit on the floor, not to blow their noses by applying a digit to one nostril while blowing down the other, and not to jab their elbows into their seating partners during formal dinners, nor place their feet in guests' dishes while standing on the dining table.
15. In accordance with the strict rules of Spanish etiquette, when Spanish monarchs die their corpses are deliberately left to rot for several days before interment in the Escorial vault, to emphasize the "ordinariness" of kings.

10 Facts about Samuel Pepys without once mentioning the Great Fire

1. He had adulterous affairs with his maid and Betty Lane, a linen-seller.
2. He was an avid reader of pornographic material.
3. He is reputed never to have had a bath in his life. In the nine years that he kept his diary he only once mentioned his wife taking a bath.
4. He thought Shakespeare was crap. On 29 September 1662 he wrote: ". . . and then to the King's Theatre, where we saw *Midsummer Night's Dream*, which I had never seen before, nor shall ever again, for it is the most insipid ridiculous play that ever I saw in my life." And on 6 January 1663: ". . . after dinner to the Duke's house, and there saw *Twelfth Night* acted well, though it is a silly play, and not related at all to the name or day."
5. Due to an unfortunate oversight, Henry VII's wife Queen Katherine lay above ground in Westminster Abbey, neglected and covered only by a loose cloth in an open wooden cask for several hundred years. It was still there in Pepys's lifetime, and he had a birthday treat when he went to visit the corpse on 23 February 1668. "I had the upper part of her body in my hands, and I did kiss her mouth, reflecting upon it that I did kiss a Queene, and this was my birthday." By the time Pepys

stole his kiss she had been dead for over 230 years.

6. He recorded an early and horrific pioneer attempt at blood transfusion, long before it dawned on anyone that blood type compatibility was important. On 23 November 1667 members of the Royal Society gathered to witness the transfusion of 12 ounces of sheep's blood into the unfortunate Reverend Arthur Coga. Pepys recorded in his diary that the man lived. "The patient speaks well, saying that he finds himself much better, as a new man . . . but he is cracked a little in his head."
7. He once noted in his diary that because his maid had forgotten to leave a chamber pot in his bedroom he had been forced in the night to "shit twice in the chimney fireplace".
8. Pepys was only 22 years old when he survived the only internal surgical operation available before the nineteenth century – lithotomy, or removal of a bladder stone, which in Pepys's case was "as big as a tennis ball". (See page 244.)
9. Although his operation did nothing to inhibit his energetic sex life, he and his wife never had children. It is assumed that the lateral perineal cut made him sterile.
10. He died of chronic inflammation of the kidneys and urinary poisoning.

10 Ingenious uses for Ordure

1. Hare dung was once used as a remedy for sagging breasts.
2. Some of the most sought-after varieties of Virginian tobacco got their flavour by being left to cure in lavatories to absorb the fumes of human ordure and urine.
3. A garden centre in Norwalk, California sells garden gnomes manufactured from recycled cow dung.
4. Class-conscious German farmers traditionally stacked piles of faeces, animal and human, in front of their farms and dwellings. The size of the pile was their way of showing off to the neighbours that they had loads of livestock and could afford a big family.
5. Visitors to the 1994 Winter Olympics were offered souvenir earrings made from elk droppings at £7 a pair.
6. Camel dung was once rubbed into the scalp to make the hair wavy. Ass or hen dung was used to cure skin blemishes, swellings or burns.
7. Cakes of animal excrement, especially pig manure, which contains ammonia, was commonly used in some parts of Britain as an alternative to soap right up until World War II. Women became so immune to the stench of dung on wash days that when soap became popular they often complained that the suds made them nauseous.
8. For centuries most poor people in Britain used cow or horse dung as fuel: although the smell was incredibly offensive, it was free, easy to collect, simple to burn and gave out a great deal of heat. When coal became more easily available in the late eighteenth and early nineteenth centuries, dung fuel became less common, but the practice continued in Cornwall. On the Isle of Arran, off the west coast of Scotland, it was still the main

source of heat in the 1930s.

9. A fashionable salad in eighteenth-century Britain comprised horse dung with mustard and cress.
10. The Alabama mail order company Endangered Feces sells paperweights made from coprolites – fossilized dinosaur droppings. Each of the 65 million-year-old four-ounce turds is certified as authentic by their own geologist, and each comes with a signed and numbered certificate of authenticity at $60 apiece.

What's in a Name: the USA's 10 most Expensive Hurricanes

1. Andrew (1992): $25 billion's worth of damage.
2. Hugo (1989): $7.2 billion's worth.
3. Becky (1965): $6.5 billion's worth.
4. Agnes (1972): $6.4 billion's worth.
5. Camille (1969): $5.2 billion's worth.
6. Diane (1955): $4.2 billion's worth.
7. New England (1938): $3.6 billion's worth.
8. Fred (1979): $3.5 billion's worth.
9. Alicia (1983): $2.4 billion's worth.
10. Carol (1954): $2.3 billion's worth.

One Man's Vision: The 10 Best Quotes attributed to former US Vice-President Dan Quayle

1. "I love California. I practically grew up in Phoenix."
2. "What a waste it is to lose one's mind. Or not to have a mind is being very wasteful. How true that is."
3. "It isn't pollution that's harming the environment. It's the impurities in our air and water that are doing it."
4. "I was recently on a tour of Latin America, and the only regret I have was that I didn't study Latin harder in school, so I could converse with those people."
5. "Mars is essentially in the same orbit . . . Mars is somewhat the same distance from the Sun, which is very important. We have seen pictures where there are canals, we believe, and water. If there is water, that means there is oxygen. If oxygen, that means we can breathe."
6. "For NASA, space is still a high priority."
7. "The Holocaust was an obscene period in our nation's history. I mean in this century's history. But we all lived in this century. I didn't live in this century."
8. "I believe we are on an irreversible trend toward more freedom and democracy – but that could change."
9. "One word sums up probably the responsibility of any vice-president, and that one word is 'to be prepared'."
10. "We don't want to go back to tomorrow, we want to go forward."

Only In America

1. In 1995 a driver who was both drunk and speeding crashed his car, then successfully sued the engineering firm responsible for designing the road, the contractor, four subcontractors and the state highway department. He received an out-of-court settlement of $35,000.
2. A convenience-store worker in West Virginia was awarded $2.52 million in 1995 after suffering emotional distress when she hurt her back while opening a pickle jar.
3. Disneyland, California was sued in 1997 by a woman who claimed that her grandchildren were traumatized when they saw Mickey Mouse climbing out of his costume.
4. In 1996 a drunken golfer from Wisconsin who fell and broke his jaw while leaving the nineteenth hole was awarded $41,540 damages.
5. In 1994 the US Supreme Court awarded $500,000 to a kidnapper who broke his ankle while running away from the police.
6. A drunken restaurant worker who fell in front of a train and lost an arm was paid $9 million compensation in 1990 by the New York Transport Authority.
7. A convicted bankrobber on parole in Oakland, California was awarded $2 million damages in 1987 when the wad of money he had recently stolen from the Savings and Loan Company exploded in his pocket, releasing tear gas and dye, resulting in burns which required hospital treatment.
8. A Californian who hurt himself diving into a swimming pool of the house he had rented in 1997 sued the owners for $66 million. Apparently they failed to warn him about the shallow end.
9. In 1993 a restaurant in Long Island was obliged to pay

$3 million damages to a customer who was stung by a bee.

10. In 1995 a teenager in New Hampshire received a $50,000 out-of-court settlement from the manufacturers of a basketball net. The complainant lost his two front teeth when they became entangled in the net while he was performing a "slam dunk".

DIPPED IN VITRIOL:
10 Writers On Writers

1. Jane Austen: "To me, Poe's prose is unreadable – like Jane Austen's. No, there is a difference. I could read his prose on a salary, but not Jane's."
   – Mark Twain
2. Ben Jonson: "Reading him is like wading through glue."
   – Alfred, Lord Tennyson
3. Alexander Pope: "There are two ways of disliking poetry. One way is to dislike it, the other is to read Pope."
   – Oscar Wilde
4. Robert Browning: "I don't think Browning was very good in bed. His wife probably didn't care for him very much. He snored and had fantasies about twelve-year-old girls."
   – W.H. Auden
5. James Joyce: "The work of a queasy undergraduate scratching his pimples."
   – Virginia Woolfe on *Ulysses*
6. Arnold Bennett: "The Hitler of the book racket."
   – Percy Wyndham Lewis
7. Thomas Gray: "He was dull in company, dull in his closet, dull everywhere . . . he was a mechanical poet."
   – Samuel Johnson
8. Ernest Hemingway: "When his cock wouldn't stand up he blew his head off. He sold himself a line of bullshit and he bought it."
   – Germaine Greer
9. Percy Bysshe Shelley: "A poor creature who has said or done nothing worth a serious man taking the trouble of remembering."
   – Thomas Carlyle

10. Dylan Thomas: "An outstandingly unpleasant man, one who cheated and stole from his friends and peed on their carpets."
– Kingsley Amis

10 Succinct Pop Reviews

1. The Beatles (1964): "Bad-mannered little shits."
   – Noël Coward
2. Let's Groove – Earth Wind & Fire (1981): "Let's not."
   – Johnny Black, *Smash Hits*
3. Run to the Hills – Iron Maiden (1982): "Don't think I wasn't tempted."
   – Red Starr, *Smash Hits*
4. All the Way Up – Belle & The Devotions (1984): "Don't tempt me."
   – Stephen Gray, *Record Mirror*
5. The Robots – Kraftwerk (1978): "Zzzzzzzzz."
   – Dean Porsche, *Zig-Zag*
6. I'm Alive – ELO (1980): "A blatant lie. Product."
   – Deanne Parsons, *Smash Hits*
7. Away From This Town – Still Life (1982): "And the further the better."
   – Robin Smith, *Record Mirror*
8. Like a Rock – Bob Seger (1986): "Exactly, Bob. Prehistoric."
   – Kevin Murphy, *Sounds*
9. Wasting Time – Strangeways (1979): "Yes, mine."
   – Robin Banks, *Sounds*
10. Forever Young – Alphaville (1984): "Should have been strangled at birth."
    – Morrissey, *Smash Hits*

10 People Who Hated Shakespeare

1. Edward Young, British poet: "Shakespeare – what trash are his works in the gross."
2. Voltaire: "This enormous dunghill."
3. Leo Tolstoy: "Crude, immoral, vulgar and senseless."
4. George Bernard Shaw: "With the single exception of Homer, there is no eminent writer, not even Sir Walter Scott, whom I despise so entirely as I despise Shakespeare when I measure my mind against his. It would be positively a relief to me to dig him up and throw stones at him."
5. Walter Savage Landor, British poet: "The sonnets are hot and pothery, there is much condensation, little delicacy, like raspberry jam without cream, without crust, without bread."
6. Dr Samuel Johnson: "Shakespeare never had six lines together without a fault. Perhaps you may find seven, but this does not refute my general assertion."
7. Robert Greene, English playwright: "An upstart now beautified with our feathers."
8. Elizabeth Forsyth, English writer: "A sycophant, a flatterer, a breaker of marriage vows, a whining and inconsistent person."
9. Charles Darwin: "I have tried lately to read Shakespeare and found it so intolerably dull that it nauseated me."
10. King George III: "Is this not sad stuff, what what?"

10 FRANCOPHOBES

1. "You must consider every man your enemy who speaks ill of your king: and you must hate a Frenchman as you hate the devil."
   – Lord Horatio Nelson
2. GUILLOTINE, n. A machine which makes a Frenchman shrug his shoulders with good reason.
   – Ambrose Bierce, *Devil's Dictionary*
3. "The French; utter cowards who force their own children to drink wine, they gibber like baboons even when you try to speak to them in their own wimpy language . . . racial characteristics; sawed-off cissies who eat snails and slugs and cheeses that smell like people's feet."
   – P.J. O'Rourke, *National Lampoon, 1976*
4. "I remember being much amused last year, when landing at Calais, at the answer made by an old traveller to a novice who was making his first voyage. 'What a dreadful smell,' said the uninitiated stranger, enveloping his nose in his pocket handkerchief. 'It is the smell of the continent, sir,' replied the man of experience. And so it was."
   – Mrs Frances Trollope
5. "France is a dog-hole."
   – William Shakespeare (*All's Well That Ends Well*)
6. "I do not dislike the French from the vulgar antipathy between neighbouring nations, but for their insolent and unfounded airs of superiority."
   – Horace Walpole

7. "There's always something fishy about the French!
   Whether Prince or Politician
   We've a sinister suspicion
   That behind their savoir-faire
   They share
   A common contempt
   For every mother's son of us."
   – Noël Coward, from *Conversation Piece*
8. "France is the largest country in Europe, a great boon for drunks who need room to fall . . ."
   – Alan Coren, *The Sanity Inspector*, 1974
9. "Frenchmen are like grains of gunpowder – each by itself smutty and contemptible, but mass them together and they are horrible indeed."
   – Samuel T. Coleridge
10. "The ignorance of French society gives one a rough sense of the infinite."
   – Joseph E. Renan

12 Misanthropes

1. "Happiness is to vanquish your enemies, to chase them before you, to rob them of their wealth, to see their near and dear bathed in tears, to ride their horses and sleep on the white bellies of their wives and daughters."
   – Genghis Kahn
2. "If they were drowning to death, I'd put a hose in their mouth."
   – Ray Kroc, former Chief Executive Officer of McDonald's, on his competitors
3. "It is better to be feared than loved, if you cannot be both."
   – Niccolo Machiavclli
4. "The meek shall inherit the Earth, but not its mineral rights."
   – J. Paul Getty
5. "I have the heart of a child. I keep it in a jar on my shelf."
   – Robert Bloch
6. "Happiness is nothing more than good health and a bad memory."
   – Albert Schweitzer
7. "The public be damned – I'm working for my stockbrokers."
   – William H. Vanderbilt. Reply to a newspaper reporter who asked the railway magnate if the withdrawal of an

unprofitable express train was against public interest, Chicago, 1883

8. "You can get a lot more done with a kind word and a gun than with a kind word alone."
   – Al Capone
9. "Practically everyone but myself is a pusillanimous son of a bitch."
   – General George S. Patton Jnr
10. "The secret of success is sincerity. Once you can fake that you've got it made."
   – Jean Giraudoux
11. "If you can't say anything good about someone, sit right here by me."
   – Alice Roosevelt Longworth
12. "I am free of all prejudices. I hate everyone equally."
   "Start every day off with a smile; get it over with."
   – W.C. Fields

10 UNINSPIRING US PRESIDENTS

1. Andrew Jackson: "A barbarian who could not write a sentence of grammar and hardly could spell his own name."
   – John Quincy Adams
2. John Quincy Adams: "It is said he is a disgusting man to do business with. Coarse and dirty and clownish in his address and stiff and abstracted in his opinions, which are drawn from books exclusively."
   – William Henry Harrison
3. Warren G. Harding: "He writes the worst English I have ever encountered. It reminds me of a string of wet sponges . . . of tattered washing on the line . . . of stale bean soup, of college yells, of dogs barking idiotically through endless nights. It is so bad that a sort of grandeur creeps into it. It drags itself out of a dark abyss of pish, and crawls insanely up the topmost pinnacle of posh. It is rumble and bumble. It is flap and doodle. It is balder and dash.
   – H.L. Mencken
4. Calvin Coolidge: "He slept more than any other president, whether by day or night. Nero fiddled, but Coolidge only snored."
   – H.L. Mencken
5. Dwight D. Eisenhower: "Why, this fellow don't know any more about politics than a pig knows about Sunday."
   – Harry S. Truman

6. Franklin D. Roosevelt: "He had every quality that morons esteem in their heroes. He was the first American to reach the real depths of vulgar stupidity."
   – H.L. Mencken
7. Lyndon Baines Johnson: "How does one tell the president of the United States to stop picking his nose and lifting a leg to fart in front of the camera and using 'chickenshit' in every other sentence?"
   – Stuart Rosenberg, TV director
8. Jimmy Carter: "I think Jimmy Carter as president is like Truman Capote marrying Dolly Parton. The job is just too big for him."
   – Rich Little
9. Gerald Ford: "In the Bob Hope Golf Classic the participation of President Gerald Ford was more than enough to remind you that the nuclear button was at one stage at the disposal of a man who might have either pressed it by mistake or else pressed it deliberately to obtain room service."
   – Clive James
10. Ronald Reagan: "In a disastrous fire in Ronald Reagan's library, both books were destroyed. And the real tragedy is that he hadn't finished colouring it."
    –Jonathan Hunt

10 Prosaic Prime Ministers

1. George Canning: "Canning in office is like a fly in amber. Nobody cares about the fly, the only question is, how the devil did I get there?"
   – Sydney Smith
2. William Gladstone: "If Gladstone fell into the Thames it would be a misfortune. But if someone dragged him out again, it would be a calamity."
   – Benjamin Disraeli
3. Ramsay Macdonald: "I have waited fifty years to see the Boneless Wonder sitting on the Treasury Bench."
   – Winston Churchill
4. Clement Attlee: "Reminds me of nothing so much as a dead fish before it has time to stiffen."
   – George Orwell
5. Stanley Baldwin: "One could not even dignify him with the name of stuffed shirt. He was simply a hole in the air."
   – George Orwell
6. Neville Chamberlain: "A retail mind in wholesale business."
   – David Lloyd George
7. Winston Churchill: "Simply a radio personality who outlived his prime."
   – Evelyn Waugh
8. Anthony Eden: "He is not only a bore, but he bores for England."
   – Malcolm Muggeridge

9. Edward Heath: "In any civilized country, Heath would have been hanging upside down on a petrol pump years ago."
   – Auberon Waugh
10. Margaret Thatcher: "The Enid Blyton of economics. Nobody must be allowed to spoil her simple plots."
    – Robert Holme

20 OBSCURE STATISTICS

1. Britain has an estimated three-quarters of a million bedwetters.
2. An estimated 600,000 Americans are impotent from injuries to their crotches. Approximately 40 per cent of these are bicycling accidents.
3. Seven out of ten Americans have daydreams about having sex with their boss, irrespective of whether or not they are the same sex.
4. One in 13 British adults has purchased a vibrator in the last ten years.
5. According to a recent survey, one in three male motorists picks his nose while driving.
6. Every day 356,000 people are newly infected with a sexually transmitted disease.
7. Ninety-five per cent of all lavatory hot-air dryers discharge pathogenic bacteria which can cause food poisoning and a variety of skin disorders including boils and abscesses.
8. India and Bangladesh have exported more human skeletons for medical research than any other countries. The trade is now prohibited as an affront to national dignity.
9. More than 35,000 Americans have had themselves insured against being kidnapped or eaten alive by aliens.
10. To date, 15 Americans have been crushed to death while attempting to tilt soft-drink vending machines.
11. Twenty-four people in Tokyo have been killed or received serious skull fractures while bowing to each other with the traditional Japanese greeting.
12. On average every glass of London tap water has already passed through the bladders of nine other people.
13. Following a visit to the US by Diana, Princess of Wales in 1996, the

New York *Observer* reported that requests for colonic irrigation treatments had increased ten-fold.

14. People with smaller than average heads stand 18 times more risk than people with big heads of suffering premature senility from Alzheimer's.
15. Neither horses nor rabbits can vomit.
16. Impotence is legal grounds for divorce in 24 American states.
17. The typical person spends about 600 hours having sex between the ages of 20 and 70.
18. Hungary currently has the world's highest suicide rate.
19. British people spend more on laxatives per capita – about £70 million per annum – than any other nationality in Europe.
20. Irish men suffer less from dandruff than those in any other European country.

10 Last Words

1. "I don't know." – Pierre Abelard, philosopher, 1142.
2. "Wait a minute . . ." – Pope Alexander VI, Borgia, 1503.
3. "Monks. monks, monks." – King Henry VIII, 1547.
4. "Strike, man!" – Sir Walter Raleigh (to his executioner), 1618.
5. "Am I still alive?" – Julie de Lespinasse, 1776.
6. "Enough." – Immanuel Kant, 1804.
7. "Get out." – Karl Marx, 1883.
8. "Bugger Bognor." – King George V, 1936.
9. "I am Heinrich Himmler." – Heinrich Himmler, 1945.
10. "I'm all right." – H.G. Wells, 1946.